ORGANIZATIONAL BEHAVIOUR

ORGANIZATIONAL BEHAVIOUR

Kumar Pranit

genNEXT Publication

Published by

GenNext Publication
5, Ansari Road
Daryaganj, New Delhi-110002
Phone: 011-47034999, 9811692060
E-mail: gennextpublication@hotmail.com

Distribution Network
gyanbooks.com
India, USA, Canada, UK, Australia, France

ISBN: 978-93-5663-282-0 (PB)

First Published, 2024

Printed at: Gyan Press, Delhi.

Organisational Behaviour
Author: Kumar Paranit

Contents

Preface

Organizational studies, organizational behaviour, and organizational theory is the systematic study and careful application of knowledge about how people - as individuals and as groups - act within organizations. Organizational Behaviour studies encompasses the study of organizations from multiple viewpoints, methods, and levels of analysis.

Organizational Behaviour is a purposeful blend of study, hypothesis and practice, making it a practical science in the truest sense. This is reflected in this text so that readers will gain a firm understanding of what should be done (and what currently is being done) to improve the functioning of organizations and the satisfaction of people who work in them.

This volume is a concise introduction to Organizational Behaviour. It is developed specifically for courses and business students. It focuses on the core topics of the organizational behaviour and illustrates to show its application in practice. It is written for students on undergraduate and postgraduate degree programmes.

It has been developed to cover extensively various aspects of the field of organizational behaviour. The language is highly lucid so that it becomes interesting and comprehensive. This book describes the approaches to organizational behaviour, structure and design, theories, motivation, leadership theories, personality, learning, perception, stress, power and authority, organizational development and conflicts & negotiations. It's a text book that is well thought-out, easy to read and a great reference book for anything to do with organizational behaviour.

We are confident enough that this book will be a handy tool for the students of management. Your sincere feedback always encourages us to improve our way of presentation. Reader's suggestions and comments are always welcome.

About the Book

This book presents the intricacies of retailing from both academic and practical points of view. New changing business practices are actuating changes in the retail environment. Dearth of time and increase in incomes of public has created a need for new types of retail formats. This means retailers will have to have knowledge of knowing their customers and anticipating their needs. As the economic structure in India is changing so is the field of retailing. What was once an unorganized sector, have transformed into an organized sector in the last decade. Malls, supermarkets, shopping outlets have mushroomed, calling for the practical application of modern management techniques to run them effectively and efficiently. This calls for retail managers to be expert at designing, planning, marketing, pricing, and promotion. This book presents the subject of Retailing as no other book in the market does. It introduces the subject in an absorbing way, is stimulating and motivates readers. This is a must-have book for everyone engaged in retail management.

About the Author

Kumar Pranit was born in 1969. He did his Graduation in Industrial & Production Engineering in 1993 and P.G. Diploma in Human Resource Management in 1996. With a 15+ years of experience in H.R.M. including Corporate, Sales and Factory HR Functions and is working since June'07, with Priknit India Ltd., as Asstt. General Manager. He has published various Articles such as "Mistakes Sales Professionals Make", "Role of workers in implementation of TQM", "Simple ways to enhance productivity at the shop floor".

1

Organizational Behaviour: An Introduction

Organizational Behaviour (OB) is the study and application of knowledge about how people, individuals, and groups act in organizations. It does this by taking a system approach. That is, it interprets people-organization relationships in terms of the whole person, whole group, whole organization, and whole social system. Its purpose is to build better relationships by achieving human objectives, organizational objectives, and social objectives. As you can see from the definition above, organizational behaviour encompasses a wide range of topics, such as human behaviour, change, leadership, teams, etc.

ELEMENTS OF ORGANIZATIONAL BEHAVIOUR

The organization's base rests on management's philosophy, values, vision and goals. This in turn drives the organizational culture which is composed of the formal organization, informal organization, and the social environment. The culture determines the type of leadership, communication, and group dynamics within the organization. The workers perceive this as the quality of work life which directs their degree of motivation. The final outcomes are performance, individual satisfaction, and personal growth and development. All these elements combine to build the model or framework that the organization operates from.

MODELS OF ORGANIZATIONAL BEHAVIOUR

There are four major models or frameworks that organizations operate out of:

- Autocratic - The basis of this model is power with a managerial orientation of authority. The employees in turn are oriented towards obedience and dependence on the boss. The employee need that is met is subsistence. The performance result is minimal.

- Custodial - The basis of this model is economic resources with a managerial orientation of money. The employees in turn are oriented towards security and benefits and dependence on the organization. The employee need that is met is security. The performance result is passive cooperation.
- Supportive - The basis of this model is leadership with a managerial orientation of support. The employees in turn are oriented towards job performance and participation. The employee need that is met is status and recognition. The performance result is awakened drives.
- Collegial - The basis of this model is partnership with a managerial orientation of teamwork. The employees in turn are oriented towards responsible behaviour and self-discipline. The employee need that is met is self-actualization. The performance result is moderate enthusiasm.

Although there are four separate models, almost no organization operates exclusively in one. There will usually be a predominate one, with one or more areas over-lapping in the other models.

The first model, autocratic, has its roots in the industrial revolution. The managers of this type of organization operate out of McGregor's Theory X. The next three models begin to build on McGregor's Theory Y. They have each evolved over a period of time and there is no one "best" model. The collegial model should not be thought as the last or best model, but the beginning of a new model or paradigm.

SOCIAL SYSTEMS, CULTURE, AND INDIVIDUALIZATION

A social system is a complex set of human relationships interacting in many ways. Within an organization, the social system includes all the people in it and their relationships to each other and to the outside world. The behaviour of one member can have an impact, either directly or indirectly, on the behaviour of others. Also, the social system does not have boundaries...it exchanges goods, ideas, culture, etc. with the environment around it.

Culture is the conventional behaviour of a society that encompasses beliefs, customs, knowledge, and practices. It influences human behaviour, even though it seldom enters into their conscious thought. People depend on culture as it gives them stability, security, understanding, and the ability to respond to a given situation. This is why people fear change. They fear the system will become unstable, their security will be lost, they will not understand the new process, and they will not know how to respond to the new situations. Individualization is when employees successfully exert influence on the social system by challenging the culture.

Impact of Individualization on an Organization

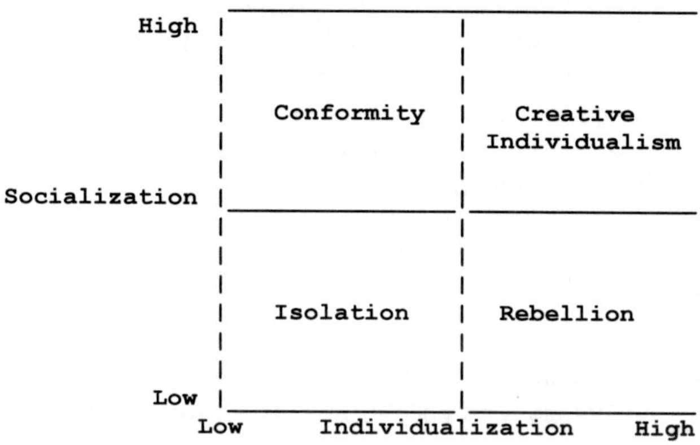

The chart above shows how individualization affects different organizations:

- Too little socialization and too little individualization create isolation.
- Too high socialization and too little individualization create conformity.
- Too little socialization and too high individualization creates rebellion.
- While the match that organizations want to create is high socialization and high individualization for a creative environment. This is what it takes to survive in a very competitive environment...having people grow with the organization, but doing the right thing when others want to follow the easy path.

This can become quite a balancing act. Individualism favours individual rights, loosely knit social networks, self respect, and personal rewards and careers. It becomes look out for number 1! Socialization or collectivism favours the group, harmony, and asks "What is best for the organization?" Organizations need people to challenge, question, and experiment while still maintaining the culture that binds them into a social system.

ORGANIZATION DEVELOPMENT

Organization Development (OD) is the systematic application of behavioural science knowledge at various levels, such as group, inter-group, organization, etc., to bring about planned change. Its objectives are a higher quality of work-life, productivity, adaptability, and effectiveness. It accomplishes this by changing attitudes, behaviours, values, strategies, procedures, and structures so that the organization can adapt to competitive actions, technological advances, and the fast pace of change within the environment.

There are seven characteristics of OD:

1. Humanistic Values: Positive beliefs about the potential of employees (McGregor's Theory Y).
2. Systems Orientation: All parts of the organization, to include structure, technology, and people, must work together.
3. Experiential Learning: The learners' experiences in the training environment should be the kind of human problems they encounter at work. The training should NOT be all theory and lecture.
4. Problem Solving: Problems are identified, data is gathered, corrective action is taken, progress is assessed, and adjustments in the problem solving process are made as needed. This process is known as Action Research.
5. Contingency Orientation: Actions are selected and adapted to fit the need.
6. Change Agent: Stimulate, facilitate, and coordinate change.
7. Levels of Interventions: Problems can occur at one or more level in the organization so the strategy will require one or more interventions.

QUALITY OF WORK LIFE

Quality of Work Life (QWL) is the favourableness or unfavourableness of the job environment. Its purpose is to develop jobs and working conditions that are excellent for both the employees and the organization. One of the ways of accomplishing QWL is through job design. Some of the options available for improving job design are:

- Leave the job as is but employ only people who like the rigid environment or routine work. Some people do enjoy the security and task support of these kinds of jobs.
- Leave the job as is, but pay the employees more.
- Mechanize and automate the routine jobs.
- And the area that OD loves - redesign the job.

When redesigning jobs there are two spectrums to follow - job enlargement and job enrichment. Job enlargement adds a more variety of tasks and duties to the job so that it is not as monotonous. This takes in the breadth of the job. That is, the number of different tasks that an employee performs. This can also be accomplished by job rotation.

Job enrichment, on the other hand, adds additional motivators. It adds depth to the job - more control, responsibility, and discretion to how the job is performed. This gives higher order needs to the employee, as opposed to job enlargement which simply gives more variety. The chart below illustrates the differences:

Job Enrichment and Job Performance

Accent on Needs	Few	Many
Higher Order	Job Enrichment	Job Enrichment and Enlargement
Lower Order	Routine Job	Job Enlargement

Variety of Tasks

The benefits of enriching jobs include:

- Growth of the individual
- Individuals have better job satisfaction
- Self-actualization of the individual
- Better employee performance for the organization
- Organization gets intrinsically motivated employees

- Less absenteeism, turnover, and grievances for the organization
- Full use of human resources for society
- Society gains more effective organizations

There are a variety of methods for improving job enrichment:

- Skill Variety: Perform different tasks that require different skill. This differs from job enlargement which might require the employee to perform more tasks, but require the same set of skills.
- Task Identity: Create or perform a complete piece of work. This gives a sense of completion and responsibility for the product.
- Task Significant: This is the amount of impact that the work has on other people as the employee perceives.
- Autonomy: This gives employees discretion and control over job related decisions.
- Feedback: Information that tells workers how well they are performing. It can come directly from the job (task feedback) or verbally form someone else.

ACTION LEARNING

An unheralded British academic was invited to try out his theories in Belgium -- it led to an upturn in the Belgian economy. "Unless your ideas are ridiculed by experts they are worth nothing," says the British academic Reg Revans, creator of action learning [L = P + Q] -- learning occurs through a combination of programmed knowledge (P) and the ability to ask insightful questions (Q).

Action learning has been widely used in Europe for combining formal management training with learning from experience. A typical program is conducted over a period of 6 to 9 months. Teams of learners with diverse backgrounds conduct field projects on complex organizational problems requiring use of skills learned in formal training sessions. The learning teams then meet periodically with a skilled instructor to discuss, analyze, and learn from their experiences.

Revans basis his learning method on a theory called "System Beta," in that the learning process should closely approximate the "scientific method." The model is cyclical - you proceed through the steps and when you reach the last step you relate the analysis to the original hypothesis and if need be, start the process again. The six steps are:

- Formulate Hypothesis (an idea or concept)
- Design Experiment (consider ways of testing truth or validity of idea or concept)
- Apply in Practice (put into effect, test of validity or truth)
- Observe Results (collect and process data on outcomes of test)
- Analyze Results (make sense of data)
- Compare Analysis (relate analysis to original hypothesis)

Note that you do not always have to enter this process at step 1, but you do have to complete the process.

Revans suggest that all human learning at the individual level occurs through this process. Note that it covers what Jim Stewart calls the levels of existence:

- We think - cognitive domain
- We feel - affective domain
- We do - action domain

All three levels are interconnected -- e.g. what we think influences and is influenced by what we do and feel.

CHANGE

In its simplest form, discontinuity in the work place is "change." Our prefrontal cortex is similar to the RAM memory in a PC -- it is fast and agile computational device that is able to hold multiple threads of logic at once so that we can perform fast calculations. However it has its limits in that it can only hold a handful of concepts at once. In addition, it burns lots of high energy glucose (blood sugar), which is expensive for the body to produce. Thus when given lots of information, such as when a change is required, it has a tendency to overload and being directly linked to the amygdala (the emotional centre of the brain) that controls our fight-or-flight response, it can cause severe physical and psychological discomfort.

Our prefrontal cortex is marvellous for insight when not overloaded. But for normal everyday use, our brain prefers to run off its "hard-drive" -- the basal ganglia, which has a much larger storage area and stores memories and our habits. In addition, it sips rather than gulps food (glucose).

When we do something familiar and predictable, our brain is mainly using the basal ganglia, which is quite comforting to us. When we use our prefrontal cortex, then we are looking for fight, flight, or insight. Too much change produces fight or flight syndromes. As change agents we want to produce "insight" into our learners so that they are able to apply their knowledge and skills not just in the classroom, but also on the job.

And the way to help people come to "insight" is to allow them to come to their own resolution. These moments of insight or resolutions are called "epiphanies" -- sudden intuitive leap of understanding that are quite pleasurable to us and act as rewards. Thus you have to resist the urge to fill in the entire picture of change, rather you have to leave enough gaps so that the learners are allowed to make connections of their own. Doing too much for the learners can be just as bad, if not worse, than not doing enough.

ROLE OF MANAGERS IN ORGANIZATIONAL BEHAVIOUR

As a field of study, organizational behaviour is built on a succession of approaches or ways of thinking about people. Since the early 1900s those who studied behaviour in organizations have attempted to prescribe ways to effectively manage employees in order to achieve the organization's goals. The early approaches, referred to as the classical view, promoted increased management coordination of tasks, strict specialization and standardization of work tasks, a strict chain of command, and centralized decision making at the manager level. During the 1920s and 1930s the next new school of thought began to emerge, which was referred to as the human relations movement. By and large this movement began with the famous Hawthorne studies at the Western Electric plant that demonstrated how psychological and social processes could affect productivity and work behaviour. This new way of thinking looked at organizational behaviour by advocating a more people-oriented style of management that was more participative and oriented toward employee needs. Contemporary organizational thought has shifted to a more integrative systems approach, which includes the consideration of external influences; the relationship of the organization with managers and employees; and organizational processes, which are the activities through which work gets accomplished. In other words, the best solution for the situation depends on many factors. The organization is depicted as a number of interrelated, interdependent, and interacting subsystems that are continually changing.

Those who managed by the classical approach emphasized the critical role of control and coordination in helping organizations to achieve goals. Those who managed by the human relations approach considered the risks of high levels of control and coordination, focusing instead on the need for flexibility. So where do today's managers fit in? A contemporary approach to management recognizes that there is no one best way to manage; management approaches need to be tailored to fit the situation.

The manager's role is to effectively predict, explain, and manage behaviour that occurs in organizations. Particularly, managers are interested in determining why people are more or less motivated or satisfied. Managers must have a capacity to observe and understand the behaviour patterns of individuals, groups, and organizations; to predict what responses will be drawn out by managerial actions; and ultimately to use this understanding and eventual predictions to effectively manage employees. Behaviour can be examined on three levels-the individual, the group, and the organization as a whole. Managers seek to learn more about what causes people-individually or collectively-to behave as they do in organizational settings. What motivates people? What makes some employees leaders and others not? How do people communicate and make decisions? How do organizations respond to changes in their external environments?

Although it may be said that the responsibility for studying organizational behaviour rests with researchers, assessing and increasing organizational effectiveness is a primary responsibility of managers. They need to collect data about the environment in which people work and describe events, behaviours, and attitudes in order to develop plans for changing and improving behaviour and attitudes. Managers can begin to understand organizational behaviour by accurately describing events, behaviours, and attitudes. How can this be accomplished?

Data can be gathered by observing situations, surveying and interviewing employees, and looking at written documents. These methods help to objectively describe events, behaviours, and attitudes-a first step in determining their causes and then acting on them.

By direct observation, for example, managers can attend meetings and then describe what is happening, such as who talks most often, what topics are discussed, or how frequently those attending the meeting ask for the managers' viewpoint on the topic. In addition, survey questionnaires could be sent to employees; these might provide concrete data about the situation, proving more useful than relying solely on personal perception of events. Sending the same questionnaire to employees each year could provide some insight into changes in behaviour and attitude over time. Employees could also be interviewed in order to examine attitudes in greater depth. Some valuable information about attitudes and opinions may also be gathered by talking informally with employees.

Finally, data could be gathered from organizational documents, including annual reports, department evaluations, memoranda, and other nonconfidential personnel files. An analysis of these documents might provide some insight into the attitudes of employees, the quality of management, group interactions, or other possible reasons behind the problems or situation.

Modern managers should give proper emphasis to modern theories of organizational behaviour to cope up with new problems concerning the conduct of individuals and groups within organizations. Old views and methods, which treat individuals as mere cogs and wheels of an organization, has been proven to be deficient in resolving the issues of productivity, industrial harmony, and conflict resolution. The autocratic, top - to - bottom system of management breeds discontent because individual employees feel alienated from their work. This alienation, in turn, will have a negative effect on individual productivity and will result in labour - management conflict in the long run. To avoid this, modern managers must excel in pro-active methods of organizational communication wherein individuals and groups within an organization are given enough opportunity to channel their views and aspirations to higher authorities.

The current trend in effective control and management of organizational behaviour is to increase the participation of individual employees in organizational decisions and processes. This approach gives importance to the inherent capacity of human beings to think critically and to make correct decisions based on prior knowledge and supplied information. However, this can only happen if managers are practicing efficient and effective communication with subordinates. The quality of this communication process can be measured in terms of increased productivity and decrease in labour - management conflict. Managers who excel in this constructive organizational communication scheme are considered experts in theories of organizational behaviour. More and more industries now are channelling their top - level human resource development towards this. The idea is to develop a lot of experts in organizational behaviour control to prepare the organization towards future expansion and market dominance.

To succeed in a competitive global environment, industries are now focusing their efforts in developing a proper balance between importance of organizational behaviour control and human resource management. A new system of leadership is necessary in motivating employees and subordinates to raise the level of job performance and increase productivity. This balance can ensure the over all development of organizations and will result in harmonious relationship between management and labour. As the basis of conflict is increasingly minimized, if not totally eliminated, industries can now concentrate their efforts in more productive endeavours, research and development, and in refining their organizational systems. This will result in expansion, thus generating positive growth not just for management but for the whole organization as well.

DEFINITION OF ORGANIZATIONAL BEHAVIOUR

Actions and attitudes of individuals and groups toward one another and towards the organization as a whole, and its effect on the organization's functioning and performance.

Organizational behaviour is the systematic study and careful application of knowledge about how people-as individuals and as groups-act within organizations. It strives to identify ways in which people can act more effectively. Organizational behaviour is a scientific discipline in which a large number of research studies and conceptual developments are constantly adding to its knowledge base. It is also an applied science, in that information about effective practices in one organization is being extended to many others. Organizational behaviour provides a useful set of tools at many levels of analysis. For example, it helps managers look at the behaviour of individuals within an organization. It also aids their understanding of the complexities involved in interpersonal relations, when two people (two co-workers or a superior-subordinate pair) interact. At the next level, organizational behaviour is valuable for examining the dynamics of relationships within small groups, both formal teams and informal groups. When two or more groups need to coordinate their efforts, such as engineering and sales, managers become interested in the intergroup relations that emerge. Finally, organizations can also be viewed, and managed, as whole systems that have interorganizational relationships (e.g., mergers and joint ventures). Organizational behaviour, as a relatively new discipline, has experienced some difficulty emerging as a clearly defined field of study and application. There is a lack of consensus regarding its unit of analysis (individual, group, or total organization), its greatest need (as a source of empirical data and integrating theory, or as a basis for applied information), its major focus (micro or macro issues), and its major contributions to date. This lack of clear definition has been compounded by the multiple criteria that can be used to assess its effectiveness. Issues here include identification of the relevant stakeholders, short or long time frame to wait for results, and reliance on soft or hard data (perceptions or records). All these issues deserve attention and clarification.

CONTRIBUTING DISCIPLINE TO ORGANIZATIONAL BEHAVIOUR

Most sciences share four goals-to describe, understand, predict, and control some phenomena. These are also the goals of organizational behaviour. The first objective is to describe, systematically, how people behave under a variety of conditions. Achieving this goal allows managers to communicate about human behaviour at work using a common language. A second goal is to understand why people behave as they do. Managers would be highly frustrated if they could only talk about behaviours of their employees, but not understand the reasons behind those actions. Therefore, inquisitive managers learn to probe for underlying explanations. Predicting future employee behaviour is another goal of organizational behaviour. Ideally, managers would have the capacity to predict which employees might be dedicated and productive or which ones might be absent, tardy, or disruptive on a certain day (so that managers could take preventive actions). The final goal of organizational behaviour is to control, at least partially, and develop some human activity at work. Since managers are held responsible for performance outcomes, they are vitally interested in being able to make an impact on employee behaviour, skill development, team effort, and productivity. Managers need to be able to improve results through the actions they and their employees take, and organizational behaviour can aid them in their pursuit of this goal. Some people may fear that the tools of organizational behaviour will be used to limit their freedom and take away their rights. Although that scenario is possible, it is not likely, for the actions of most managers today are subject to intense scrutiny. Managers need to remember that organizational behaviour is a human tool for human benefit. It applies broadly to the behaviour of people in all types of organizations, such as businesses, government, schools, and service organizations. Wherever organizations are, there is a need to describe, understand, predict, and better manage human behaviour.

Organizational behaviour is a blended discipline that has grown out of contributions from numerous earlier fields of study. These interdisciplinary influences are the root for what is increasingly recognized as the independent discipline of organizational behaviour. Organizational behaviour is an applied behavioural science that is built on contributions from a number of behavioural disciplines. The sciences of psychology, sociology, anthropology, political science, engineering, management and medicine are the primary fields of study out of which organizational behaviour has grown. Each of these sciences has had its own importance and unique influence on the discipline of organizational behaviour.

Psychology: Psychology is the science of human behaviour and dates back to the closing decades of the nineteenth century. Psychology traces its origins to philosophy and the science of physiology. Psychology is the science that seeks to measure, explain and sometimes change the behaviour of humans. Psychologists concern themselves with studying and attempting to understand individual behaviour.

Since its origin, psychology has itself become differentiated into a number of specialized fields, such as clinical, experimental, military, organizational and Psychology. The topics in organizational psychology, which include work teams, work motivation, training and development, power and leadership, human resource planning and workplace wellness, are very similar to the topics covered by organizational behaviour. Those who have contributed and continue to add to the knowledge of OB are learning theorist, personality theorists, counselling psychologists and most important, industrial and organizational psychologists. Industrial and organizational psychologists concern themselves with problems of fatigue, boredom, perception, learning motivation, job satisfaction, personality, performance appraisals, employee selection, job designing, work stress etc.

Medicine: It is the applied science of healing or treatment of diseases to enhance an individual's health and well-being. Medicine embraces concern for both physical and psychological health with the concern for the concern mental health dating back at least sixty years. More recently, as the war against acute diseases is being won, medical attention has shifted from the acute diseases such as influenza to the more chronic, such as hypertension. Individual behaviour and lifestyle patterns play a more important role in treating chronic diseases than in treating acute diseases. These trends have contributed to the growth of wellness programmes in the context of corporate medicine. These programmes have led to the increasing attention to medicine in organizational behaviour.

Sociology: Sociology, the science of society, has made important contributions to knowledge about group and inter group dynamics in the study of organizational behaviour. Because sociology takes the society rather than the individual as a point of departure, the sociologist is concerned with the variety of roles within a society or culture, the norms and standards of behaviour that emerge within societies and groups, and the examination of the consequences of compliant and deviant behaviour within social group. Sociologists have made their greatest contributions to organizational behaviour through their study of group behaviour in organizations, particularly formal and complex organizations. Some of the areas within organizational behaviour that have received inputs from sociologist are group dynamics, design of work teams, organizational culture, formal organizations theory and structure, organizational culture, formal organization theory and structure, organizational technology, bureaucracy, communications, power, conflict and inter group behaviour.

Social Psychology: Social psychology is a branch of psychology which borrows concepts from psychology and sociology. Social psychology focuses on the influence of people on one another. Social psychologists have made significant contributions in the area of measuring, understanding and changing attitudes; communication patterns; the way in which group activities can satisfy individual needs, and group decision-making processes.

Engineering: Engineering has made important contributions to our understanding of the design of work. By taking basic engineering ideas and applying them to human behaviour in work organizations, Fredrick Taylor had a profound influence on the early years of the study of organizational behaviour. Taylor's engineering background led him to place special emphasis of human productivity and efficiency in work behaviour. His notions of performance standards and differential piece- rate system have contributed to the growth of organizational behaviour.

Management: Originally called administrative science, is a discipline concerned with the study of overseeing activities and supervising people in organizations. It emphasizes the design, implementation, and management of various administrative and organizational systems. Management is the first discipline to take the modern corporation as the unit of analysis, and this viewpoint distinguishes the discipline's contribution to the study of organizational behaviour.

Anthropology: It is the science of human learned behaviour and is especially important to understand organizational culture. Anthropologists study societies to learn about human beings and their activities. Their work on cultures and environments has helped us understand differences in fundamental values, attitudes, and behaviour between people in different countries and within different organizations. Cultural anthropology focuses on the origins of culture and the patterns of behaviour as culture is communicated symbolically. Current research in this tradition has examined the effects of efficient cultures on organization performance and how pathological personalities may lead to dysfunctional organizational cultures. Much of our current understanding of organizational culture, organizational environments, and differences between national cultures is the result of anthropologists.

Political Science: Political scientists study the behaviour of individual and groups within a political environment. Political scientists have become increasingly aware that organizations are political entities and if we are able to accurately explain and predict the behaviour of people in organizations, we need to bring a political perspective to our analysis. The contributions of political scientists are significant to the understanding of behaviour in organizations.

CHALLENGES AND OPPORTUNITIES FOR ORGANIZATIONAL BEHAVIOUR

In the last few decades, the challenges facing organizations to effectively utilize and develop skills, knowledge, and "human capital" of their employees have been increasing. Among these challenges, those stemming from changing pressures or forces in the social and cultural, global, technological, and work environments stand out. To appreciate the way changes in the environment affect behaviour in organizations, it is useful to model an organization from an open-systems perspective. In an open system, an organization takes in resources from its external environment, where they are bought by customers.

The activities of most organizations can be modelled using the open-systems view. At the input stage, companies such as Ford, General Electric, Ralph Lauren acquire resources such as raw materials, component parts, skilled employees, robots, and computer-controlled manufacturing equipment. The challenge is to create a set of OBs and procedures that allow employees to identify and purchase high-quality resources at a favourable price. An organizational procedure is a rule or routine an employee follows to perform some task in the most effective way.

Once the organization has gathered the necessary resources, conversion begins. At the conversion stage, the organization's workforce, using appropriate skills, tools, techniques, machinery, and equipment, transforms the inputs into outputs of finished goods and services, such as cars, appliances, clothing, and hamburgers. The challenge is to develop the set of Organizational behaviours and procedures that results in high-quality goods and services produced at the lowest possible cost.

At output stage, the organization releases finished goods and services to its external environment where customers purchase and use them to satisfy their needs. The challenge is to develop the set of Organizational Behaviours and procedures that attract customers to a company's products and who come to believe in the value of a company's goods and services and thus become loyal customers. The money the organization obtains from the sales of its outputs to customers allows the organization to acquire more resources so that the cycle can begin again. The system just described is said to be open because the organization draws from and interacts with the external environment to secure resources, and then disposes of its outputs by selling its products to customers. Only by continually altering and improving its Organizational Behaviours and procedures to respond to changing environmental forces can an organization adapt and prosper over time. Organizations that fail to recognize the many changing forces in the environment lose their ability to acquire resources, to sell their products, and so they often disintegrate and disappear over time.

The challenges and opportunities of organizational behaviour could be understood through the following areas:

1. Understanding Global Organizational Behaviour: Globalization reflects a business orientation based on the belief that the world is becoming more homogeneous and that distinctions between national markets are not only fading, but, for some products will eventually disappear. International firms have found it necessary to institute formal global strategic planning to provide a means for top management to identify opportunities and threats from all over the world, formulate strategies to handle them and stipulate how to finance the strategies of these implementation. Keeping these changes in mind the challenges are to understand global organizational behaviour. The issues include:
   - The creation of a global village
   - Work force diversity
   - Improving quality and productivity to match global

standards
- Improving people skills
- Moving towards employee empowerment
- Improving ethical behaviour
- Multiculturalism and diversity.

2. Working with people from different cultures: To work effectively with people from different cultures, you need to understand how their culture and religion have shaped them and how they will respond to particular styles in management. What motivates people from one culture may not be appealing for people form another culture and this makes the work of a manager more challenging.
3. Movement of jobs to countries with low cost labour: In a global economy, jobs tend to flow to places where lower costs of labour provide business firms with a comparative advantage. Jobs are moving from U.S.A and U.K and other developed countries to developing countries like India and China. This is a threat to managers from developed counties while it is an opportunity for developing countries especially like India for we have a talented people with good knowledge of the English language.
4. Workforce Diversity: While globalization focuses on differences between people form different countries, workforce diversity addresses differences among people within a given country. Workforce diversity means that organizations are becoming more heterogeneous in terms of gender, age race etc.

2

Personality and Emotions Perception

INTRODUCTION

When we talk of personality, we don't mean a person has charm, a positive attitude toward life, a smiling face, or has won the "miss world" context. When psychologists talk of personality, they mean a dynamic concept describing the growth and development of a person's whole psychological system. The word personality has an interesting derivation.

It can be traced to the Latin words "per sonare" which translates as "to speak through". The Latin term was used to denote the masks worn by actors in ancient Greece and Rome. This Latin meaning is particularly relevant to the contemporary analysis of personality. Personality traditionally refers to how people influence others through their external appearances and actions. But for the psychologists personality includes:

- Eternal appearances and behaviour
- The inner awareness of self as a permanent organizing force, and
- The particular organization of measurable traits, both inner and outer.

Personality is an individual difference that lends consistency to a person's behaviour. Personality is defined as a relatively stable set of characteristics that influence an individual's behaviour. For our purposes, you should think of personality as the sum total of ways in which an individual reacts and interacts with others. This is most often described in terms of measurable personality traits that a person exhibits.

DEFINITION OF PERSONALITY

Though psychologists and social scientists unanimously agree to the importance of personality, they are unable to come out with a unanimous definition. Many authorities on the subject have defined personality in different ways. Some of the definitions are reproduced below:

Probably the most meaningful approach would be to include both the person and the role as Floyd L Ruch does in his definition. He states that: "the human personality includes:

- External appearance and behaviour or social stimulus value
- Inner awareness of self as a permanent organizing force
- The particular pattern or organization of measurable traits, both "inner and "outer"."

Gordon Allport gave the most frequently used definition of personality nearly 70 years ago. He said personality is "the dynamic organization within the individual of those psychophysical systems that determine his unique adjustments to his environment". J.B Kolasa defines personality as - "Personality is a broad, amorphous designation relating to fundamental approaches of persons to others and themselves. To most psychologists and students of behaviour, this term refers to the study of the characteristic traits of an individual, relationships between these traits and the way in which a person adjusts to other people and situations".

According to Gluck - "Personality is a pattern of stable states and characteristics of a person that influences his or her behaviour toward goal achievement. Each person has unique ways of protecting these states".

James D Thompson and Donald Van Houten define personality as - "a very diverse and complex psychological concept. The word "personality" may mean something like outgoing, invigorating interpersonal abilities ... but we must also recognize and explain the fact that development results in man acquiring a distinctiveness or uniqueness which gives him identity which enables him and us to recognize him as apart from others. These distinguishing characteristics are summarized by the term personality". From the above definitions we can say that personality is a very diverse and complex psychological concept. It is concerned with external appearance and behaviour, self, measurable traits, and situational interactions. The words of Clyde Kleeckholn and H. A Murray can be used to sum up the meaning of this complex term personality whey they said "that to some extent, a person's personality is like all other people's, like some other people's, like no other people's ".

MAJOR DETERMINANTS OF PERSONALITY

What determines personality? Of all the complexities and unanswered questions in the study of human behaviour, this question may be the most difficult. People are enormously complex; their abilities and interests and attitudes are diverse. An early argument in personality research was whether an individual's personality was the result of heredity or environment. Was the personality predetermined at birth, or was it the result of the individual's interaction with his or her environment? Personality appears to be a result of both influences. Additionally, today we recognize another factor - the situation. The problem lies in the fact the cognitive and psychological processes, plus many other variables, all contribute to personality. The determinants of personality can perhaps best be grouped in five broad categories: biological, cultural, family, social and situational.

BIOLOGICAL FACTORS

The study of the biological contributions to personality may be studied under three heads:

Heredity: Heredity refers to those factors that were determined at conception. Physical stature, facial attractiveness, sex, temperament, muscle composition and reflexes, energy level, and biological rhythms are characteristics that are considered to be inherent from one's parents. The heredity approach argues that the ultimate explanation of an individual's personality is the molecular structure of the genes, located in the chromosomes.

Research on animals has showed that both physical and psychological characteristics can be transmitted through heredity. But research on human beings is inadequate to support this viewpoint. However, psychologists and geneticists have accepted the fact that heredity plays an important role in one's personality.

Brain: The second biological approach is to concentrate on the role that the brain plays in personality. Though researchers make some promising inroads, the psychologists are unable to prove empirically the contribution of human brain in influencing personality. The most recent and exciting possibilities come from the work done with electrical stimulation of the brain (ESB) and split-brain psychology. Preliminary results from the electrical stimulation of the brain (ESB) research give indication that better understanding of human personality and behaviour might come Personality from the study of the brain. Work with ESB on human subjects is just beginning. There seem to be definite pleasurable and painful areas in the human brain. This being true, it may be possible physically to manipulate personality through ESB.

Biofeedback: Until recently, physiologists and psychologists felt that certain biological functions such as brainwave patterns, gastric secretions, and fluctuations in blood pressure and skin temperature were beyond conscious control. Now some scientists believe that these involuntary functions can be consciously controlled through biofeedback. In BFT the individual learns the internal rhythm of a particular body process through electronic signals feedback from equipment that is wired to the body area. From this biofeedback the person can learn to control the body process in question. More research is needed on biofeedback before any definitive conclusions can be drawn. But its potential impact could be extremely interesting for the future.

Physical features: A vital ingredient of the personality, an individual's external appearance, is biologically determined. The fact that a person is tall or short, fat or skinny, black or white will influence the person's effect on others and this in turn, will affect the self-concept. Practically all would agree that physical characteristics have at least some influence on the personality. According to Paul H. Mussen "a child's physical characteristics may be related to his approach to the social environment, to the expectancies of others, and to their reactions to him. These, in turn, may have impacts on personality development". If personality characteristics were completely dictated by heredity, they would be fixed at birth and no amount of experience could alter them. But personality characteristics are not completely dictated by heredity. There are other factors, which also influence personality.

CULTURAL FACTORS

Among the factors that exert pressures on our personality formation are the culture in which we are raised, our early conditioning, the norms among our family, friends and social groups and other influences we experience. Traditionally, cultural factors are usually considered to make a more significant contribution to personality than biological factors. The culture largely determines attributes toward independence, aggression, competition, and cooperation. According to Paul H. Mussen "each culture expects, and trains, its members to behave in the ways that are acceptable to the group. To a marked degree, the child's cultural group defines the range of experiences and situations he is likely to encounter and the values and personality characteristics that will be reinforced and hence learned". Culture requires both conformity and acceptance from its members. There are several ways of ensuring that members comply with the dictates of the culture. The personality of an individual to a marked extent is determined by the culture in which he or she is brought up. It follows that a person reared in a western culture has a different personality from a person reared in our Indian culture.

FAMILY FACTORS

Whereas the culture generally prescribes and limits what a person can be taught, it is the family, and later the social group, which selects, interprets and dispenses the culture. Thus, the family probably has the most significant impact on early personality development. A substantial amount of empirical evidence indicates that the overall home environment created by the parents, in addition to their direct influence, is critical to personality development. For example, children reared in a cold, unstimulating home are much more likely to be socially and emotionally maladjusted than children rose by parents in a warm, loving and stimulating environment. The parents play an especially important part in the identification process, which is important to the person's early development. According to Mischel, the process can be examined from three different perspectives.

- Identification can be viewed as the similarity of behaviour including feelings and attitudes between child and model.
- Identification can be looked at as the child's motives or desires to be like the model.
- It can be viewed as the process through which the child actually takes on the attributes of the model.

From all three perspectives, the identification process is fundamental to the understanding of personality development. The home environment also influences the personality of an individual. Siblings (brothers and sisters) also contribute to personality.

SOCIAL FACTORS

There is increasing recognition given to the role of other relevant persons, groups and especially organizations, which greatly influence an individual's personality. This is commonly called the socialization process. Socialization involves the process by which a person acquires, from the enormously wide range of behavioural potentialities that are open to him or her. Socialization starts with the initial contact between a mother and her new infant. After infancy, other members of the immediate family -

father, brothers, sisters and close relatives or friends, then the social group - peers, school friends and members of the work group, play influential roles. Socialization process is especially relevant to organizational behaviour because the process is not confined to early childhood, taking place rather throughout one's life. In particular, evidence is accumulating that socialization may be one of the best explanations for why employees behave the way they do in today's organizations.

SITUATIONAL FACTORS

Human personality is also influenced by situational factors. The effect of environment is quite strong. Knowledge, skill and language are obviously acquired and represent important modifications of behaviour. An individual's personality, while generally stable and consistent, does change in different situations. The different demands of different situations call forth different aspects of one's personality. According to Milgram "Situation exerts an important press on the individual. It exercises constraints and may provide push. In certain circumstances it is not so much the kind of person a man is, as the kind of situation in which he is placed that determines his actions". We should therefore not look at personality patterns in isolation.

PERSONALITY CHARACTERISTICS IN ORGANIZATIONS

Managers should learn as much as possible about personality in order to understand their employees. Hundreds of personality characteristics have been identified. We have selected eight characteristics because of their particular influences on individual behaviour in organizations. They are:

- Locus of Control
- Machiavellianism Personality
- Self-esteem
- Self-efficacy
- Self-monitoring
- Positive/Negative affect
- Risk Taking
- Type A Personality

LOCUS OF CONTROL

Some people believe they are masters of their own fate. Other people see themselves as pawns of fate, believing that what happens to them in their lives is due to luck or chance. An individual's generalised belief about internal (self) versus external (situation or others) control is called locus of control.

- Internals: Those who believe they control their destinies have been labeled internals. Internals (those with an internal locus of control) have been found to have higher job satisfaction, to be more likely to assume managerial positions, and to prefer participative management styles. In addition, internal's have been shown to display higher work motivation, hold stronger beliefs that effort leads to performance, receive higher salaries and display less anxiety than externals (those with an external locus of control).
- Externals: Externals are those individuals who believe that what happens to them is controlled by outside forces such as luck or chance. Externals prefer a more structured work setting and they may be more reluctant to participate in decision making. They are more compliant and willing to follow directions. Research on locus of control has strong implications for organizations. A large amount of research comparing internals with externals has consistently shown that individuals who rate high in externality are less satisfied with their jobs, have higher absenteeism rates, are more alienated from the work setting, and are less involved on their jobs than internals. Why are externals more dissatisfied? The answer is probably because they perceive themselves as having little control over those organizational outcomes that are important to them. Knowing about locus of control can prove valuable to managers. Because internals believe they control what happens to them, they will want to exercise control in their work environment. Allowing internals considerable voice is how work is performed is important. Internals will not react well to being closely supervised. Externals, in contrast, may prefer a more structured work setting, and they may be more reluctant to participate in decision-making.

Therefore, internals do well on sophisticated tasks - which includes most managerial and professional jobs - that require complex information processing and learning. Additionally, internals are more suited to jobs that require initiative and independence of action. In contrast, externals should do well on jobs that are well structured and routine and where success depends heavily on complying with the directions of others.

Machiavellianism

Niccolo Machiavelli was a sixteenth century Italian statesman. He wrote "The Prince", a guide for acquiring and using power. The primary method for achieving power that he suggested was manipulation of others. Machiavellianism then is a personality characteristic indicating one's willingness to do whatever it takes to get one's way. An individual high in Machiavellianism is pragmatic, maintains emotional distance and believes that ends can justify means. "If it works use it", is consistent with a high-Mach perspective.

High-Machs believe that any means justify the desired ends. They believe that manipulations of others are fine if it helps to achieve a goal. Thus, high-Machs are likely to justify their manipulative behaviour as ethical. They are emotionally detached from other people and are oriented toward objective aspects of situations.

R Christie and F.L Geis, have found that high-Mach's flourish -

- When they interact face to face with others rather than indirectly;
- When the situation has a minimum number of rules and regulations thus allowing latitude for improvisation; and
- When emotional involvement with details irrelevant to winning distracts low-Mach's.

A high-Mach individual behaves in accordance with Machiavelli's ideas, which include the notion that it is better to be feared than lived. High-Machs tend to use deceit in relationships have a cynical view of human nature and have little concern for conventional notions of right and wrong. They are skilled manipulators of other people, relying on their persuasive abilities. High-Machs are suitable in jobs that require bargaining skills or where there are substantial rewards for winning (example commissioned sales).

Self-Esteem

Self-esteem is an individual's general feeling of self-worth. Individuals with high self-esteem have positive feelings about themselves, perceive themselves to have strength as well as weaknesses, and believe their strengths are more important than their weaknesses. Individuals with low self-esteem view themselves negatively. They are more strongly affected by what other people think of them, and they compliment individuals who give them positive feedback while cutting down people who give them negative feedback.

Research on self-esteem (SE) offers some interesting insights into organizational behaviour.

i. High-SEs: People with High SEs
   - Believe they possess more of the ability they need in order to succeed at work,
   - Will take more risks in job selection and are more likely to choose unconventional jobs,
   - Are more satisfied with their jobs.

ii. Low-SEs: - People with low SEs
   - Are more susceptible to external influence,
   - Depend on the receipt of positive evaluations from others,
   - Tend to be concerned with pleasing others and therefore, are less likely to take unpopular stands, and

Are less satisfied with their jobs.

Self-esteem may be strongly affected by situations. Success tends to raise self-esteem, whereas failure tends to lower it. Given that high self-esteem is generally a positive characteristic, managers should encourage employees to raise their self-esteem by giving them appropriate challenges and opportunities for success.

Self-Efficacy

Self-efficacy refers to an individual's belief that he or she is capable of performing a task. The higher your self-efficacy, the more confidence you have in your ability to succeed in a task. So, in difficult situations, we find that people with low self-efficacy are more likely to lessen their effort or give up altogether whereas those with high self efficacy will try harder to master the challenge. In addition, individuals high in self-Personality efficacy seem to respond to negative feedback with increased effort and motivation; those low in self-efficacy are likely to lessen their effort when given negative feedback. Individuals with high self-efficacy believes that they have the ability to get things done, that they are capable of putting forth the effort to accomplish the task, and that they can overcome any obstacles to their success. There are four sources of self-efficacy:

- Prior experiences;

- Behaviour models - witnessing the success of others;
- Persuasion from other people; and
- Assessment of current physical and emotional capabilities.

Believing in one's own capability to get something done is an important facilitator of success. There is strong evidence that self-efficacy leads to high performance on a wide variety of physical and mental tasks. Managers can help employees develop their self-efficacy. This can be done by providing performance, and rewarding employee's achievements.

Self-Monitoring

A characteristic with great potential for affecting behaviour in organizations is selfmonitoring. Self-monitoring refers to an individual's ability to adjust his or her behaviour to external situational factors. High self-monitors pay attention to what is appropriate in particular situations and to the behaviour of other people, and they behave accordingly. Low self-monitors, in contrast, are not as vigilant to situational cues and act from internal states rather than paying attention to the situation. As a result, the behaviour of low self-monitors, because their behaviour varies with the situation appear to be more unpredictable and less consistent. High self-monitors are capable of presenting striking contradictions between their public persona and their private self. Low self-monitors can't disguise themselves this way.

Positive/Negative Effect

Individuals who focus on the positive aspects of themselves, other people, and the world in general are said to have positive effect. In contrast, those who accentuate the negative in themselves, others, and the world are said to possess negative affect. Employees with positive effect are absent from work less often. Individuals with negative effect report more work stress. Negative individual effect produces negative group effect and this leads to less cooperative behaviour in the work group. Managers can do several things to promote positive effect, including allowing participative decision making and providing pleasant working conditions.

Risk-Taking

People differ in their willingness to take chances. High-risk-taking managers made more rapid decisions and used less information in making their choices than the low-risktaking managers. While it is generally correct to conclude that managers in organizations are risk aversive, there are still individual differences on this dimension. As a result, it makes sense to recognise these differences and even to consider aligning risk-taking propensity with specific job demands. For example, a high-risk-taking propensity may lead to more effective performance for a stockbroker but these personality characteristics might prove a major obstacle for an auditor.

Type A and Type B Personality

Type A behaviour pattern is a complex of personality and behavioural characteristics, including competitiveness, time urgency, social status insecurity, aggression, hostility and a quest for achievements. Type A personality individual is "aggressively involved in a chronic, struggle to achieve more and more in less and less time, and if required to do so, against the opposing efforts of other things or other persons".

Type A personality:

- Are always moving, walking, and eating rapidly:
- Feel impatient with the rate at which most events take place;
- Strive to think or do two or more things simultaneously;
- Cannot cope with leisure time; and
- Are obsessed with numbers, measuring their success in terms of how much of everything they acquire.

The alternative to the Type A behaviour pattern is the Type B behaviour pattern. People with Type B personalities are relatively free of the Type A behaviours and characteristics. Type B personalities are "rarely harried by the desire to obtain a wildly increasing number of things or participate in an endless growing series of events in an ever decreasing amount of time".

Type B personality:

- Never suffer from a sense of time urgency with its accompanying impatience;
- Feel no need to display or discuss either their achievements or accomplishments unless such exposure is demanded by the situation;
- Play for fun and relaxation, rather than to exhibit their superiority at any cost; and
- Can relax without guilt.

Organizations can also be characterised as Type A or Type B

organizations. Type A individuals in Type B organizations and Type B individuals in Type A organizations experience stress related to a misfit between their personality type and the predominant type of the organization.

TRANSACTIONAL ANALYSIS

Transactional Analysis (TA) is a social-psychology developed by Eric Berne and based loosely on the theories of Sigmund Freud. Over the past four decades Eric Berne's theory has evolved to include applications to psychotherapy, counseling, education, and organizational development.

Transactional Analysis is one of the most accessible theories of modern psychology. Transactional Analysis was founded by Eric Berne, and the celebrated 'parent adult child' theory is still being developed today. Transactional Analysis has wide applications in clinical, therapeutic, organizational and personal development, encompassing communications, management, personality, relationships and behaviour.

Transactional Analysis is a powerful tool in the hands of organizational development specialists. Through presenting the basic concepts of transactional analysis and using it as the basic theory to undergird the objectives of their clients, organizational development specialists build a common strategy with which to address the particular needs of organizations and to build a functional relationship, as well as eliminate dysfunctional organizational behaviors.

ROOTS

Throughout history people have believed that each man and woman has a multiple nature. In the early 20th century, Sigmund Freud first established that the human psyche is multi-faceted. Since then, new theories continue to be put forward, all concentrating on the essential conviction that each one of us has parts of our personality which surface and affect our behaviour according to different circumstances.

In the 1950's Eric Berne began to develop his theories of Transactional Analysis. He said that verbal communication, particularly face to face, is at the centre of human social relationships and psychoanalysis. His starting-point was that when two people encounter each other, one of them will speak to the other. This he called the Transaction Stimulus. The reaction from the other person he called the Transaction Response. The person sending the Stimulus is called the Agent. The person who responds is called the Respondent. Transactional Analysis became the method of examining the transaction wherein: 'I do something to you, and you do something back'. Berne also said that each person is made up of three alter ego states, i.e. Parent, Adult and Child. These terms have different definitions than in normal language.

Parent

This is our ingrained voice of authority, absorbed conditioning, learning and attitudes from when we were young. We were conditioned by our real parents, teachers, older people, next door neighbours, aunts and uncles. Our Parent is made up of a huge number of hidden and overt recorded playbacks. Typically embodied by phrases and attitudes starting with 'how to', 'under no circumstances', 'always' and 'never forget', 'don't lie, cheat, steal', etc, etc. Our parent is formed by external events and influences upon us as we grow through early childhood. We can change it, but this is easier said than done.

Child

Our internal reaction and feelings to external events form the 'Child'. This is the seeing, hearing, feeling, and emotional body of data within each of us. When anger or despair dominates reason, the Child is in control. Like our Parent we can change it, but it is no easier.

Adult

Our 'Adult' is our ability to think and determine action for ourselves, based on received data. The adult in us begins to form at around ten months old, and is the means by which we keep our Parent and Child under control. If we are to change our Parent or Child we must do so through our adult.

In other words; Parent is our 'Taught' concept of life, Adult is our 'Thought' concept of life, and Child is our 'Felt' concept of life.

When we communicate we are doing so from one of our own alter ego states, our Parent, Adult or Child. Our feelings at the time determine which one we use, and at any time something can trigger a shift from one state to another. When we respond, we are also doing this from one of the three states, and it is in the analysis of these stimuli and responses that the essence of Transactional Analysis lies. At the core of Berne's theory is the rule that effective transactions (ie successful communications) must be complementary. They must go back from the receiving ego state to the sending ego state.

If a crossed transaction occurs, there is an ineffective communication. Worse still either or both parties will be upset. In order for the relationship to continue smoothly the agent or the respondent must rescue the situation with a complementary transaction. In serious break-downs, there is no chance of immediately resuming a discussion about the original subject matter. Attention is focused on the relationship. The discussion can only continue constructively when and if the relationship is mended.

Here are some simple clues as to the ego state sending the signal. You will be able to see these clearly in others, and in yourself:

MODERN TRANSACTIONAL ANALYSIS THEORY

Transactional Analysis is a theory which operates as each of the following:

- A theory of personality
- A model of communication
- A study of repetitive patterns of behaviour

Transactional Analysis developed significantly beyond these Berne's early theories, by Berne himself until his death in 1970, and since then by his followers and many current writers and experts.

Today there is greater understanding of Transactional Analysis. More and more people are taking the four to five year part-time training courses to qualify, and increasingly universities are accrediting these courses for masters degrees. Those taking training include psychiatrists, organizational and management consultants, teachers, social workers, designers, engineers and the clergy.

There are some key concepts in Transactional Analysis which are outlined here.

TA: CONTRACTING

Transactional Analysis is a contractual approach. A contract is "an explicit bilateral commitment to a well-defined course of action" Berne E. (1966). Which means that all parties need to agree:

- Why they want to do something
- With whom
- What they are going to do
- By when
- Any fees, payment or exchanges there will be

Contracts need to be outlined in positive words i.e. what is wanted, rather than what is not wanted. Our minds tend to focus on the negative and so this encourages failure. We have contracts about employment, how much will we be paid and when, what holidays we are due, what deductions there will be etc. In order to ensure placements are effective then different, but similar, details are required. Naturally, these details will vary dependent on the setting in which we work.

All parties need to state what are they are prepared to do. Are they able and willing to undertake what is being asked, is this appropriate? Does it fit within any statements of purpose and function? Is it legal? Do they have the competence to deliver this? Do they want to? What does each party want of the others?

In short contracts need to be: measurable, manageable and motivational. Measurable means that the goals need to be tangible. That each party involved in the contract will be able to say in advance how they will know when the goal has been achieved. The goal will be specific and behavioural and clearly defined. The contract will also need to be manageable and feasible for all those concerned.

TA: EGO STATES

Berne devised the concept of ego states to help explain how we are made up, and how we relate to others. They categorise the ways we think, feel and behave and are called Parent, Adult, and Child. Each ego state is given a capital letter to denote the difference between actual parents, adults and children.

Parent ego state

This is a set of feelings, thinking and behaviour that we have copied from our parents and significant others. As we grow up we take in ideas, beliefs, feelings and behaviours from our parents and caretakers. If we live in an extended family then there are more people to learn and take in from. When we do this, it is called introjecting and it is just as if we take in the whole of the care giver. For example, we may notice that we are saying things just as our father, mother, grandmother may have done, even though, consciously, we don't want to. We do this as we have lived with this person so long that we automatically reproduce certain things that were said to us, or treat others as we might have been treated.

Adult ego state

The Adult ego state is about direct responses to the here and now. We deal with things that are going on today in ways that are not unhealthily influenced by our past. The Adult ego state is about being spontaneous and aware with the capacity for intimacy. When in our Adult we are able to see people as they are, rather than what we project onto them. We ask for information rather than stay scared and rather than make assumptions. Taking the best from the past and using it appropriately in the present is an integration of the positive aspects of both our Parent and Child ego states. So this can be called the Integrating Adult.

Child ego state

The Child ego state is a set of behaviours, thoughts and feelings which are replayed from our own childhood. The process of analysing personality in terms of ego states is called structural analysis. It is important to remember that ego states do not have an existence of their own, they are concepts to enable understanding. Therefore it is important to say "I want some fun" rather than "My Child wants some fun". We may be in our Child ego state when we say this, but saying "I" reminds us to take responsibility for our actions.

TA: DESCRIPTIVE MODEL

This model shows how we function or behave with others. The model used here is divided up into nine and we have used S. Temple's (1999) term "mode" as it differentiates it from the structural ego state model mentioned above.

Ineffective modes

Negative Controlling Parent - communicates a "You're not OK" message, and is punitive.

Negative Nurturing Parent - communicates a "You're not OK" message. When in this mode the person will often do things for others which they are capable of doing for themselves. When in this mode the person is engulfing and overprotective.

Negative Adapted Child - expresses an "I'm not OK" message. When in this mode the person over-adapts to others and tends to experience such emotions as depression, unrealistic fear and anxiety.

Negative Free Child - in this mode the person runs wild with no restrictions or boundaries. In this mode they express a "You're not OK" message.

Effective modes

Positive Nurturing Parent - communicates the message "You're OK". When in this mode the person is caring and affirming.

Positive Controlling Parent - communicates the message "You're OK". This is the boundary setting mode, offering constructive criticism, whilst being caring but firm.

Positive Adapted Child - communicates an "I'm OK" message. From this mode we learn the rules to help us live with others.

Positive Free Child - communicates an "I'm OK" message. This is the creative, fun loving, curious and energetic mode.

Accounting mode - communicates "We're OK" messages. The Adult is able to assess reality in the here and now. When the Accounting mode is in the executive position it is possible to choose which of the other effective modes to go into, dependent on the situation. This is then called Accounting Mode. When using the descriptive behavioural model the term Accounting Mode helps to differentiate it from the structural model where it is referred to as Adult. When stable in this Accounting Mode we are taking account of the present context and situation and deciding the most appropriate mode to come from. We are then able to respond appropriately rather than flipping into archaic or historic ways of being, thinking and behaving which are likely to be inappropriate and unhelpful.

TA: DIAGNOSIS

It is helpful to be able to assess or diagnose which ego state in the structural model, or which mode in the descriptive model, somebody is in. In this way we can respond appropriately as well as ensure which mode we are addressing. However, when we work with other staff or are relating with young people, we are responding on the behavioural level. It is not always possible, or appropriate, to be undertaking more in-depth types of diagnosis.

TA: STROKES

In Transactional Analysis we call compliments and general ways of giving recognition strokes. This name came from research which indicated that babies require touching in order to survive and grow. It apparently makes no difference whether the touching induces pain or pleasure - it is still important. On the whole we prefer to receive negative strokes than no strokes at all, at least that way we know we exist and others know we exist.

We all have particular strokes we will accept and those we will reject. For example, if we have always been told we are clever, and our brother is creative, then we are likely to accept strokes for being clever, but not for being creative. From this frame of reference only one person in the family can be the creative one and so on. Stroking can be physical, verbal or nonverbal. It is likely that the great variety of stroke needs and styles present in the world results from differences in wealth, cultural mores, and methods of parenting.

TA: LIFE POSITIONS

Life positions are basic beliefs about self and others, which are used to justify decisions and behaviour.

When we are conceived we are hopefully at peace, waiting to emerge into the world once we have grown sufficiently to be able to survive in the outside of the womb. If nothing untoward happens we will emerge contented and relaxed. In this case we are likely to perceive the world from the perspective of I am OK and You are OK.

TA: WORKING STYLES

These are ways in which we defend against the injunctions. These are very helpful to us and when we understand them we can work to their strengths through choice, rather than because subconsciously we believe we have to do things this way to be okay. The names of five working styles have been developed, these are:

- Be perfect
- Be strong
- Try hard
- Please others
- Hurry up

TA: GAMES

We are sure that every one of us must have been in the situation where we have said, "Why does this always keep happening to me" or "I always keep meeting people who hurt me and then go off and leave me". Sometimes it may be that we like to help people and then it goes wrong as the person we were trying to help says that we didn't do it well enough and that we got it wrong. We might think "Well, I was only trying to help" and feel got at.

When similar situations keep happening over and over again then the term Transactional Analysis uses for this is a game. A game is a familiar pattern of behaviour with a predictable outcome. Games are played outside Games are learned patterns of behaviour, and most people play a small number of favourite games with a range of different people and in varying intensities.

First Degree games are played in social circles generally lead to mild upsets not major traumas.

Second Degree games occur when the stakes may be higher. This usually occurs in more intimate circles, and ends up with an even greater negative payoff.

Third Degree games involve tissue damage and may end up in the jail, hospital or morgue.

Games vary in the length of time that passes while they are being played. Some can take seconds or minutes while others take weeks months or even years. People play games for these reasons:

· To structure time

· To acquire strokes

· To maintain the substitute feeling and the system of thinking, beliefs and actions that go with it

· To confirm parental injunctions and further the life script

· To maintain the person's life position by "proving" that self/ others are not OK

· To provide a high level of stroke exchange while blocking intimacy and maintaining distance

· To make people predictable. Adult awareness and they are our best attempt to get our needs met - although of course we don't.

Dealing with games

There are various ways to stop a game, including the use of different options than the one automatically used. We can:

· Cross the transaction by responding from a different ego state than the one the stimulus is designed to hook.

· Pick up the ulterior rather than the social message.

· The opening message to the game always entails a discount. There are further discounts at each stage of the game. By detecting discounts we can identify game invitations and defuse them with options. (A discount is when we minimise, maximise or ignore some aspect of a problem which would assist us in resolving it).

· Replace the game strokes. Loss of strokes to the Child ego state means a threat to survival. We get a great many strokes from games, even if they are negative. However, if we don't obtain sufficient positive strokes, or give ourselves positive strokes, we will go for quantity rather than quality of strokes and play games to get them. This loss of strokes is also a loss of excitement that the game has generated.

MEASURING PERSONALITY

Several methods can be used to assess personality. These include projective tests, behavioural measures and self-report questionnaires. These measures of personality are explained below: -

THE PROJECTIVE TESTS

In these tests, individuals are shown a picture, abstract image, or photo and are asked to describe what they see or to tell a story about what they see. The rationale behind projective tests is that each individual responds to the stimulus in a way that reflects his or her unique personality. The Rorschach inkblot test, Thematic Apperception test (TAT), sentence completion method are projective tests commonly used to assess personality.

Research evidence concerning the validity of projective techniques as a whole is very disappointing. Projective tests continue to suffer from a lack of objectivity in scoring and an absence of adequate norms. Nevertheless, in clinical practice, projective tests continue to be popular and valued diagnostic tool.

BEHAVIOURAL MEASURES

There are behavioural measures of personality as well. Using an observational technique known as behavioural assessment, psychologist can count and record the frequency of particular behaviours. For example, we might assess a person's sociability; by counting the number of times he or she approaches strangers at a party. The behaviour is scored in some manner to produce an index of personality. Although much can be learned from observation, it has the following shortcomings -

- It is time-consuming and expensive.
- What is observed may be misinterpreted.
- Two observers can view the same event and interpret it differently.
- The presence of the observer can alter the behaviour being

observed.

SELF-REPORT QUESTIONNAIRE

The most common method of assessing personality is the self-report questionnaire. Individuals respond to a series of questions, usually in an agree/disagree or true/false format. The widely recognized self-report questionnaire are:

Minnesota Multiphasic Personality Inventory (MMPI)

Myers-Briggs Type Indicator (MBTI): Minnesota Multiphasic Personality Inventory (MMPI): The MMPI is comprehensive and assesses a variety of traits, as well as various neurotic or psychotic disorders. Used extensively in psychological counselling to identify disorders, the MMPI is a long questionnaire. It is useful in the screening, diagnosis and clinical description of abnormal behaviour, but does not reveal differences among normal personalities very well.

The Myers-Briggs Type Indicator (MBTI): Another popular self-report questionnaire is the Myers-Briggs Type Indicator (MBTI). It is essentially a 100 -question personality test that asks people how they usually feel or act in particular situations. Katharine Briggs and her daughter, Isabel Briggs Myers, developed the Myers-Briggs Type Indicator to put Jung's type theory into practical use. The MBTI is used extensively in organizations as a basis for understanding individual differences. The MBTI has been used in career counselling, team building, conflict management and understanding management styles.

Based on the answers individuals give to the test, they are classified as:

- Extroverted or Introverted (E or I)
- Sensing or Intuitive (S or N)
- Thinking or Feeling (T or F) and
- Perceiving or Judging (P or J)

There are four basic preferences in type theory and two possible choices for each of the four preferences. The combination of these preferences makes up an individual's psychological type.

MATCHING PERSONALITIES AND JOBS

Obviously, individual personalities differ. So, too do jobs. Following this logic, efforts have been made to match the proper personalities with the proper jobs. John Holland's "personality-job fit theory" is concerned with matching the job requirements with personality characteristics. The personality-job fit theory identifies 6 personality types and proposes that the fit between personality type and occupational environment determines satisfaction and turnover.

Holland has developed a Vocational Preference Inventory Questionnaire that contains 160 occupational titles. Respondents indicate which of these occupations they like or dislike, and these answers are used to form personality profiles. Six major personality types have been identified.

TRAIT THEORIES

INTRAPSYCHIC THORY

Based on the work of Sigmund Freud, Intrapsychic theory emphasises the unconscious determinants of behaviour.

The Components of Personality

Freud proposed a new conception of the personality, one that contains three systems - the id, the ego, and the superego. These systems do not exist physically; they are only concepts, or ways of looking at personality.

1. Id: The id is the only part of the personality that is present at birth. It is inherited, primitive, inaccessible and completely unconscious. The id contains
   - The life instincts, which are sexual instincts and the biological urges such as hunger and thirst, and
   - The death instinct, which accounts for our aggressive and destructive impulses. The id operates according to the pleasure principle; that is, to seek pleasure, avoid pain and gain immediate gratification of its wishes. The id is the source of the libido, the psychic energy that fuels the entire personality; yet the id cannot act on its own. It can only wish, image, fantasize, and demand.
2. Ego: The ego is the logical, rational, realistic part of the personality. The ego evolves from the id and draws its energy from the id. One of the ego functions is to satisfy the id's urges. But the ego, which is mostly conscious, acts according to the reality principle. It must consider the constraints of the real world in determining appropriate times, places, and object for gratification of the id's wishes.

3. Superego: when the child is age 5 or 6 the superego - the moral component of the personality - is formed. The superego has two parts -

- The "conscience" consists of all the behaviours for which we have been punished and about which we feel guilty;
- The "ego ideal" contains the behaviours for which we have been praised and rewarded and about which we feel pride and satisfaction.

In its quest for moral perfection, the superego sets moral guide that define and limit the flexibility of ego.

- Defence Mechanisms: A defence mechanism is a technique used to defend against anxiety and to maintain self-esteem, but it involves self-deception and the distortion of reality. We use defence mechanisms to protect us from failure and from guilt arousing desires or actions. All of us use defence mechanisms to some degree; it is only their overuse that is considered abnormal.
- Repression: According to Freud, repression is the most important and frequently used defence mechanism. Repression operates in two ways:
  — It can remove painful or threatening memories, thoughts, ideas or perceptions from consciousness and keep them in the unconscious.
  — It can prevent unconscious but disturbing sexual and aggressive impulses from breaking into consciousness.
- Projection: We use projection when we attribute our own undesirable impulses, thoughts, personality traits or behaviour to others, or when we minimize the undesirable in ourselves and exaggerate it in others. Projection allows us to avoid acknowledge our unacceptable traits and thereby to maintain our self-esteem, but it seriously distorts our perception of the external world. For example (1) A sexually promiscuous wife may accuse her husband of being unfaithful. (2) A dishonest man may think everyone is out to cheat him.
- Denial: It is a refusal to acknowledge consciously or to believe that a danger or a threatening condition exists. For example (1) Smokers use denial when they refuse to admit that cigarettes are a danger to their health. (2) Many people who abuse alcohol

and drugs deny that they have a problem. Yet denial is sometimes useful as a temporary means of getting through a crisis until a more permanent adjustment can be made, such as when people initially deny the existence of a terminal illness.

- Rationalization: It occurs when we unconsciously supply a logical, rational, or socially acceptable reason rather than the real reason for an action or event. Rationalization can be used to justify past, present, or future behaviours or to soften the disappointment connected with not attaining a desired goal. When we rationalize, we make excuses for or justify, our failures and mistakes.
- Regression: Sometimes, when frustrated or anxious, we may use regression and revert to behaviour that might have reduced anxiety at an earlier stage of development. For example, an adult may have a temper tantrum, rant and rave or through things.
- Reaction Formation: is at work when people express exaggerated ideas and emotions that are the opposite of their disturbing, unconscious impulses and desires. In reaction formation the conscious thought or feeling masks the unconscious one. For example, a former chain smoker becomes irate and complains loudly at the faintest whiff of cigarette smoke.
- Displacement: Occurs when we substitute a less threatening object or person for Personality the original object of a sexual or aggressive impulse. For example, if your boss makes you angry, you may take out your hostility on your wife.
- Sublimation: With sublimation, we re-channel sexual or aggressive energy into pursuits or accomplishments that society considers acceptable or even praiseworthy. For example, an aggressive person may re-channel the aggression and become a football player. Freud viewed sublimation as the only completely healthy ego defence mechanism.

PSYCHO-ANALYTICAL SOCIAL LEARNING

Evaluating Freud's Contribution: Freud's theory is so comprehensive that its elements must be evaluated separately. As we have seen, Freud believed that his concepts of the unconscious and the principles by which it operates were his most important work. In fact the primary aim of psychoanalysis is to bring unconscious thoughts, wishes and desires to consciousness. Leading scholars today do not dispute the existence of unconscious processes. However, they do not see the unconscious as envisioned by Freud and they disagree as to how sophisticated or simple it might be.

Freud is a towering figure in the world of psychology, but today he does not loom as large as in decades past. There are very strict Freudians left, and for most psychoanalysts, Freud's techniques constitute only a part of their therapeutic arsenal. Sigmund Freud has been both worshipped and ridiculed, but his standing as a pioneer in psychology cannot be denied.

- Social Learning Theory: The main focus of social learning approach is on the patterns of behaviour the individuals learn in coping with environment. Some behaviour patterns are learned or acquired through direct experience. Responses can also be acquired or learned without direct reinforcement. Individuals can also learn by observing what happens to other people and just be being told about something, as well as direct experiences. So, for example much of what we have learned comes from watching models - parents, teachers, peers, bosses etc. This view that we can learn through both observation and direct experience has been called social-learning theory.

  Social-learning theory acknowledges the existence of observational learning and the importance of perception in learning. People respond to how they perceive and define consequences, not to the objective consequences themselves. The influence of models is central to the social-learning process. Four processes have been found to determine the influence that a model will have on an individual. They are-

- Attentional Processes: People tend to be most influenced by models that are attractive and important to us. As the model influences them they learn from the model by paying attention to them.

- Retention Processes: A model's influence will depend on how well the individual remembers the model's action after the model is no longer available.

- Motor Reproduction Processes: After a person has seen a new behaviour by observing the model, the watching must be converted to doing. This process then demonstrates that the individual can perform the modelled activities.

- Reinforcement Processes: Individuals will be motivated to exhibit the modelled behaviour if positive incentives or rewards are provided. Behaviours that are reinforced will be given more attention, learned better, and performed more often. Reinforcement that controls the expression of learned behaviour may be:
- Direct: It refers to the social approval or disapproval or alleviation of aversive conditions, and other tangible rewards.
- Vicarious: It refers to observation of someone else receiving reward or punishment for similar behaviour.
- Self-administered: It refers to evaluation of one's own performance with self-praise.

Of all these, self-administered reinforcement theory plays a vital role in social learning theory.

Evaluation of Social Learning Theory: Social learning theory has made a significant contribution to personality theory.

- It enables us to look more clearly at human actions as reactions to specific conditions or circumstances rather than merely symbolic manifestations of internal and unconscious forces.
- It emphasis on the environmental variables that elicit specific behaviours.

Social learning theory has been criticised on two grounds:

- It overemphasise the importance of situational factors in behaviour.
- The experimental methods used by social learning theorists are particularly sensitive to the impact of situational variables and are apt to emphasise change in behaviour.

JOB FIT THEORY

The personality-job Fit Theory assumes that examining a person's personality will give insight into their adaptability in an organization. By matching the personality with the company we can achieve a better synergy and avoid problems like high turnover and low job satisfaction. The person-job fit theory is a study of personality attributes and the requirements of the job. The matching of the job requirements with personality characteristics is given in John Holland's Personality-job fit theory. This theory is based on the notion of fit between an individual's personality characteristics and his or her occupational environment. Holland presents six personality types and proposes that satisfaction and the propensity to leave a job depends on the degree to which individuals successfully match their personality to an occupational environment. Holland has developed a vocational reference inventory questionnaire that contains 160 occupational titles. Respondents indicate which of these occupations they like or dislike, and their answers are used to form personality profiles. The person-job fit theory argues that satisfaction is highest and turnover lowest when personality and occupation are in agreement. Social individuals should be in social jobs, conventional people in conventional jobs and so forth. A realistic person in a realistic job is in a more congruent situation than is a realistic person in an investigative job.

CONCLUSION

When psychologists talk of personality, they mean a dynamic concept describing the growth and development of a person's whole psychological system. Personality is defined as a relatively stable set of characteristics that influence an individual's behaviour. Personality is a very diverse and complex psychological concept. It is concerned with external appearance and behaviour, self, measurable traits, and situational interactions. Personality appears to be a result of heredity and environment. Additionally, today we recognize another factor - the situation. Managers should learn as much as possible about personality in order to understand their employees. Several methods can be used to assess personality. These include projective tests, behavioural measures and self-report questionnaires.

Note: For a case study visit Goodrich Corporation's site. Goodrich is a supplier of aerospace components, systems and services to the commercial and general aviation airplane markets. The company primarily operates in the US. It is headquartered in Charlotte, North Carolina and employs about 25,000 people. www.goodrich.com

3

Motivation

First, productivity is a function of each of the employees' unique personalities. Second, employees' behaviours are influenced by the environments in which they find themselves. For example, an employee's behaviour (and productivity) will be influenced by a dirty, hot, noisy, or dangerous worksite. Finally, an employee's behaviour will be a function of that employee's innate drives or felt needs and the opportunities he or she has to satisfy those drives or needs in the workplace.

Employees' performance is, of course, partially determined by the opportunities given them to demonstrate their abilities. If employees are never given opportunities to utilize all of their skills, then the employer may never have the benefit of their total performance. Work performance is also contingent upon employee abilities. If employees lack the learned skills or innate talents to do a particular job, then performance will be less than optimal. A third dimension of performance is motivation.

A generalized model of motivation posits a set of innate drives and felt needs for each employee. The employee brings these drives and needs to the workplace and they influence the employee's workplace behaviour and productivity. These drives and needs create a tension within the employee if left unsatisfied. This tension may be both physical (manifested through the symptoms of stress) and psychological. The employee thus engages in whatever behaviours are necessary to reduce this tension. If the behaviour undertaken is appropriate, it may be assumed that the tension is reduced and that tension-reducing behaviours are ceased.

NEEDS: an internal state of disequilibrium or deficiency which has the capacity to energize or trigger a behavioural response.

As seen in the discussion above, motivation is a dynamic process; people may be motivated by different things (needs and drives) during different periods of their lives. In the following sections, we will discuss both content and process theories of motivation.

Content theories focus on the differences among different employees' needs. Process theories focus on the choices individual employees get to make regarding their actions.

THEORIES OF MASLOW

Motivational theories dealing with the needs of employees fall under the general rubric of Content Theories of Motivation. Content theories posit that workers' behaviours are a function of the workers' abilities to satisfy their felt needs at the workplace. A basic assumption of all need theories is that, when need deficiencies exist, individuals are motivated into action in order to satisfy them. The best known of the Content Theories of Motivation is Maslow's Hierarchy of Needs. (Abraham Maslow)

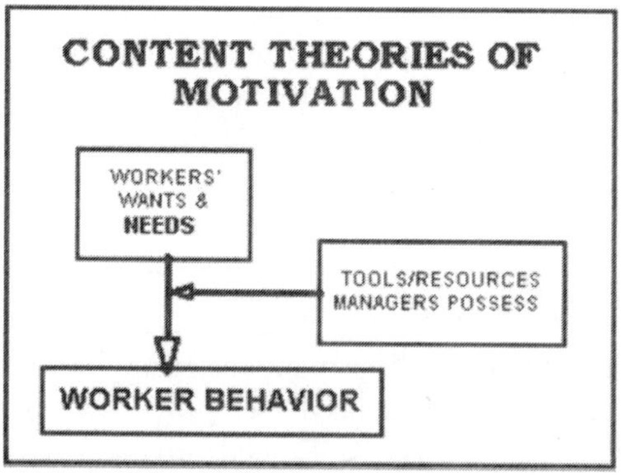

Maslow's Hierarchy of Needs is based on the assumption that people are motivated by a series of five universal needs. These needs are ranked, according to the order in which they influence human behaviour, in hierarchical fashion.

- Physiological needs are deemed to be the lowest- level needs. These needs include the need for food, oxygen, sex, and drink.

— So long as physiological needs are unsatisfied, they exist as a driving or motivating force in a person's life. A hungry person has a felt need. This felt need sets up both psychological and physical tensions that manifest themselves in overt behaviours directed at reducing those tensions (getting something to eat). Once the hunger is sated, the tension is reduced, and the need for food ceases to motivate. At this point (assuming the needs for sex, drink, and other physiological requirements are also satisfied) the next higher order need becomes the motivating need.

- Thus, safety needs -- the needs for shelter and security -- become the motivators of human behaviour.

  — Safety needs include a desire for security, stability, dependency, protection, freedom from fear and anxiety, and a need for structure, order, and law. In everyday life, we may see this as a need to be able to fall asleep at night, secure in the knowledge that we will awake alive and unharmed. In the workplace this needs translates into a need for at least a minimal degree of employment security; the knowledge that we cannot be fired on a whim and that appropriate levels of effort and productivity will ensure continued employment.

- Social needs include the need for belongingness and love.

  — Generally, as gregarious creatures, human have a need to belong. In the workplace, this need may be satisfied by an ability to interact with one's coworkers and perhaps to be able to work collaboratively with these colleagues.

- After social needs have been satisfied, ego and esteem needs become the motivating needs.

  — Esteem needs include the desire for self-respect, self-esteem, and the esteem of others. When focused externally, these needs also include the desire for reputation, prestige, status, fame, glory, dominance, recognition, attention, importance, and appreciation.

- The highest need in Maslow's hierarchy is that of self-actualization; the need for self-realization, continuous self-development, and the process of becoming all that a person is capable of becoming.

Douglas MacGregor (of Theory X and Theory Y fame) used to following example to illustrate the motivating potential of unfulfilled needs in Maslow's Theory:

Consider your own need for air. Except as you are deprived of it, it has no appreciable motivating effect upon your behaviour. Money is usually considered relatively unimportant for satisfying higher-level needs. The general belief is that most workers, because of adequate levels of pay, are mainly concerned about higher-level needs. Douglas MacGregor, in attempting to explain the extent to which one may observe Theory X - type behaviour in many organizations, suggests that organizations do little to satisfy their employee's higher-order needs (Social and Esteem). In general, a pay cheque allows employees to satisfy their lower order needs (Physiological and Safety).

HERZBERG'S TWO FACTOR THEORY

MOTIVATON-HYGIENE THEORY

The motivation of employees is important to organizations since it is one of several factors that significantly affects the productivity of employees. Raising the level of motivation increases profitability through greater creativity and commitment in employees.

Herzberg's Two Factor Theory, also known as the Motivation-Hygiene Theory, was derived from a study designed to test the concept that people have two sets of needs:

- Their needs as animals to avoid pain
- Their needs as humans to grow psychologically

Herzberg's Study

Herzberg's study consisted of a series of interviews that sought to elicit responses to the questions:

- Recall a time when you felt exceptionally good about your job. Why did you feel that way about the job? Did this feeling affect your job performance in any way? Did this feeling have an impact on your personal relationships or your well- being?
- Recall a time on the job that resulted in negative feelings? Describe the sequence of events that resulted in these negative feelings.

RESEARCH RESULTS

It appeared, from the research, that the things making people happy on the job and those making them unhappy had two separate themes.

SATISFACTION (MOTIVATION)

Five factors stood out as strong determiners of job satisfaction:

- Achievement
- Recognition
- Work itself
- Responsibility
- Advancement

The last three factors were found to be most important for bringing about lasting changes of attitude. It should be noted, that recognition refers to recognition for achievement as opposed to recognition in the human relations sense.

DISSATISFACTION (HYGIENE)

The determinants of job dissatisfaction were found to be:

- Company policy
- Administrative policies
- Supervision
- Salary

- Interpersonal relations
- Working conditions

It appears that the central theme of the satisfiers (also called motivators) is one having to do with the relationship the employee has with his or her job; job content. The theme of the dissatisfiers appears to be related to the environment or context of the job. These dissatisfiers seem to have little effect on positive job attitudes (in some of the literature, these dissatisfiers were called hygiene or maintenance factors).

TWO DIMENSIONS

At the psychological level, the two dimensions of job attitudes appear to reflect a two-dimensional need structure:

- One need structure for the avoidance of unpleasantness, and
- A parallel need system for personal growth

For Herzberg, motivation results from personal growth and is based on an innate need to grow. In other words, people find satisfaction in work that is interesting and challenging. A desire to fulfill our potential drives us to seek growth and provides the incentive to achieve. According to Herzberg, the idea that the work one does is significant leads, ultimately, to satisfaction with the the work itself. Employees will be motivated to do work that they percieve to be significant.

From a philosophical perspective, it is Herzberg's position that it is the responsibility of society's dominant institutions to provide for the growth and well being of people. In our society, one such dominant organization is the business institution. Therefore it is the responsibility of business and industry to provide the means for growth and self actualization.

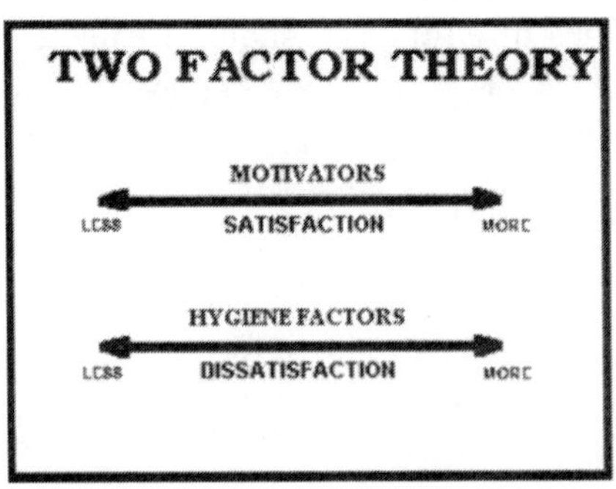

Herzberg's theory thus posits that there are two classes of factors that influence employee motivation; intrinsic factors and the extrinsic factors. The intrinsic factors were also called the motivator factors and were related to job satisfaction. The extrinsic factors were called hygiene factors and were related to job dissatisfaction.

Motivators (intrinsic factors) led to job satisfaction because of a need for growth and self actualization, and hygiene (extrinsic) factors led to job dissatisfaction because of a need to avoid unpleasantness. The negative or positive KITA or "kick in the a**" approach to employee motivation yields short- range results, but rarely generates any actual motivation. In fact, to call it an "approach to motivation" is to clearly misunderstand motivation as Herzberg understood it. KITA yields movement -- the avoidance of pain -- not motivation.

Positive KITA, in the form of raises and incentives reduces time spent at work, inflates wages and benefits, and overemphasizes human relations. K-I-T-A techniques fail to instill self-generating motivation in workers. Job content factors, such as achievement and responsibility, are motivators, while job environment factors are hygiene or KITA factors. Motivators are the key to satisfaction.

APPLICABILITY

In an era of increasing competition, it is important for organizations to effectively utilize all available resources; including human resources. In the workplace, the motivation of employees is important to the organization as it is one of the variables that affects the employee productivity. Fundamental to Herzberg's position is the notion that motivation is a result of personal growth and is based on an innate need to grow. What this means is that people find satisfaction in work that is interesting and challenging.

JOB ENRICHMENT

Job Enrichment: The idea of job enrichment is probably the most significant contribution of Herzberg's theory. Meaningful tasks allow for growth, and job enrichment is a relatively simple method for facilitating this growth:

- Adding different tasks to a job to provide greater involvement and interaction with the task.

Adding tasks can raise the level of challenge in any particular job to a level commensurate with the abilities of an employee. It might be argued that, if a job can not be enriched and it is not challenging to the person in that position, then that person ought to be replaced by someone who will find the job challenging.

JOB LOADING

Job Loading: There are two forms of job loading.

- Horizontal job loading: adding tasks to a job but not adding any responsibility or challenge -- the meaningless of the job is simply increased. Horizontal loading ought to be avoided!
- Vertical job loading: adding meaningful tasks that will lead to growth -- additional tasks that permit growth and provide motivating factors.

Examples of vertical job loading:

- Increasing accountability
- Removing controls
- Making periodic reports available to workers
- Granting job freedom
- Granting job authority
- Introducing new and challenging tasks assigning specific or specialized tasks

By providing motivators and removing hygienes, management can facilitate the growth of employees. This is essential to both the individual and the organization.Growth makes the employee more valuable to the organization because of his/her ability to perform higher order duties.

ANSWERING THE CRITICS OF THE THEORY

Critics of Herzberg's theory argue that the sample population was small and limited to a group of professionals. Numerous replication studies have been performed to check the validity of the original results. Mostly, the results are comparable to the results obtained in the original experiment and indicate that motivators are the primary cause of job satisfaction. There is also the criticism that the study applies only to middle management professionals (the original sample consisted of 200 middle management professionals).

However, an application of Maslow's concepts suggests that people work to achieve what they do not have. As such, the set of motivators can differ from person to person. Instead of saying that Herzberg's findings only apply to middle level professionals, it would be more correct to say that Herzberg's findings apply to people that have needs and wants similar to the test subjects.

When attempting to motivate employees, it is important to know their needs. Effective motivation results from a determination of what will motivate employees and then providing the factors that address those needs.

THEORY OF MCCELLAND

THE THEMATIC APPERCEPTION TEST (TAT) AND MCCLELLAND'S ACHIEVEMENT MOTIVATION THEORY

Motivation research has long considered human motives and needs. However, isolating people's motivational needs can be a difficult process because most people are not explicitly aware of what their motives are.

In attempting to understand employee motivation, Abraham Maslow proposed a hierarchy of needs. David McClelland furthered this idea in his learned needs theory. McClelland's experimental work identified sets of motivators present to varying degrees in different people. He proposed that these needs were socially acquired or learned. That is, the extent to which these motivators are present varies from person to person, and depends on the individual and his or her background.

McClelland's experiment -- the Thematic Apperception Test (TAT) -- consisted of showing individuals a series of pictures and asking them to give brief descriptions of what was happening in the pictures. The responses were analyzed in terms of the presence or absence of certain themes. The themes McClelland and his associates were looking for revolved around the following motivators: achievement, affiliation and power.

According to David McClelland, regardless of culture or gender, people are driven by three motives:

- Achievement,
- Affiliation
- Influence

Since McClelland's first experiments, over 1,000 studies relevant to achievement motivation have been conducted. These studies strongly support the theory.

ACHIEVEMENT

The need for achievement is characterized by the wish to take responsibility for finding solutions to problems, master complex tasks, set goals, get feedback on level of success.

AFFILIATION

The need for affiliation is characterized by a desire to belong, an enjoyment of teamwork, a concern about interpersonal relationships, and a need reduce uncertainty.

POWER

The need for power is characterized by a drive to control and influence others, a need to win arguments, a need to persuade and prevail.

According to McClelland, the presence of these motives or drives in an individual indicates a predisposition to behave in certain ways. Therefore, from a manager's perspective, recognizing which need is dominant in any particular individual affects the way in which that person can be motivated.

UNDERSTANDING MOTIVES

High achievement motivation

Specifically, achievement motivation is defined as a non-conscious concern for achieving excellence through individual efforts. Such individuals set challenging goals for themselves, assume personal responsibility for goal accomplishment, are highly persistent in the pursuit of these goals, take calculated risks to achieve the goals, and actively collect and use information for purposes of feedback.

High achievement motivated managers are also strongly inclined to be personally involved in performing their organizational tasks. However, they may also be reluctant to delegate authority and responsibility. Thus, high achievement motivation may be expected to result in poor performance of high- level executives in large organizations.

High achievement motivation is predicted to contribute to effective entrepreneurship and effective leadership of small task-oriented groups.

Achievement motivation is positively related to the leadership of small task-oriented groups and small entrepreneurial firms and negatively related to the effectiveness of high- level managers in complex organizations or in political situations.

High power motivation

Power motivation is defined as the concern for acquiring status and having an impact on others. McClelland used power motivation as a measure of social influence behaviours. Clearly, since most management activities require the use of social influence behaviours and since power motivation measures an individual's desire to influence, the power motive is important for leadership effectiveness.

David McClelland proposed the Leader Motive Profile Theory (LMP theory) in which he argued that a high power motivation, greater than the affiliation motive, is predictive of leader effectiveness.

Highly power-motivated individuals obtain great satisfaction from the exercise of influence. Consequently, their interest in the exercise of leadership is sustained.

High power motivation is predicted to result in effective managerial performance in middle and high-level positions. However, unless constrained in some manner, some power-motivated managers may also be predicted to exercise power in an aggressive manner for self-aggrandizing purposes, to the detriment of their organizations.

High affiliation motivation

Affiliative motivation is defined as a nonconscious concern for establishing, maintaining, and restoring close personal relationships with others. Individuals with high affiliative motivation tend to be non-assertive, submissive, and dependent on others.

Such managers are expected to manage on the basis of personal relationships with subordinates. This may result in them showing favouritism toward some.

As managers, highly affiliative individuals are predicted to be reluctant to monitor the behaviour of subordinates, give negative feedback to others, or discipline their subordinates. However, when the power motive is higher than the affiliative motive, individuals are disinclined to engage in dysfunctional management behaviours such as submissiveness, reluctance to monitor and

discipline subordinates, and favouritism.

Need for Achievement and Entrepreneurship

Originally, the need for achievement was the greatest concern for McClelland. He was particularly interested in this need and associated behaviours because most organizations want their employees to achieve. The 'need achievement' refers to an unconscious disposition to energize and drive. High Achievement individuals are constantly 'competing with standards of excellence'. Further, they are attracted to tasks of moderate difficulty.

McClelland further described the profile of an entrepreneur as someone high in (Achievement) and low in (Power), while good managers have high Power and low Achievement.

Over four decades of research into the characteristics of entrepreneurs has established that the essential need for achievement for entrepreneurship is learned at an early age. Persons with a high 'need achievement' have a general predisposition towards entrepreneurial activity.

Adults are assumed to possess all three motivations to one degree or another, however, one of the motives is usually dominant. Managers need to identify what motivates others and to create appropriately motivating conditions for them.

People with achievement motives are motivated by standards of excellence, delineated roles and responsibilities and concrete, timely feedback. Those with affiliation motives are motivated when they can accomplish things with people they know and trust. And the power motive is activated when people are allowed to have an impact, impress those in power, or beat competitors.

PORTER & LAWLER MODEL

Layman Porter and Edward Lawler developed a complex model of motivation that integrated ideas of the Equity and Expectancy Theories. Porter and Lawler suggest there are five components that affect motivation: efforts, perception, performance, reward and satisfaction. When value of expected rewards is perceived, efforts are followed by performance. Performance is admitted by rewards (both intrinsic and extrinsic). If rewards equal desired ones, they lead to satisfaction. A satisfied employee is motivated to perform well in the future and increase his or her efforts. If rewards are regarded as unequal or unfair, they make an individual unsatisfied and thus less motivated to perform well in the future. So, in case a reward is perceived as unfair, it is followed by decreased efforts of an employee. The theorists argued that motivation is a cyclical process and presented the model reflecting interdependence of its basic components.

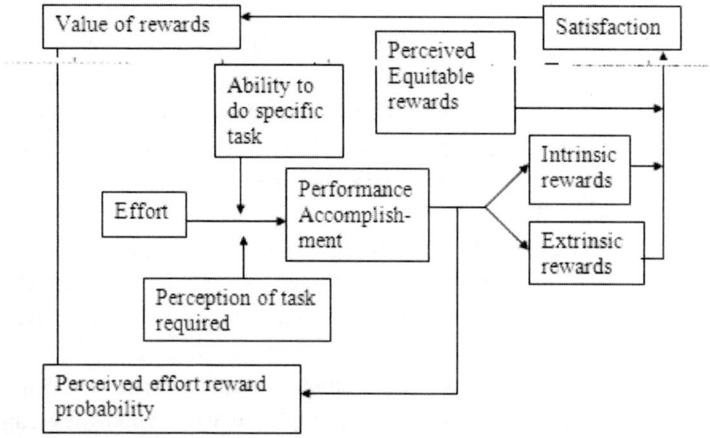

Fig: The Porter-Lawler Model

The model elicits three groups of factors that influence main components effecting motivation:

1. Factors to shape an effort:
    - Perceived value of rewards. An individual estimates attractiveness of a reward. If a reward is perceived as positive, a person becomes interested to put efforts to do the job.
    - Probability an effort will achieve performance. Performance depends on an individual's efforts; thus, an individual decides if his or her efforts will be enough to perform well.
    - Probability an effort will achieve result. Performance is a result of efforts. A reward is given only if performance of an individual is successful. An individual decides if his or her efforts are enough to be properly rewarded.
2. Factors to affect effort-and-performance relationship:
    - Abilities. Efforts of an employee depend on his or her individual differences, i.e. personality traits, skills, intelligence, education, experience, etc.
    - Role perceptions. Efforts that an employee puts forth to perform successfully are connected with the type of behaviour and activities in which the individual is engaged in doing the job. The behaviour and activities to be chosen

depend on how a worker perceives his or her role in implementing the task.

3. Factors to form performance-and-satisfaction relationship:
   - Extrinsic and intrinsic rewards. An employee should necessarily be rewarded in case his or her performance was successful. Both extrinsic (e.g. money, material rewards) and intrinsic (e.g. self-esteem, recognition, etc) rewards are desirable.
   - Perceived equity of rewards. Rewards should meet the individual's expectation. An employee expects to get something desirable and needed (i.e., rewards that will equal to that of a coworker doing the same job).

The Porter-Lawler Model provides managers with visual explanation of how a person is motivated. Employees perform well when they can reasonably expect that their performance will be fairly and desirably rewarded. To make individuals perform well, managers should try to understand employees. To do it, managers should make an effort to decide, from employees' viewpoint, upon:

- What could be perceived a valuable reward for acting well?
- What efforts are needed to do the required job?
- Would employees' inputs be equal to their outcomes?
- How do employees assess probability they will get the desired reward if they make an effort?

Motivated employees always try to find better ways to do their job. They are more productive, responsible and quality-oriented. Thus, a manager's main task is to properly motivate their work employees. Modern theories of motivation (both process and content) give company managers a powerful tool to drive their workers into action.

APPLICATION OF MOTIVATION CONCEPT

At lower levels of Maslow's hierarchy of needs, such as Physiological needs, money is a motivator, however it tends to have a motivating effect on staff that lasts only for a short period (in accordance with Herzberg's two-factor model of motivation). At higher levels of the hierarchy, praise, respect, recognition, empowerment and a sense of belonging are far more powerful motivators than money, as both Abraham Maslow's theory of motivation and Douglas McGregor's Theory X and theory Y (pertaining to the theory of leadership) demonstrate.

Maslow has money at the lowest level of the hierarchy and shows other needs are better motivators to staff. McGregor places money in his Theory X category and feels it is a poor motivator. Praise and recognition are placed in the Theory Y category and are considered stronger motivators than money.

- Motivated employees always look for better ways to do a job.
- Motivated employees are more quality oriented.
- Motivated workers are more productive.

The average workplace is about midway between the extremes of high threat and high opportunity. Motivation by threat is a dead-end strategy, and naturally staff are more attracted to the opportunity side of the motivation curve than the threat side. Motivation is a powerful tool in the work environment that can lead to employees working at their most efficient levels of production.

The assumptions of Maslow and Herzberg were challenged by a classic study[4] at Vauxhall Motors' UK manufacturing plant. This introduced the concept of orientation to work and distinguished three main orientations: instrumental (where work is a means to an end), bureaucratic (where work is a source of status, security and immediate reward) and solidaristic (which prioritises group loyalty).

Other theories which expanded and extended those of Maslow and Herzberg included Kurt Lewin's Force Field Theory, Edwin Locke's Goal Theory and Victor Vroom's Expectancy theory. These tend to stress cultural differences and the fact that individuals tend to be motivated by different factors at different times. According to the system of scientific management developed by Frederick Winslow Taylor, a worker's motivation is solely determined by pay, and therefore management need not consider psychological or social aspects of work. In essence scientific management bases human motivation wholly on extrinsic rewards and discards the idea of intrinsic rewards.

In contrast, David McClelland believed that workers could not be motivated by the mere need for money-- in fact, extrinsic motivation (e.g., money) could extinguish intrinsic motivation such as achievement motivation, though money could be used as an indicator of success for various motives, e.g., keeping score. In keeping with this view, his consulting firm, McBer & Company, had as its first motto "To make everyone productive, happy, and free." For McClelland, satisfaction lay in aligning a person's life with their fundamental motivations.

Elton Mayo found out that the social contacts a worker has at the workplace are very important and that boredom and repetitiveness of tasks lead to reduced motivation. Mayo believed that workers could be motivated by acknowledging their social needs and making them feel important. As a result, employees were given freedom to make decisions on the job and greater attention was paid to informal work groups. Mayo named the model the Hawthorne effect. His model has been judged as placing undue reliance on social contacts at work situations for motivating employees.

Note: For a case study visit company's site of BorgWarner Inc. BorgWarner is a product leader in highly engineered components and systems for vehicle powertrain applications worldwide. The company primarily operates in the US and Europe. It is headquartered in Auburn Hills, Michigan and employs about 13,800 people. www.borgwarner.com

4

Attitudes, Values and Work Ethics

INTRODUCTION

Attitudes are individuals' general affective, cognitive and intentional responses toward objects, other people, themselves, or social issues. Attitudes are evaluative statements - either favourable or unfavourable - concerning objects, people or events. They reflect how one feels about something. As individuals, we respond favourably or unfavourably towards many things: co-workers, bosses, our own appearances etc. The importance of attitudes lies in their link to behaviour. When an employee says, "I like my job" he or she is expressing their attitude about work.

MEANING OF ATTITUDES

Attitude is defined as a more or less stable set of predisposition of opinion, interest or purpose involving expectancy of a certain kind of experience and readiness with an appropriate response. Attitudes are also known as "frames of reference". They provide the background against which facts and events are viewed. It becomes necessary to know the attitudes of members of an organization because they have to perceive specific aspects like pay, hours of work, promotion etc., of their job life in the wider context of their generalised attitudes. An attitude is also a cognitive element; it always remains inside a person. Everyone's psychological world is limited and thus everyone has a limited number of attitudes. In business organization, employees have attitudes relating to world environment, job security etc. The individual's attitudes towards these factors are indicative of his apathy or enthusiasm towards the activities and objectives of the organization.

CHARACTERISTICS OF ATTITUDES

- An attitude is the predisposition of the individual to evaluate some objects in a favourable or an unfavourable manner.
- The most pervasive phenomenon is "attitude". People at work place have attitudes about lots of topics that are related to them. These attitudes are firmly embedded in a complex psychological structure of beliefs.
- Attitudes are different from values. Values are the ideals, whereas attitudes are narrow, they are our feelings, thoughts and behavioural tendencies toward a specific object or situation.
- Attitude is a predisposition to respond to a certain set of facts.
- Attitudes are evaluative statements - either favourable or unfavourable concerning the objects, people or events.

An attitude is "a mental state of readiness, organized through experience, exerting a specific influence upon a person's response to people, objects and situation with which it is related". Attitudes thus state one's predispositions towards given aspects of world. They also provide an emotional basis of one's interpersonal relations and identification with others. Managers in work organizations need to know and understand employee's attitudes in order to manage effectively. Attitudes do influence behaviour of people and their performance in organizations.

FUNCTIONS OF ATTITUDE

Attitudes are known to serve at least four important functions in an organization setting:

- Attitudes determine meaning: Much of what is seem in the environment and in other people's behaviour is determined by attitudes. If one has a overall favourable attitude towards a person, one tends to judge his activities as "good" or "superior". On the other hand, negative attitudes or prejudices generally prompt disagreement with the individual concerned or failure to appreciate the good work done by him.
- Attitudes reconcile contradictions: It is not uncommon to come across people who hold contradictory opinions. With the proper attitude as a background, intelligent people can reconcile or rationalise the same actions, which to others are obvious contradictions. For example when a worker takes a little rest a

superior considers it "idling".

- Attitudes organize facts: As already seen, objective events can be differently perceived by different people because of different attitudes. Meanings can be concocted and falsely communicated to others by changing the attitudes of the recipients towards wider social issues.
- Attitudes select facts: From the plethora of environmental facts and stimuli, one tends to select those, which are in consonance with one's cherished beliefs and attitudes. Attitudes, thus, act as a screen or filter.

COMPONENTS OF ATTITUDES

The three components of attitudes are:

COGNITIVE COMPONENT

This component includes the beliefs an individual has about a certain person, object, or situation. The belief that "discrimination is wrong" is a value statement. Such an opinion is the cognitive component of an attitude. Learned beliefs, such as "you need to work long hours to get ahead in this job", lead to attitudes that have an impact on behaviour in the workplace. The cognition component of an attitude, reflects a persons perceptions or beliefs. Cognitive elements are evaluative beliefs and are measured by attitude scales or by asking about thoughts. The statement "I believe Japanese workers are industrious," reflect the cognitive component of an attitude. The cognitive component sets the stage for the more critical part of attitude - its affective component.

AFFECTIVE COMPONENT

This component refers to the person's feelings that result from his or her beliefs about a person, object or situation. A person who believes hard work earns promotions may feel anger or frustration when he or she works hard but is not promoted. The affective component becomes stronger as an individual has more frequent and direct experience with a focal object, person or situation. Affect is the emotional component of an attitude. It refers to an individual's feeling about something or someone. Statements such as "I like this" or "I prefer that" reflect the affective component of an attitude. Affect is measured by physiological indicators such as galvanic skin response (changes in electrical resistance of skin which indicate emotional arousal) and blood pressure. These indicators show changes in emotions by measuring physiological arousal. If an individual is trying to hide his or her feelings, this might be shown by a change in arousal.

BEHAVIOURAL COMPONENT

This component refers to the individual's behaviour that occurs as a result of his or her feeling about the focal person, object or situation. An individual may complain, request a transfer, or be less productive because he or she feels dissatisfied with work. The behavioural component of an attitude refers to an intention to behave in a certain way toward someone or something. For example, our attitudes towards women in management may be inferred from an observation of the way we behave toward a female supervisor. We may be supportive, passive or hostile depending on our attitude. The behavioural component of an attitude is measured by observing behaviour or by asking a person about behaviour or intentions.

Viewing attitudes as made up of three components - cognition, affect and behaviour - is helpful toward understanding their complexity and the potential relationship between attitude and behaviour. The object of an attitude is represented as a prototype in a person's memory. Then an individual uses an attitude as a schema for evaluating an object. The person may assess the object as good or bad, positive or negative, favoured or not; then the person determines the strategy to take toward it. The accessibility of an attitude, or ease with which it is activated, affects its implementation. Personal experience with the object and the repeated expression of the attitude increases it accessibility. In this way, attitude-related information helps process complex information.

SOURCES OF ATTITUDES

Attitudes, are acquired from parents, teachers, and peer group members. We model our attitudes after those we admire, respect or fear. We observe the way family and friends behave, and we shape our attitudes and behaviour to align with theirs. People also imitate the attitudes of popular individuals and those they admire and respect. Attitudes are an integral part of the world of work. It is important for managers to understand the antecedents to attitudes as well as their consequences. Managers also need to understand the different components of attitudes, how attitudes are formed, and the major attitudes that affect work behaviour and how to use persuasion to change attitudes.

TYPES OF ATTITUDES

A person can have thousands of attitudes, but most of the research in OB has been concerned with three attitudes: Job satisfaction, job involvement, and organizational commitment.

- Job Satisfaction: Satisfaction results when a job fulfils or facilitates the attainment of individual values and standards and dissatisfaction occurs when the job is seen as blocking such attainment. This attitude has received extensive attention by researchers and practitioners because it was at one time believed to be the cause of improved job performance. The term "job satisfaction" refers to an individual's general attitude toward his or her job. A person with a high level of job satisfaction holds positive attitudes toward the job; a person who is dissatisfied with his or her job holds negative attitudes about the job. Now, because of managers' concern for creating both a humane and high performance workplace, researchers continue to search for definite answers about the causes and consequences of job satisfaction.
- Job Involvement: Job involvement is the degree to which a person identifies with his or her job, actively participates in it and considers his or her performance important to self-worth. Employees with a high level of job involvement strongly identify with and really care about the kind of work they do. High levels of job involvement have been found to be related to fewer absences and lower resignation rates.
- Organizational Commitment: Organizational commitment is the degree to which an employee identifies with a particular organization and its goals, and wishes to maintain membership in the organization. High organizational commitment means identifying with one's employing organization.

ATTITUDE FORMATION

Attitudes are learned. Individuals acquire attitudes from several sources but the point to be stressed is that the attitudes are acquired but not inherited. Our responses to people and issues evolve over time. Two major influences on attitudes are direct experience and social learning.

1. Direct Experience: Attitudes can develop from a personally rewarding or punishing experience with an object. Direct experience with an object or person is a powerful influence on attitudes. Research has shown that attitudes that are derived from direct experience are stronger, are held more confidently

and are more resistant to change than are attitudes formed through indirect experience. One reason that attitudes derived from direct experience are so powerful is because of their availability. This means that the attitudes are easily accessed and are active in our cognitive processes. When attitudes are available, we can call them quickly into consciousness. Attitudes that are not learned from direct experience are not as available, and therefore we do not recall them easily.

a. Classical Conditioning: One of the basic processes underlying attitude formation can be explained on the basis of learning principles. People develop associations between various objects and the emotional reactions that accompany them.

b. Operant Conditioning: Attitudes that are reinforced, either verbally or nonverbally, tends to be maintained. Conversely, a person who states an attitude that elicits ridicule from others may modify or abandon the attitude.

c. Vicarious Learning: In which a person learns something through the observance of others can also account for attitude development particularly when the individual has no direct experience with the object about which the attitude is held. It is through vicarious learning processes that children pick up the prejudices of their parents.

2. Social Learning: In social learning, the family, peer groups and culture shape an individual's attitudes in an indirect manner. Substantial social learning occurs through modelling, in which individuals acquire attitudes by merely observing others. For an individual to learn from observing a model, four processes must take place:

   a. The learner must focus attention on the model. Attitudes, Values and Work Ethics

   b. The learner must retain what was observed from the model.

   c. Behavioural reproduction must occur; that is, the learner must practise the behaviour.

   d. The learner must be motivated to learn from the model.

Social learning can take place through the following ways:

a. The Family: A person may learn attitudes through imitation of parents. If parents have a positive attitude towards an object and the child admires his parents, he is likely to adopt a similar attitude, even without being told about the object, and even without having direct experience. Children also learn to adopt certain attitudes by the reinforcement they are given by their parents when they display behaviours that reflect an appropriate attitude.

b. Peer Groups: Peer pressure moulds attitudes through group acceptance of individuals who express popular attitudes and through sanctions, such as exclusion from the group, placed on individuals who espouse (promote) unpopular attitudes.

c. Modelling: Substantial social learning occurs through modelling, in which individuals acquire attitudes by merely observing others. The observer overhears other individuals expressing an opinion or watches them engaging in a behaviour that reflects an attitude, and the observer adopts this attitude.

COGNITIVE DISSONANCE THEORY

Leon Festinger, in 1957, proposed the theory of cognitive dissonance. According to this theory, people want their belief to be consistent with one another and want their behaviours to be consistent with their beliefs. When people become aware of inconsistency among their beliefs or between their attitudes and their behaviour, they experience "cognitive dissonance", an unpleasant state of arousal that motivates them to re-establish consistency by changing one of their attitudes or by changing their behaviours. Thus, if a person behaves in a way that runs counter to his or her attitude, cognitive dissonance is created in that person. He or she then attempts to reduce the dissonance by changing either the attitude or the behaviour.

Cognitive dissonance refers to any incompatibility that an individual might perceive between two or more of his or her attitudes or between his or her behaviour and attitudes. Festinger argues that any form of inconsistency is uncomfortable and that individuals will attempt to reduce the dissonance and hence, the discomfort. Therefore, individuals will seek a stable state where there is a minimum of dissonance.

COPING WITH DISSONANCE

No individual can completely avoid dissonance. So how do people cope with dissonance?

According to Festinger, the desire to reduce dissonance would be determined by the importance of the elements creating the dissonance; the degree of influence the individual believes he or she has over the elements and the rewards that may be involved in dissonance.

1. Importance of the Elements: If the elements creating the dissonance are relatively unimportant, the pressure to correct this imbalance will be low.
2. Degree of Influence: The degree of influence that individuals believe they have over the elements will have an impact on how they will react to the dissonance. If they perceive the dissonance to be an uncontrollable, they are less likely to be receptive to attitude change.
3. Rewards: Rewards also influence the degree to which individuals are motivated to reduce dissonance. High rewards accompanying high dissonance tend to reduce the tension inherent in the dissonance.

These moderating factors suggest that just because individuals experience dissonance they will not necessarily move directly toward consistency, that is, toward reduction of this dissonance. If the issues underlying the dissonance are of minimal importance, if an individual perceives that the dissonance is externally imposed and is substantially uncontrollable by him or her, or if rewards are significant enough to off set the dissonance, the individual will not be under great tension to reduce the dissonance.

VALUES

Another source of individual differences is value. Values exist at a deeper level than attitudes and are more general and basic in nature. We use them to evaluate our own behaviour and that of others. Value is an enduring belief that a specific mode of conducts or end state of existence is personally and socially preferable to the alternative modes of conduct or end states of existence. Once it is internalised it becomes consciously or unconsciously, a standard or criterion for guiding action, for developing and maintaining attitudes toward relevant objects and situation, for justifying one's own and others' actions and attitudes for morally judging oneself and others and for comparing oneself with others. Value, therefore, is a standard or yardstick to guide actions, attitudes, evaluations and justifications of the self and others.

Ronald D White and David A Bednar have defined value as a "concept of the desirable, an internalised criterion or standard of evaluation a person possesses. Such concepts and standards are relatively few and determine or guide an individual's evaluations of the many objects encountered in everyday life". Values are tinged with moral flavour, involving an individual's judgement of what is right, good or desirable. Thus values:

- Provide standards of competence and morality.
- Are fewer in number than attitudes.
- Transcend specific objects, situations or persons.
- Are relatively permanent and resistant to change.
- Are more central to the core of a person.

Individuals learn values as they grow and mature. They may change over the life span of an individual develops a sense of self. Cultures, societies, and organizations shape values.

IMPORTANCE OF VALUES

Values are important to the study of organizational behaviour because they lay the foundation for the understanding of attitudes and motivation and because they influence our perceptions. Individuals enter an organization with preconceived notions of what "ought" and what "ought not' to be. For example, If Jeevan enters IG Ferns and Curtains with a view that salary on piece-rate system is right and on time-rate basis is wrong. He is likely to be disappointed if the company allocates salary on time-rate basis. His disappointment is likely to breed his job dissatisfaction. This will, in turn, adversely affect his performance, his attitude and in turn, behaviour would be different if his values are aligned with the company's reward/ pay policy.

FORMATION OF VALUES

Values are learned and acquired primarily through experiences with people and institutions. Parents, for example, will have substantial influence on their children's values. A parent's reaction to everyday events demonstrates what is good and bad, acceptable and unacceptable and important and unimportant. Values are also taught and reinforced in schools, religious organizations, and social groups. As we grow and develop, each source of influence contributes to our definition what is important in life. Cultural mores have influence of the formation of values. Basic convictions of what is good or bad are derived from one's own culture.

TYPES OF VALUES

Allport and his associates categorized values into six types:

- Theoretical: Interested in the discovery of truth through reasoning and systematic thinking.
- Economic: Interest in usefulness and practicality, including the accumulation of wealth.
- Aesthetic: Interest in beauty, form and artistic harmony.
- Social: Interest in people and love as a human relationship.
- Political: Interest in gaining power and influencing people.
- Religious: Interest in unity and understanding the cosmos as a whole.

Instrumental and Terminal Values: Rokeach distinguishes between two types of values: Instrumental and Terminal.

Instrumental Value: Instrumental values reflect the means to achieve goals; that is, they represent the acceptable behaviour to be used in achieving some end state. Instrumental values identified by Rokeach include ambition, honesty, self-sufficiency and courageousness. Instrumental value refers to a single belief that always takes the form: It is believed that such and such a mode of conduct (example Honesty, courage, etc.) is personally and socially preferable in all situations with respect to all objects. An instrumental value is a tool or means for acquiring a terminal value.

Terminal Value: Terminal values, in contrast, represent the goals to be achieved, or the end states of existence. Rokeach identified happiness, love, pleasure, self-respect, and freedom among the terminal values.

Terminal value takes a comparable form: It is believed that such and such an end state of existence (example salvation, or world at peace etc.) is personally and socially worth striving for. A terminal value is an ultimate goal in a desired status or outcome.

Work Values

Work values are important because they affect how individuals behave on their jobs in terms of what is right and wrong. The work values most relevant to individuals are: -

1. Achievement: Achievement is a concern for the advancement of one's career. This is shown in such behaviours as working hard and seeking opportunities to develop new skills.

2. Concern for Others: Concern for others reflects caring, compassionate behaviour such as encouraging other employees or helping others work on difficult tasks. These behaviours constitute organizational citizenship.
3. Honesty: Honesty is accurately providing information and refusing to mislead others for personal gain.
4. Fairness: Fairness emphasizes impartiality and recognises different points of view. Although individuals vary in their value systems, when they share similar values at work, the results are positive. This means that organizations recruiting job candidates should pay careful attention to individual's values.

MEANING OF ETHICS

Ethics is the study of moral values and moral behaviour. Ethical behaviour is acting in ways consistent with one's personal values and the commonly held values of the organization and society. Ethical issues are a major concern in organizations. There is evidence that paying attention to ethical issues pays off for companies. Doing the right thing can positively affect an organization's performance.

Managers must confront the ethical challenges that are encountered in organizations. Some organizations manage ethical issues well. Despite the positive way some organizations handle ethical issues, there is plenty of evidence that unethical conduct does occur in other organizations. How can people in organizations rationally think through ethical decisions so that they make the "right" choice? Ethical theories give us a basis for understanding, evaluating, and classifying moral arguments and then defending conclusions about what is right and wrong.

ETHICAL THEORIES

Ethical theories can be classified into the following types:

1. Consequential Theories: Consequential theories of ethics emphasize the consequences or results of behaviour. John Stuart Mill's Utilitarianism, a well-known consequential theory suggests that right and wrong is determined by the consequences of the action. "Good" is the ultimate moral value, and we should maximize the most good for the greatest number of people. But do good ethics makes for good business? Right actions do not always produce good consequences, and good

consequences do not always follow from right actions. Using the "greatest number" criterion can we imply that minorities be excluded. Should an issue that may be important for a minority but unimportant for the majority is ignored? These are but a few of the dilemmas raided by utilitarianism.

2. Rule-based Theories: In contrast, rule-based theories of ethics emphasize the character of the act itself, not its effects, in arriving at universal moral rights and wrongs. Moral rights, the basis for legal rights, are associated with such theories. Companies and business enterprises are more prone to subscribe to consequential ethics than rule-based ethics, in part due to the persuasive arguments of the Scottish political economist Adam Smith. He believed that the self-interest of human beings is God's providence, not the government's. Smith set forth a doctrine of natural liberty, presenting the classical argument for open market competition and free trade. Within this framework, people should be allowed to pursue what is in their economic self-interest, and the natural efficiency of the market place would serve the well being of society. However, Immanuel, Kant argued that individuals should be treated with respect and dignity, and that they should not be used as a means to an end. He argued that we should put over selves in the other person's position and asks if we would make the same decision if we were in the other person's situation.

3. Cultural Theories: The theory emphasises respect for different cultural values. Cultural relativism contends that there are no universal ethical principles and that people should not impose universal ethical principles and that people should not impose their own ethical standards on others. Local standards should be the guides for ethical behaviour. This theory operates under the old adage "when in Rome do as the Romans do". Strict adherence to cultural relativism can lead individuals to deny their accountability for their own decisions and to avoid difficult ethical dilemmas.

CONTEMPORARY ETHICAL ISSUES IN ORGANIZATIONS

In contemporary organizations, people face ethical and moral dilemmas in many diverse areas. The key areas are:-

i. White-Collar Crime: Corporate criminal behaviours have resulted in big financial scandals. White-collar crime may occur in more subtle forms as well. Using work hours for conducting personal business, sending out personal mail using the company resources. Inflating expenses etc., are all practices some individuals would consider unethical. Whether the impact is large or small, white-collar crimes are important issues in organizations.

ii. Employee Rights: Managing the rights of employees at work creates many ethical dilemmas in organizations. Some of these dilemmas are privacy issues, drug testing etc. The use of employee data from computerized information systems presents many ethical concerns. Safeguarding employee's right to privacy and at the same time preserving access to the data for those who need it requires that the manager balance competing interests.

iii. Sexual Harassment: Sexual harassment is unwelcome sexual attention, whether verbal or physical, that affects an employee's job conditions or created a hostile working environment. Sexual harassment costs the company in the form of absenteeism, turnover, and loss of productivity. Companies may be required to pay damages to victims of sexual harassment. Besides, the company may face negative publicity because of sexual harassment cases.

iv. Romantic Involvements: Hugging, kissing, sexual innuendos, and repeated requests for dates may constitute sexual harassment for some, but they are prelude to romance for others. This situation carries with it a different set of ethical dilemmas for organizations. Conflicts occur within an organization when romantic involvements at work become disruptive. Moreover, employers are liable for acts of their employees and can thus be held liable for sexual harassment. Other employees might claim that the subordinate who is romantically involved with the supervisor gets preferential treatment. Romantic involvements at work can create a conflict of interest. A comprehensive policy should require anyone who might be experiencing a conflict of interest to report it to his or her manager. The policy should also include an explanation of how unwelcome romantic advances can turn into sexual harassment.

v. Organizational Justice: Another area in which moral and ethical dilemmas may arise for people at work concerns organizational justice, both distributive and procedural.

   a. Distributive Justice: Concerns the fairness of outcomes individuals receives.

   b. Procedural Justice: Concerns the fairness of the process by which outcomes is allocated. The ethical questions here do not concern the just or unjust distribution of organizational resources. Rather, the ethical questions in procedural justice concern the process. Has the organization used the correct procedures in allocating resources? Have the right considerations such as competence and skill, been brought to bear in the decision process?

vi. Whistle blowing: Whistle-blowers are employees who inform authorities of wrongdoings of their companies or co-workers. Whistle blowing is important because committed organizational members sometimes engage in unethical behaviour in an intense desire to succeed. Organizations can manage whistle blowing by communicating the conditions that are appropriate for the disclosure of wrongdoing. Clearly delineating wrongful behaviour and the appropriate ways to respond are important organizational actions.

vii. Social Responsibility: Corporate social responsibility is the obligation of an organization to behave in ethical ways in the social environment in which it operates. Socially responsible actions are expected of organizations. Current concerns including protecting the environment, promoting worker safety, supporting social issues, investing in the community etc. Managers must encourage both individual ethical behaviour and organizational social responsibility.

TYPES OF MANAGEMENT ETHICS

Managerial ethics, are standards of conduct or moral judgement used by managers of organizations in caring out their business. Archi B Carroll, notes that three major levels of moral or ethical, judgement characterize managers: immoral management, amoral management, and moral management.

IMMORAL MANAGEMENT

Immoral management not only lacks ethical principles but also is actively opposed to ethical behaviour. This perspective is characterized by principal or exclusive concern for company gains, emphasis on profits and company success at virtually any price, lack of concern about the desires of others to be treated fairly, views of laws as obstacles to be overcome, and a willingness to "cut corners".

MORAL MANAGEMENT

In contrast to immoral management, moral management strives to follow ethical principles and percepts. While moral managers also desire to succeed, they seek to do so only within the parameters of ethical standards and the ideals of fairness, justice, and due process. As a result, moral managers pursue business objectives that involve simultaneously making a profit and engaging in legal and ethical behaviours.

AMORAL MANAGEMENT

The amoral management approach is neither immoral nor moral but, rather, ignores or is oblivious to ethical considerations. There are two types of amoral management:

- Intentional: A moral managers do not include ethical concerns in their decision-making, or behaviour, because they basically think that general ethical standards are more appropriate to other areas of life than to business.
- Unintentional: Amoral managers also do not think about ethical issues in their business dealings, but the reason is different. These managers are basically inattentive or incentive to the moral implications of their decision-making, actions, and behaviour. Overall amoral managers pursue profitability as a goal and may be generally well meaning, but intentionally or unintentionally they pay little attention to the impacts of their behaviours on others.

IMPROVING ETHICAL BEHAVIOUR

Unethical behaviour by employees can affect individuals, work teams and even the organization. Organizations thus depend on individuals to act ethically. The ethical issues that individuals face at work are complex. Following is the summary of ethical issues.

1. Stealing: Taking things that don't belong to you.
2. Lying: Saying things you know aren't true.

3. Fraud and deceit: Creating or perpetuating false impressions.
4. Conflict of interest and influence buying: Bribes, payoff and kickbacks.
5. Hiding versus divulging information: Concealing information that another party has a right to know, or failing to protect personal or proprietary information.
6. Cheating: Taking unfair advantage of a situation.
7. Personal decadence: Aiming below excellence in terms of work performance (e.g., careless or sloppy work).
8. Interpersonal abuse: Behaviours that are abusive of others (e.g., sexism, racism, emotional abuse).
9. Organizational abuse: Organizational practices that abuse members (e.g., inequitable compensation, misuses of power).
10. Rule violations: Breaking organizational rules.
11. Accessory to unethical acts: Knowing about unethical behaviour and failing to report it.
12. Ethical dilemmas: Choosing between two equally desirable or undesirable options.

Members of organizations are increasingly finding themselves facing ethical dilemmas, situations where they are required to define right and wrong conduct. What constitutes good ethical behaviour has never been clearly defined. And in recent years the line differentiating right from wrong has become more blurred. Employees see people all around them engaging in unethical practices. When caught these people giving excuses like "everyone does it", or "I never thought I would get caught". Managers and their organizations are responding to this problem from a number of directions. They are writing and distributing codes of ethics to guide employees through ethical dilemmas and they are creating protection mechanisms for employees who reveal internal unethical practices.

Today's manager needs to create an ethically healthy climate for his or her employees, where they can do their work productivity and confront a minimal degree of ambiguity regarding what constitutes right and wrong behaviours. Making ethical decisions is part of each manager's job. It has been suggested by K.R. Andrews that ethical decision-making requires three qualities of individuals:

1. The competence to identify ethical issues and evaluate the consequences of alternative courses of action.

2. The self-confidence to seek out different opinions about the issue and decide what is right in terms of a particular situation.
3. Tough-mindedness - the willingness to make decisions when all that needs to be known cannot be known and when the ethical issue has no established unambiguous solution.

Values and Ethics: Sometimes some people consider values and ethics synonymous and use them interchangeably. However, the two have different meanings. The major distinction between the two is that values are beliefs that affect an individual's judgemental ideas about what is good or bad. The ethics is the way the values are acted out. Ethical behaviour is acting in ways consistent with one's personal values and the commonly held values of the organization and society.

Values and Attitudes: Both values and attitudes are tinged with morale. There are some similarities and some dissimilarity between the two:

Similarities: The similarities between values and attitudes are:

1. Both are learned or acquired from the same sources - experience with people, objects and events.
2. Both affect cognitive process and behaviour of people. Attitudes, Values and Work Ethics
3. Both are endurable and difficult to change.
4. Both influence each other and more often than not, are used interchangeably.

Work Attitudes and Job Satisfaction: Attitudes at work are important because, directly or indirectly, they affect work behaviour. Although many work attitudes are important, two attitudes in particular have been emphasized. Job satisfaction and organizational commitment are key attitudes of interest to managers.

1. Job Satisfaction: Job satisfaction is a pleasurable or positive emotional state resulting from the appraisal of one's job or hob experiences. The most important factors conductive to job satisfaction are:
   i. Mentally Challenging Work: Employees tend to prefer job that give them opportunities to use their skills and abilities and offer a variety of tasks, freedom and feedback on how well they are doing. Under conditions of moderate challenge, most employees will experience pleasure and satisfaction.

ii. Personality-Job Fit: People with personality types congruent with their chosen vocations should find they have the right talents and abilities to meet the demands of their jobs; and because of this success, have a greater probability of achieving high satisfaction from their work. It is important, therefore to fit personality factors with job profiles.

iii. Equitable Rewards: Employees want pay systems and promotion policies that they perceive as being just, unambiguous, and in line with their expectations. When pay is seen as fair based on job demands, individual skill level, and industry pay standards, satisfaction is likely to result. Similarly, employees seek fair promotion policies and practices. Promotions provide opportunities for personal growth, more responsibilities and increased social status. Individual's who perceive that promotion decisions are made in a fair and just manner are likely to experience job satisfaction.

iv. Supportive working conditions: Employees prefer physical conditions that are comfortable and facilitating doing a good job. Temperature, light, noise and other environmental factors should not be extreme and provide personal comfort. Further, employees prefer working relatively close to home, in clean and relatively modern facilities and with adequate tools and equipment.

v. Supportive Colleagues: Employees have need for social interaction. Therefore, having friendly and supportive co-workers and understanding supervisor's leads to increase job satisfaction. Most employees want their immediate supervisor to understand and friendly, offers praise for good performance, listens to employees' opinions and show a personal interest in them. An individual may hold different attitudes toward various aspects of the job. For example, an employee may like his job responsibilities but be dissatisfied with the opportunities for promotion. Characteristics of individuals also affect job satisfaction. Those with high negative affectivity are more likely to be dissatisfied with their jobs.

Are satisfied workers more productive? Or, are more productive workers more satisfied?

The link between satisfaction and performance has been widely explored. Research shows weak support for both views, but not simple, direct relationship between satisfaction and performance have been found. However, we can say that satisfied workers are more likely to want to give something back to the organization because they want to reciprocate their positive experiences.

2. Organizational Commitment: - The strength of an individual's identification with an organization is known as organizational commitment. There are two kinds of organizational commitment.

    i. Affective Commitment: Affective commitment is an employee's intention to remain in an organization because of a strong desire to do so. It consists of three factors:

        - A belief in the goals and values of the organization.
        - A willingness to put forth effort on behalf of the organization.
        - A desire to remain a member of the organization.

        Affective commitment encompasses loyalty, but it is also a deep concern for the organization's welfare.

    ii. Continuance Commitment: Continuance commitment is an employee's tendency to remain in an organization because the person cannot afford to leave. Sometimes, employees believe that if they leave, they will lose a great deal of their investments in time, effort and benefits and that they cannot replace these investment.

Organizational commitment is related to lower rates of absenteeism, higher quality of work, and increased productivity. Managers should be concerned about affective commitment because committed individuals expend more task-related effort and are less likely than others to leave the organization. Job satisfaction and organizational commitment are two important work attitudes that managers can strive to improve among their employees. And these two attitudes are strongly related; so increasing job satisfaction is likely to increase commitment as well.

CONCLUSION

Attitudes are individuals' general affective, cognitive and intentional responses toward objects, other people, themselves, or social issues. Attitudes are evaluative statements - either favourable or unfavourable - concerning objects, people or events. Attitudes thus state one's predispositions towards given aspects of world. They also provide an emotional basis of one's interpersonal relations and identification with others. Attitudes are known to serve at least four important functions in an organization setting. Attitudes are learned. Individuals acquire attitudes from several sources but the point to be stressed is that the attitudes are acquired but not inherited. Values are learned and acquired primarily through experiences with people and institutions. In contemporary organizations, people face ethical and moral dilemmas in many diverse areas. Job satisfaction and organizational commitment are two important work attitudes that managers can strive to improve among their employees.

Note: For a detailed example of this chapter visit Big 5 Sporting Goods Corporation site. Big 5 Sporting Goods Corporation (Big 5) is a retailer of sporting goods and accessories. The company primarily operates in the US. It is headquartered in El Segundo, California and employs 8,900 people; this figure includes part-time employees. www.big5sportinggoods.com

5

Foundations of Group Behaviour

INTRODUCTION

We define "group" as more than two employees who have an ongoing relationship in which they interact and influence one another's behaviour and performance. The behaviour of individuals in groups is something more than the sum total of each acting in his or her own way. Learning capabilities represent the set of core competencies, which are defined as the special knowledge, skills, and technological know-how that differentiate an individual or an organization from his/its competitors and enable them to adapt to their environment. Learning capacities are the fuel for individuals or organizational success.

DEFINITION OF GROUPS

We define "group" as more than two employees who have an ongoing relationship in which they interact and influence one another's behaviour and performance. The behaviour of individuals in groups is something more than the sum total of each acting in his or her own way. In other words, when individuals are in groups, they act differently than they do when they are alone.

Groups can be either formal or informal.

1. Formal Groups: A formal group is set up by the organization to carry out work in support of the organization's goals. In formal groups, the behaviours that one should engage in are stipulated by and directed toward organizational goals. Examples include a bookkeeping department, an executive committee, and a product development team. Formal group may be command groups or task groups.

i. Command Group: A command group consists of a manager and the employees who report to him or her. Thus, it is defined in terms of the organization's hierarchy. Membership in the group arises from each employee's position on the organizational chart.

ii. Task Group: A task group is made up of employees who work together to complete a particular task or project. A task group's boundaries are not limited to its immediate hierarchical superior. It can cross command relationships. A employee's membership in the group arises from the responsibilities delegated to the employee - that is, the employee's responsibility to carry out particular activities. Task group may be temporary with an established life span, or they may be open ended.

2. Informal Groups: An organization's informal groups are groups that evolve to meet social or affiliation needs by bringing people together based on shared interests or friendship. Thus, informal groups are alliances that are neither formally structured nor organizationally determined. These groups are natural formations in the work environment that appear in response to the need for social contact. Many factors explain why people are attracted to one another. One explanation is simply proximity; when people work near one another every day, they are likely to form friendships. That likelihood is even greater when people also share similar attitudes, personalities, or economic status.

   i. Friendship Groups: Groups often develop because the individual members have one or more common characteristics. We call these formations friendship groups. Social alliances, which frequently extend outside the work situation, can be based on similar age, hold same political view, attended the same college etc.

   ii. Interest Groups: People who may or may not be aligned into common command or task groups may affiliate to attain a specific objective with which each is concerned. This is an interest group.

   iii. Reference Groups: Sometimes, people use a group as a basis for comparison in making decisions or forming opinions. When a group is used in this way, it is a reference group. Employees have reference groups inside or outside the organization where they work. For most people, the family is the most important reference groups. Other important reference groups typically include coworkers, friends, and members of the person's religious organization. The employee need not admire a group for it to serve as a reference group. Some reference groups serve as a negative reference; the employee tries to be unlike members of these groups.

iv. Membership Groups: When a person does belong to a group (formal and informal groups to which employees actually belong) the group is called a membership group (or affiliation group) for that person. Members of a group have some collection of benefits and responsibilities that go beyond the group serving as a reference point. In a membership group, each member would be expected to contribute to the group's well being and would enjoy the benefit arising from the group member's friendship.

REASONS FOR FORMING GROUPS

Formal and informal groups form in organizations for different reasons. Formal groups are sometimes called official or assigned groups and informal groups may be called unofficial or emergent groups. Organizations routinely form groups. If we assume management decisions are rational, groups must benefit organizations in some way. Presumably, the use of groups can contribute to achieving and maintaining a sustainable competitive advantage. Groups can do this if they enable an organization to fully tap the abilities and energy of its human resources. Furthermore, with regard to informal groups, people form groups to meet their individual needs.

1. Performance: Group effort can be more efficient and effective than individual efforts because they enable employees to specialize and contribute a variety of strengths. Organizations structure employees into functional and task groups so that they can develop and apply expertise in particular functions, products, problems or customers. The other factor contributing to performance is motivation, and groups can enhance this as well. When employees work in groups, the group is an important force for creating and enforcing standards for behaviour.

2. Cooperation: Carrying out an organization's mission is something

no single person can do alone. However, for several people to accomplish a mutual goal, they must cooperate. Group dynamics and characteristics can enhance cooperation among employees, especially when members identify themselves as group and are rewarded for group success.

3. Satisfaction: If satisfaction improves motivation (and therefore performance), organizations as well as individual employees can benefit from employees' satisfaction derived from group membership. A major source of this satisfaction is that people have needs for being with others and being liked by them. The way people satisfy this category of needs is participating in groups focusing on social activity. Group membership may also be a means for satisfying needs for security, power and esteem.

STAGES OF GROUP DEVELOPMENT

In interpreting behaviour of a particular group, it is important to recognize not only a broad pattern of development but also the unique characteristics of the particular group and the circumstances that contribute to (or detract from) its development. The way in which a particular group develops depends in part on such variables as the frequency with which group members interact and personal characteristics of group members. However, it was believed groups pass through a standard sequence of five stages.

1. Forming: When a group is initially formed, its members cannot accomplish much until they agree on what their purpose is, how they will work together and so on. Answering such questions brings group members face to face with the first obstacle to maturity: uncertainty, anxiety, and disagreement over power and authority. In this stage, the focus is on the interpersonal relations among the members. Members assess one another with regard to trustworthiness, emotional comfort, and evaluative acceptance. Thus, the forming stage is characterized by a great deal of uncertainty about the group's purpose, structure and leadership. Members are testing the waters to determine that type of behaviour is acceptable. This stage is complete when members have begun to think of themselves as part of a group.
2. Storming: The storming stage is one of inter-group conflict.

Members accept the existence of the group, but resist the constraints the group imposes on individuality. Further, there is conflict over who will control the group. After a group leader has emerged, the remaining group members must sort out where they fit in the group. Even if all the group members must sort out where they fit in the group. Even if all the group members accept the leader, the group enters a phase of conflict and challenge. One or more followers may test the leader. The group may split into factions supporting and opposing the leader. If the group gets stuck in this phase of development, group members may engage in battles over turf and expend their energies on a variety of political tactics. When this stage is complete, a relatively clear hierarchy of leadership exists within the group.

3. Norming: In this stage, close relationships develop and the group demonstrates cohesiveness. Entering and conducting the cohesion phase requires intervention by a group member who is emotionally unaffected by power and authority issues. Typically, such a person encourages group members to confront these issues openly. If the group engages in this process, the cohesion phase usually passes quickly. Group members recognize where they fit in, and the group agrees on how it will operate. A new leader may emerge, or the existing leader may become more aware of how much others in the group contribute. The norming stage is complete when the group structure solidifies and the group has assimilated a common set of expectations of what defines correct member behaviour.

4. Performing: The fourth stage is performing. The structure at this point is fully functional and accepted. Group energy has moved from getting to know and understand each other to performing the task at hand. Members' attention is directed to self-motivation and the motivation of other group members for task accomplishment. Some members focus on the task function of initiating activity and ensure that the work of the group really gets moving. Other members contribute to motivation and commitment within the group through maintenance functions such as supporting, encouraging and recognizing the contributions of members or through establishing the standards that the group may use in evaluating

its performance.

5. Adjourning: For permanent work groups, performing is the last stage in their development. However for temporary groups, there is an adjourning stage. In this stage, the group prepares for its disbandment. High task performance is no longer the group's top priority. Instead, attention is directed toward wrapping up activities.

CHARACTERISTICS OF GROUPS

Groups in organizations are more than collections of individual employees. We can distinguish effective groups in terms of role structures, norms, cohesiveness, leadership, status, tasks and size. These characteristics act as a means of understanding why some groups perform better than others.

1. Role Structures: Each person in a group has a role, or a pattern of expected behaviours associated with a certain position in the group. Each group member's role is a part of the group's overall role structure, that is the set of roles and relationships among roles that has been defined and accepted by group members. Roles develop through a combination of group processes and individual processes.
   i. Group members have an expected role for each individual. In formal groups, the organization has expectations for what employees in each position should do.
   ii. Through verbal and behavioural messages, group members communicate their expectations: a sent role. For expected roles in formal groups, the organization often spells out its expectations in job descriptions.
   iii. The individual group member's perceptions of these communication results in a perceived role.
   iv. The group member's response, acting out (or not acting out) the perceived role is the enacted role. The way the role is enacted influences the group's future role expectations. A group is most likely to be effective if its members understand and accept roles that are consistent with high perform.
2. Norms: The standards that a work group uses to evaluate the behaviour of its members are its norms of behaviour. These

norms may be written or unwritten, verbalized or not verbalized, implicit or explicit. So long as individual members of the group should do, or they may specify what members of a group should not do. Norms may exist in any aspect of work group life. They may evolve informally or unconsciously within a group, or they may arise in response to challenges. Norms reflect the culture of the particular group, so they vary from one group to another. When the group's norms are consistent with the organization's goals, they can contribute to organizational effectiveness. The degree to which norms have an impact depends on the extent to which group members comply with them and the group's enforcement of them.

Individual Adjustment: The degree to which group members accept norms is called individual adjustment. The impact of individual adjustment on the group depends on whether norms are pivotal or peripheral. Pivotal norms define behaviour that is absolutely required for continued membership in the group. Peripheral norms define behaviour that is desirable - but not essential - for continued group membership. Combining these types of norms with the choice of whether to accept them results in four possible levels of individual adjustment:

- Acceptance of both kinds of norms is "conformity" to the group.
- Rejection of both kinds of norms results in "open revolution".
- Accepting only pivotal norms amounts to "creative individualism".
- Accepting only peripheral norms amounts to "subversive rebellion".

Enforcement of Norms: To function effectively, groups enforce their norms in various ways.

i. The group may increase communication with a non-conforming member.
ii. If that does not work, the group may ignore the non-conforming member and exclude him or her from activities.
iii. In extreme cases, group members may resort to physical coercion or expulsion.

3. Cohesiveness: The commitment of members to a group and the strength of their desire to remain in the group constituted

the group's cohesiveness. It is the "interpersonal glue" that makes the members of a group stick together is group cohesion. Group cohesion can enhance job satisfaction for members and improve organizational productivity. Highly cohesive groups at work may not have many interpersonal exchanges away from the workplace. However, they are able to control and manage their membership better than work groups low in cohesion.

This is due to the strong motivation in highly cohesive groups to maintain good, close relationships with other members.

Factors Affecting Cohesiveness: Individuals tend to consider a group attractive if it meets the following conditions:

- The group's goals are clear and compatible with members' goals.
- The group has a charismatic leader.
- The group has a reputation for successfully accomplishing its task.
- The group is small enough that members can air their opinions and have them evaluated.
- The members support one another and help each other overcome barriers to growth and development.

Furthermore, cohesiveness may be easier to establish in a group whose membership is homogeneous. Groups also tend to be highly cohesive when they perceive a threat that gives group members a "common enemy".

4. Leadership: A key role in determining the success of the group is the role of the leader. Effective leadership can shape a group into a powerful force for accomplishing what individual members could not or would not do alone. Organizations need to cultivate effective group leaders whose goals support the organization's objectives.
5. Status: Status is the degree of worth and respects that other members of the group accord individual group members. Status may arise from the person's job or behaviour in the group. Often, a group member's status is linked to the person's position in the organization. Someone near the top of the organizations hierarchy has a higher status. Status may also be based on age, gender, education level, seniority, race or other

characteristics.

i. The status of group members can enhance effectiveness if the high-status members have the most to contribute to the group's objectives. However, if status causes a person to have influence beyond his or her ability to contribute to group goals, the group's effectiveness will suffer.

6. Tasks: The productivity and satisfaction of group members also depend on the kinds of tasks the group carries out. Major ways to describe group tasks are in terms of type and performance requirements.

Task Type: The type of task carried out by a group is defined by the major kinds of activity involved. Tasks may be classified as follows:

- Production tasks: Tasks requiring the group to produce and present ideas, images or arrangements.
- Discussion tasks: tasks requiring the group to evaluate issues and
- Problem-solving tasks: Tasks requiring the group to decide on a course of action for resolving a particular problem.
- Performing Requirements: The performing requirements of a task may be of following types:
- Disjunctive Tasks: Tasks that can be completed through individual efforts of group members.
- Conjunctive Tasks: These are tasks where each person's efforts are tightly linked to the efforts of others. Group members are highly interdependent.
- Additive Tasks: Are tasks where productivity is measured by adding together the output of each group member.

CHARACTERISTICS OF MATURE GROUPS

The description of a well-functioning effective groups characterizes a mature group. Such a group has four distinguishing characteristics:

1. Purpose and Mission: The purpose and mission may be assigned to a group or may emerge from within the group. Even in the case of an assigned mission, the group may re-examine, modify, revise, or question the mission. It may also embrace the mission as stated. The mission statement is converted into a specific

agenda, clear goals, and a set of critical success factors. Stating the purpose and mission in the form of specific goals enhances productivity over and above any performance benefits achieved through individual goal setting.

2. Behavioural Norms: Behavioural norms, which evolve over a period of time, are well-understood standards of behaviour within a group. They are benchmarks against which team members are evaluated and judged by other group members. Some behavioural norms become written rules while other norms remain informal, although they are no less well understood by group members.

3. Group Cohesion: It enables a group to exercise effective control over its members in relationship to its behavioural norms and standards. Goal conflict in a group, unpleasant experiences, and domination of a subgroup are among the threats to a group's cohesion. Groups with low levels of cohesion have greater difficulty exercising control over their members and enforcing their standards of behaviour. Group cohesion is influenced by a number of factors, most notably time, size, the prestige of the team, external pressure, and internal competition. Group cohesion evolves gradually over time through a group's normal development.

4. Status Structure: Status structure is the set of authority and task relations among a group's members. The status structure may be hierarchical or egalitarian (democratic), depending on the group. Successful resolution of the authority issue within a team results in a well-understood status structure of leader-follower relationship. Where leadership problems arise, it is important to find solutions and build team leader effectiveness.

   External Conditions Imposed on the Group: Groups are a subset of a larger organization system. Therefore, the organization will impose some conditions on the group. These external conditions are:

5. Authority Structures: Organizations have authority structures that define who reports to whom, who makes decisions, and what decisions individuals or groups are empowered to make. So, while someone who emerges informally from within the group might lead a work group, the formally designated leader (appointed by management) has authority that others in the

group don't have.

6. Organizational Culture: Every organization has an unwritten culture that defines standards of acceptable and unacceptable behaviour for employees. Members of work groups have to accept the standards implied in the organization's dominant culture if they are to remain in good standing.
7. Formal Regulations: Organizations create rules, procedures, policies and other forms of regulations to standardize employee behaviour. The more formal regulations that the organization imposes on all its employees, the more the behaviour of work group members are consistent and predictable.
8. Organizational Resources: When organizations have limited resources, so do their work groups. What a group actually accomplishes is, to a large degree, determined by what it is capable of accomplishing. The presence or absence of resources such as money, time, raw materials and equipment - which are allocated to the group by the organization - has a large bearing on the group's behaviour.
9. Physical Work Setting: The physical work setting imposed on the group by eternal parties has an important bearing on work group behaviour. They physical setting creates both barriers and opportunities for work group interaction. Workers will not be able to waste time if their superiors work close to them.
10. Reward System: Since work groups are part of the larger organizational system, group members will be influenced by how the organization evaluates performance and what behaviours are rewarded.

GROUP STRUCTURE

Work groups are not unorganized mobs. They have a structure that shapes the behaviour of members and makes it possible to explain and predict a large portion of individual behaviour within the group as well as the performance of the group itself. Group structure includes: -

1. Leadership: A major responsibility in working with groups is the recognition of leadership forces. Almost every work group has a formal leader. This leader can play an important part in the group's success. He is appointed by management and can exercise legitimate sanctioned power. The formal leader

possesses the power to discipline and/or fire members of his work group. Informal leaders, on the other hand, tend to emerge gradually as group members interact. They emerge from within the group according to the nature of the situation at hand. The primary function of a leader (informal / formal) is to facilitate the accomplishment of group goals. He aids the group in accomplishing its goals. To survive, the group must gear its efforts to achieve its primary goals. Leader, constantly evaluates, directs and motivates member behaviour towards overall goals.

2. Roles: A role is a set of activities expected of a person occupying a particular position within the group. It is a pattern of behaviour that is expected of an individual when he interacts with others. The understanding of role behaviour would be dramatically simplified if each of us chose one role and play it out regularly and constantly. However, Individuals play multiple roles adjusting their roles to the group in which they are. So different groups impose different role requirements on individuals.

   Characteristics of Roles:

   i. Roles are impersonal. It is the position that determines the expectations not the individual.
   ii. An organizational role is the set of expected behaviours for a particular position vis-à-vis a particular job.
   iii. It is fairly difficult to pin down roles in exact terms. It is the most complex organized response pattern the human being is capable of making.
   iv. Roles are learned quickly and can result in major changes in behaviour.

   Role Identity: Role identity is certain attitudes and behaviour consistent with a role. People have the ability to shift roles rapidly when they recognize that the situation and its demands clearly require major changes. For example, when a worker holds a position in a workers union is promoted as supervisor, his attitude will change from pro-union to pro-management.

   Role Perception: Role perception is an individual's view of how he or she is supposed to act in a given situation. Based on an interpretation of how we believe we are supposed to behave, we engage in certain types of behaviour.

Role Expectations: Role expectations are defined as how others believe you should act in a given situation. How you behave is determined to a large extent by the role defined in the context in which you are acting.

Role Conflict: Role conflict is a situation in which an individual is confronted by divergent role expectations. Role conflict, like other forms of conflict, can be a major source of stress. Excessive stress can cause problems for individual employees and for the organizations that employ them.

3. Norms: Norms are shared ways of looking at the world. Groups control members through the use of norms. A norm is a rule of conduct that has been established by group members to maintain consistency in behaviour. Norms tell members what they ought and ought not to do under certain circumstances. From an individual's standpoint they tell what is expected of you in certain situations. Norms differ among groups, communities, and societies, but they all have norms.

   According to Hackman, Norms have five characteristics: -

   i. Norms summarize and simplify group influence processes. They resolve impersonal differences in a group and ensure uniformity of action.
   ii. Norms apply only to behaviour - not to private thoughts and feelings.
   iii. Norms are usually developed gradually, but the process can be shortened if members so desire.
   iv. Not all norms apply to everyone. High status members often enjoy more freedom to deviate from the "letter of the law" than do other members.

Types of Norms

A work group's norms are unique to each work group. Yet there are some common classes of norms that appear in most work groups.

i. Performance-related processes: Work groups typically provide their members with explicit cues on how hard they should work, how to get the job done, their level of output etc. These norms deal with performance-related processes and are extremely powerful in affecting an individual employee's performance.
ii. Appearance Factors: Some organizations have formal dress

codes. However, even in their absence, norms frequently develop to dictate the kind of clothing that should be worn to work.

iii. Allocation of Resources: These norms cover pay, assignment of difficult jobs, and allocation of new tools and equipment.

iv. Informal Social arrangement: These norms can originate in the group or in the organization and cover pay assignment of difficult jobs, and allocation of new tools and equipment.

Factors Influencing Conformance to Norms

As a member of a group, you desire acceptance by the group. Because of your desire for acceptance, you are susceptible to conforming to the group's norms. Considerable evidence shows that groups can place strong pressures on individual members to change their attitudes and behaviours to conform to the group's standard. However, conformity to norms is not automatic it depends on the following factors:

i. Personality Factors: Research on personality factors suggests that the more intelligent are less likely to conform than the less intelligent. Again, in unusual situations where decisions must be taken on unclear items, there is a greater tendency to conform to the group's norms. Under conditions of crisis, conformity to group norms is highly probable.

ii. Situational Factors: Group size, communication patterns, degree of group unanimity etc., are the situational factors influencing the conformity to norms.

iii. Intra-group Relationships: A group that is seen as being creditable will evoke more compliance than a group that is not.

iv. Compatible Goals: When individual goals coincide with group goals, people are more willing to adhere to group norms.

4. Status: Status is a socially defined position or rank given to groups or group members by others. Individual group members are also distinguished by the amount of status they have within the group, that is, the degree of worth and respect they are accorded by group members. Status is an important factor in understanding human behaviour because it is a significant motivator and has major behavioural consequences when individuals perceive a disparity between what they believe their status to be and what others perceive it to be.

Formal Status: Status may be formally imposed by organizations through position and titles. We are all familiar with the trappings of high organizational status - large offices with impressive views, fancy titles, high pay etc.

Informal Status: Status may be informally acquired by such characteristics as education, age, gender, skill and experience. Anything can have status value if others in the group evaluate it as status conferring.

Status is an important characteristic of groups because it affects group structure and dynamics. Status figures in the allocation of roles among group members. In general, high-status group members get high status roles such as group leader or expert, whereas low-status group members get low-status roles. Furthermore, group members tend to pay more attention to input from high-status group members, including their contributions to group decisions.

5. Size: The size of a group can have profound implications on how the group behaves internally and with regard to other groups. It is an important factor determining the number of interactions of individuals in a group. In a small group face-to-face interaction is quite easy and uncomplicated. Members can easily communicate with other group members. Research evidence confirms the fact that small groups are effective. On the other hand, in large groups members have a better chance of finding people they like to work with. The potential for greater variety of talents is also greater. But the disadvantages of size are more than offset its advantages. Larger group offer greater opportunities for differences between and among individuals.

Composition: Most group activities require a variety of skills and knowledge. Given this requirement, it would be reasonable to conclude that heterogeneous groups would be more likely to have diverse abilities and information and should be more effective. When a group is heterogeneous in terms of gender, personalities, opinions, abilities, skills and perspectives, there is an increased probability that the group will possess the needed characteristics to complete its tasks effectively. The group may be more conflict laden and less expedient as diverse positions are introduced and assimilated, but the evidence generally supports the conclusion that heterogeneous groups perform more effectively than do those that are homogeneous

Conclusion: In interpreting behaviour of a particular group, it is important to recognize not only a broad pattern of development but also the unique characteristics of the particular group and the circumstances that contribute to (or detract from) its development. The behaviour of individuals in groups is something more than the sum total of each acting in his or her own way. Groups help in building synergy is necessary for an organization's success.

GROUP DECISION MAKING

Managers like to believe that they are accomplished in such group activities like group decision making, goal setting and problem solving. However-their ability to implement such techniques is often hindered by their lack of understanding of the dynamics of group-decision making processes. As a result, these managers often end up perpetuating problems that they themselves create through their insensitivity to the needs of other group members. Hence, instead of achieving a consensus, such managers take decision by the use of their authority. Sometimes, they lead the group towards decision making by minority rule or by majority rule. The better way to achieve consensus would be for them to track how decisions are made and ensure that they are achieved by consultations with group members. The various methods of group decision making are given below:

1. Decision by Lack of Response: The most common group decision-making method is the decision by lack of response. In this method, someone suggest an idea and before anyone else has said anything about it, without any deliberations it is rejected. In other words, all ideas that have been simply bypassed have in a sense been rejected by the group. The idea has been rejected because the 'rejections' is a simply a common decision not to support the idea. This method is also called the 'plop' method because the suggestion of the proposer has been 'plopped'.
2. Decision by Authority Rule: Many groups have a power structure that makes it clear that the leader (chairman or someone in authority) will make the ultimate decision. In this case the group can generate ideas and hold free discussion, but the chairman or the leader may say that he has heard the discussion and has decided upon a given plan. The authority

rule method produces a bare minimum of involvement by the group and unless the leader is very proficient he will not be able to take good decisions.

3. Decision by Minority Rule: A single person can enforce a decision, particularly if he is the chairman and does not give in to the opposition. A common form of minority rule is for two or more members to come to a quick and powerful agreement on a course of action and implement it through the chairman or other powerful members of the group. Usually in the decision by minority rule, one, two or three people employ the tactics that produce action and therefore must be considered decisions but which are taken without the consent of the majority.
4. Decision by Majority Rule: Under this system, it is felt that if the majority of participants feels the same way, it is often assumed that, that decision is the best. On the surface, this method seems completely sound but often it turns out that decisions made by this method are not well implemented, even by the group that made the decision. This is so because of two kinds of psychological barriers:

- The minority feels that there was an insufficient discussion or that their point of view were not properly understood and they may therefore feel misunderstood and sometimes resentful.
- The minority members feel that voting (done to understand majority preference) has resulted in two camps and that their camp has lost. As there are time constraints in coming to a group decision and because there is not perfect system, a decision by consensus is one of the most effective methods. This method is time consuming. Recognising the several types of group decision-making is only part of the process. Managers must be specific in their approach to the one that is best in their own situation.

TECHNIQUES FOR GROUP DECISION MAKING

The most common form of group decision making takes place in face-to-face interacting groups. Interacting groups often censor themselves and pressure individual members toward conformity of opinion. Once a manager has determined the technique that a group decision approach should be used, he or she can determine the technique best suited to the decision situation. Seven techniques are summarized below:

1. Brainstorming: Brainstorming is a good technique for generating alternatives. The idea behind brainstorming is to generate as many ideas as possible, suspending evaluation until all of the ideas have been suggested. Participations are encouraged to build upon the suggestions of others, and imagination is emphasized. Brainstorming is meant to overcome pressures for conformity in the interacting group that retard the development of creative alternatives. Groups that use brainstorming have been shown to produce significantly more ideas than groups that do not. In typical brainstorming session, about 6 to 10 people sit and discuss the problem. The group leader states the problem in a clear manner so that all participants understand it. No criticism is allowed, and all the alternatives are recorded for later discussion and analysis. One recent trend is the use of electronic brainstorming instead of verbal brainstorming in groups. Electronic brainstorming overcomes two common problems that can produce group-brainstorming failure:
   - Production Blocking: While listening to others, individuals are distracted from their own ideas. This is referred to as production blocking.
   - Evaluation Apprehension: Some individuals suffer from evaluation apprehension in brainstorming groups. They fear that others might respond negatively to their ideas. Brainstorming, however, is merely a process for generating ideas.
2. Nominal Group Technique (NGT): The nominal group technique restricts discussion or interpersonal communication during the decision-making process, hence the term nominal. Group members are all physically present, as in a traditional committee meeting, but members operate independently. NGT has the following discrete steps:
   i. Individuals silently list their ideas.
   ii. Ideas are written on a chart one at a time until all ideas are listed.
   iii. Discussion is permitted, but only to clarify the ideas. No criticism is allowed.
   iv. A written vote is taken

NGT is a good technique to use in a situation where group members fear criticism from others. The chief advantage of the NGT method is that it permits the group to meet formally but does not restrict independent thinking, as does the interacting group.

3. Delphi Technique: The Delphi technique originated at the Rand Corporation to gather the judgements of experts for use in decision-making. Delphi method is similar to the nominal group technique except it does not require the physical presence of the group's members. Experts at remote locations respond to a questionnaire. A coordinator summarizes the responses to the questionnaire, and the summary is sent back to the experts. The experts then rate the various alternatives generated, and the coordinator tabulates the results. The following steps characterize the Delphi technique:
    - The problem is identified and members are asked to provide potential solutions through a series of carefully designed questionnaire.
    - Each member anonymously and independently completes the questionnaire.
    - Results of the questionnaire are compiled at a central location, transcribed, and reproduced.
    - Each member receives a copy of the results.
    - After viewing the results, members are again asked for their solutions.

The advantages of the Delphi Technique are as follows:

1. The Delphi technique is valuable in its ability to generate a number of independent judgements without the requirement of a face-to-face meeting.
2. The Delphi technique can be used for decision making among geographically scattered groups.
3. The cost of bringing experts together at a central location is avoided.

    The Disadvantages of the Delphi Technique are mentioned below:

    - The Delphi technique is extremely time consuming, it is frequently not applicable where a speedy decision is necessary.
    - The method may not develop the rich array of alternatives

as the interacting of

- nominal group technique does.
- Ideas that might surface from the heat of face-to-face interaction may never arise.

4. Electronic Meetings: This method, blends the nominal group technique with sophisticated computer technology. Issues are presented to participants and they type their responses onto their computer screen. Individual comments, as well as aggregate votes, are displayed on a projection screen.

   The advantages of electronic meetings are

   - Participants can anonymously type any message they want and it flashes on the screen for all to see at the push of a participant's keyboard.
   - It allows people to be brutally honest without penalty.
   - It is fast because discussions don't go off the point and many participants can "talk" at once.

   The disadvantages of electronic meetings are

   - Those who can type fast can outshine those who are verbally eloquent but poor typists;
   - Those with the best ideas don't get credit for them; and
   - The process lacks the information richness of face-to-face oral communication.

5. Quality Circles and Quality Teams: Quality circles are small groups that voluntarily meet to provide input for solving quality or production problems. Quality circles are often generated from the bottom up; that is, they provide advice to managers, who still retain decision-making authority. As such, quality circles are not empowered to implement their own recommendations. They operate in parallel fashion to the organization's structure, and they rely on voluntary participation. Quality teams, in contrast, are included in total quality management and other quality improvement efforts as part of a change in the organization's structure. Quality teams are generated from the top down and are empowered to act on their own recommendations. Quality Circles and quality teams are methods for using groups in the decision-making process. The next method, self-managed teams take the concept of participation one step further.

6. Self-Managed Teams: Self-managed teams make many of the

decisions that were once reserved for managers, such as work scheduling, job assignments and staffing. Unlike quality circles, whose role is an advisory one, self-managed teams are delegated authority in the organization's decision-making process.

i. Before choosing a group decision-making technique, the manager carefully evaluates the group members and the decision situation. Then the best method for accomplishing the objectives of the group decision-making process can be selected.

For example:

- The need for expert input would be best facilitated by the Delphi Technique.
- If the goal is generating a large number of alternatives.
- Decisions that concern quality or production would benefit from advice of quality circles.
- If group members were reluctant to contribute ideas, the nominal group technique would be appropriate.
- A manager who wants to provide total empowerment of a group should consider self-managed.

UNDERSTANDING WORK TEAMS

A team is a relatively permanent work group whose members must coordinate their activities to achieve one or more common objectives. The objectives might include advising others in the organization, producing goods or services, and carrying out a project. Because achievement of the team's objectives requires coordination, team members depend on one another and must interact regularly. A work team generates positive synergy through coordinated effort. Their individual efforts result in a level of performance that is greater than the sum of those individual inputs. Teams have far-reaching impact in the today's workplace. They have become an essential part of the way business is being done. Teams imply a high degree of coordination among their members, along with a shared belief that winning (achieving team goals) is not only desirable but the very reason for the team's existence. Any team is therefore a group, but only some groups have the high degree of interdependence and commitment to success we associate with a team. Although the desire to achieve high levels of commitment and coordination is common among organizations using teamwork, the nature of specific teams varies considerably.

Two major dimensions along which teams differ are differentiation of team roles and integration into the organization.

- Differentiation: is the extent to which team members are specialized relative to others in the organization.
- Integration: is the degree to which the team must coordinate with managers, employees, suppliers and customers outside the team.

TYPES OF TEAMS

Based on their objectives teams may be classified as problem-solving teams, self-managed teams and cross-functional teams.

- Problem-Solving Teams: Problem-solving teams consists of groups of 5 - 10 employees from the same department who meet for a few hours each week to discuss ways of improving quality, efficiency and the work environment. These members share ideas or offer suggestions on how work processes and methods can be improved. Problem-solving teams meet regularly to discuss their quality problems, investigate causes of the problems recommend solutions and take corrective actions.
- Self-Managed Work Teams: A self-managed team includes collective control over the pace of work, determination of work assignments, organization of breaks, and collective choice of inspection procedures. Fully self-managed work teams even select their own members and have the members evaluate each other's performance. As a result, supervisory positions take on decreased importance and may even be eliminated. These teams do their own scheduling, rotate jobs on their own, establish production targets, set pay scales that are linked to skills, fire coworkers and do the hiring.
- Cross-Functional Teams: Cross-functional teams are made up of employees from about the same hierarchical level, but from different work areas, who come together to accomplish a task. Cross-functional teams are an effective way to allow people from diverse areas within an organization (or even between organization) to exchange information, develop new ideas and solve problems and coordinate complex projects. These teams are not easy

to manage. Their early stages of development are often very time consuming as members learn to work with diversity and complexity. It takes time to build trust and teamwork, especially among people from different backgrounds, with different experiences and perspectives. There are two types of cross-functional teams. They are:

- Task force - It is nothing other than a temporary cross-functional team.
- Committees - Composed of groups made up of members from across departmental lines.

CONCLUSION

We define "group" as more than two employees who have an ongoing relationship in which they interact and influence one another's behaviour and performance. The behaviour of individuals in groups is something more than the sum total of each acting in his or her own way. When individuals are in groups, they act differently than they do when they are alone. Formal and informal groups are formed in organizations for different reasons. The way in which a particular group develops depends in part on such variables as the frequency with which group members interact and personal characteristics of group members. It is therefore important for us to understand in an orderly manner how groups help managers change human behaviour in different organizational situations.

Note: For a very good case study regarding this topic, reader can visit company's website of Safeway Inc. Safeway is a food and drug retailer. The company operates in the US and Canada. It is headquartered in Pleasanton, California and employs about 197,000 people; this figure includes part-time employees. www.safeway.com

6

Positive Emotion in Organizations

The fundamental tenet of 'Positive Organization Scholarship' is that organizational management and decision settings need to be reframed in a positive light. It follows therefore that managers need to shift their focus to the positive aspects of organizational functioning and achievement, rather than dwell on the defensive measures needed to deal with real and imagined negative contingencies. A corollary of this view, first advanced by Staw et al., and more recently confirmed by Lyubomirsky et al., is that such organizations need also to be characterized by positive, rather than negative emotion. More recently, Ashkanasy and Daus have described these organizations in terms of a 'healthy emotional climate'. Consistent with this proposition and based on a multi-level model of emotions in organizations, we outline in this chapter how organizations can engender positive emotion, and conclude that positive emotion is a necessary precondition of positive organizational behaviour.

Although Isen and Baron identified the importance of mild positive affect in organizational behaviour 15 years ago, since then much of the literature that has dealt with emotions in the workplace has focused on negative emotions. For example, Fitness studied 'anger in the workplace', Ashkanasy and Nicholson studied the 'climate of fear', while Frost focused on 'toxic emotions', including their antecedents and consequences, and prescriptions for dealing with toxic emotions. In this chapter, we return to the spirit of Isen and Baron's seminal article and emphasize the link between positive emotion and exceptional performance in organizational contexts. Also, and consistent with Isen, we argue that positive emotions are associated with individual and group creativity. More recently, Lyubomirsky et al. found, in an extensive meta-analysis, that positive affect leads to more successful outcomes than negative affect across a range of contextual domains, including in the workplace. The theory of positive affect in organizations that we set out here thus provides a basis upon which to understand how and when organizations can foster positive emotion, and why positive emotions should be associated with positive behaviour. The multi-level perspective we present in this chapter to address these issues is based on the 5-level model of emotion in organizations described by Ashkanasy:

- Level 1. Neuropsychological and cognitive correlates of positive emotion at the within-person level of analysis;
- Level 2. Individual differences in positive emotion at the between persons level of analysis;
- Level 3. Communication of positive emotion at the dyadic (relationships) level of analysis;
- Level 4. Promulgation of positive emotion at the group level of analysis; and
- Level 5. Creation of a positive emotional climate at the organizational level of analysis.

ANTECEDENTS OF POSITIVE EMOTIONS IN .ORGANIZATIONS

The majority of research on the antecedents of positive emotions focuses on the cognitive appraisal process that initiates emotional reactions to positive events. The nature of the specific events that trigger positive emotions in the organizational environment has only recently been considered, however. To address this in the specific context of the workplace, we base our discussion on Weiss and Cropanzano's Affective Events Theory (AET), and use this as a basic framework to describe the situational determinants of positive emotion in workplace settings.

Weiss and Cropanzano argue that events and conditions in the workplace that facilitate the attainment of workplace goals constitute positive 'affective events', and it is these events that ultimately determine the occurrence of moods and emotions. Such emotions and moods can lead to the formation of more long-term attitudes, reflected in job satisfaction and affective commitment, or even organizational. The seminal contribution of AET is that it represents an attempt to understand why employees' moment to moment moods fluctuate in the workplace environment. A further outcome of AET is the importance of accumulation of hassles and uplifts. Thus, rather than the intensity of major events being the source of attitudes and behaviour at work, according to AET, emotions are determined more by the frequency with which hassles or uplifts occur. This conclusion implies in respect of negative emotions that people are more capable of handling once-off incidents than they are of dealing with ongoing hassles. Afurther corollary of this is that the accumulation of negative events can be offset by positive support from colleagues, friends, and family. Finally, this idea is consistent with Isen and Baron's contention that 'positive affect states induced by seemingly minor, everyday events can have significant effects on social behaviour and cognitive processes that can be important for the functioning of organizations'.

It is clear from AET that contextual factors play a pivotal role as determinants of employees' fluctuating moods and emotions in the workplace. It is also important, however, first to understand the internal neurological and cognitive mechanisms that determine the impact of positive affective events on organizational behaviour.

LEVEL 1: POSITIVE EMOTION AT THE WITHIN-PERSON LEVEL OF ANALYSIS

Neuropsychological correlates of positive emotion

At the most basic level of understanding, neurobiological processes underlie the experience of emotion, including perception, and understanding and display of positive emotional expression. Mirroring the emphasis on negative emotions in organizational research, however, much of the literature in emotions research in general has been oriented towards the negative emotions. LeDoux, for example, based his pioneering work on a study of fear. More recently, it has become clear that positive emotion is perceived, integrated and expressed by discrete neurobiological mechanisms that are quite distinct from the mechanisms associated with negative emotion. In particular, recent research has revealed that positive environmental stimuli are recognized by the basal ganglia region of the brain, while negative or aversive environmental stimuli are processed primarily by the amygdala. The basal ganglia are programmed to encode sequences of behaviour that, over time, have been repeated and rewarded - or at least not punished. The affective representations that are encoded by the basal ganglia support not only the execution of habitual behaviours but the prediction of what comes next in a sequence of thoughts or actions. These implicit skills are essential because they allow us to make automatic the sequences of thought and action that lead to adaptive success.

Further, basal ganglia activation has been found to be associated with the experience of positive emotions in response to positive environmental stimuli. As such, and as Brieter and Rosen have shown, degeneration of the basal ganglia is associated with depression and a lack of motivation to adaptive environmental demands. The ability to perceive and integrate positive emotional stimuli thus has important implications for adaptive social functioning, and is mediated by the basal ganglia.

Isen argues further that positive affect is a key facilitator of creativity. Consistent with the neuropsychological view noted earlier in this chapter, Isen and her colleagues posit that this process is mediated by the neurotransmitter dopamine. In their theory, dopamine levels in the blood are increased as a result of positive emotions, and the presence of this neurotransmitter in the anterior cingulate cortex is responsible for more creative and flexible cognitions.

In effect, there is strong evidence that positive and negative affect are driven by distinct neural circuits. Moreover, in support of Ashkanasy's multi-level model, Isen argues that the impact of positive affect on creativity at the group and organizational level derives from fundamental differences in mechanisms underlying the production of positive and negative affect, and differences in the impact of positive and negative affect on cognitive functioning. In the following, we describe theoretical frameworks for understanding the differential impact of positive and negative mood on cognitive processing.

Cognitive Correlates of Positive Emotion

Several cognitive mechanisms have been proposed to underlie the differential impact of positive and negative affect on cognitive functioning. Affect influences both the content of cognition, and the strategies that people use to process information. As such, positive and negative mood have different effects on the content and processes of cognition.

Content effects

The content effects of mood have received considerable attention in affect and cognition research. The primary finding here relates to the notion of 'mood congruence', which holds that individuals in a positive mood are likely to evaluate situational cues as correspondingly optimistic or positive, so that their associated judgments and decisions are also more likely to be positive. For example, people in a positive mood tend to form more positive impressions of others, and to make more optimistic risk assessments. People in a negative mood, on the other hand, are more likely to make more pessimistic risk assessments, and to evaluate other people and situations more negatively. A number of cognitive theories of affect congruence have been proposed. For example Bower's 'Affect Priming Theory' and Schwarz and Clore's 'Affectas- Information Model'.

Affect priming is based on an associative network model of mental representation. Fundamental to this model is the assumption that affective and cognitive representations are linked in an associative semantic network. Affect can infuse judgments by facilitating or priming access to related cognitive categories. As such, judgment and decision processes that rely on recall processes may be affected by positive affect. Consequently, when in a positive mood, managers are likely to be more optimistic, entrepreneurial, and to take more risks as their perception and assessment of situations is positively biased.

The affect-priming account suggests an indirect influence of affect on judgments, via the priming of affect-congruent semantic categories. The affect-as-information model suggests on the other hand that mood may also have direct informational effects, serving as a heuristic cue from which to infer judgments. When presented with a judgmental target, instead of deriving a response from a constructive, elaborate information search, people may simply ask themselves, 'How do I feel about it?' and base their judgments on this affective response.

Moderators of Affect-Congruence

While there is much empirical support for both content and processing effects of moods, there are many instances where affect infusion may not occur, and neither the affect priming nor the affect-as-information accounts can explain all such instances. Furthermore, there are cases in which the mood congruence literature and the mood and information processing literature make opposite predictions for the outcome of mood on cognition and behaviour. In response to this discrepancy, Forgas proposed the Affect Infusion Model (AIM) to explain the individual, situational and task differences that moderate the impact of moods and emotions on cognition and behaviour, via their impact on processing strategy. The primary assumption of the AIM is process mediation: the nature and extent of mood effects depends on the information processing strategy used for a particular task. The second assumption of the AIM is effort minimization: people should adopt the least effortful processing strategy capable of producing a response, all other things being equal. Mood congruence effects are most likely when some degree of open, constructive processing is used (heuristic and substantive strategies), and less likely when closed strategies are used (direct access and motivated processing).

LEVEL 2: POSITIVE EMOTION AT THE BETWEEN-PERSON (INDIVIDUAL DIFFERENCE) LEVEL OF ANALYSIS

Level 2 of the Ashkanasy model encompasses the between-person effects. In this section, we look at individual difference factors that moderate the frequency, intensity, and duration of the experience of positive affect. We address in particular trait affect and emotional intelligence.

Trait affect

Trait affect represents a personal disposition to be in a long-term positive or negative affective state. Fox and Spector and Staw and Barsade examined the effect of trait affect, and found that it plays a small but significant role as a determinant of personal outcomes in organizational settings. Of course, when negative trait affect becomes chronic, the result is burnout, with more severe consequences for the individual concerned. More recently, Judge and Larsen proposed a theory of job satisfaction based on trait affect, where they found that positive affect is an important precursor of job satisfaction.

Emotional intelligence

A second dimension of individual difference that we discuss is the relatively recent concept of emotional intelligence. This variable relates to individual differences in an individual's ability to perceive, to use (assimilate), to understand, and to manage or regulate their own and others' moods and emotions. Differences in emotional intelligence account for between-person variation in an individual's affective responses to affective events in the workplace, and the way that positive and negative emotions affect their cognitions and behaviours in the workplace. Fisher and Ashkanasy note that much had been expected of the emotional intelligence concept in terms of its relationship with positive organizational outcomes, but the impact of emotional intelligence on positive organizational outcomes continues to be unclear. While emotional intelligence is consistently correlated with trait positive affect and wellbeing, scholars continue to determine its relationship with work attitudes and outcomes. Ashkanasy et al. present a list of some key findings that appear to be providing a clearer picture of emotional intelligence, however. These are that emotional intelligence:

- Appears to be distinct from, but positively related to, other intelligences;
- Is an individual difference, where some people are more endowed, and others are less so;

- Develops over a person's life span and can be enhanced through training;
- Involves, at least in part, a person's abilities to identify and to perceive emotion (in self and others); and
- Includes skills to understand and to manage emotions successfully.

Emotional intelligence thus addresses an individual's ability to perceive emotion accurately, and to deal with it appropriately. Thus, while emotional intelligence does not ostensibly address positive emotion, Boyatzis and McKee make the case that emotional intelligence is a form of adaptive resilience, where high emotional intelligence employees are able to deal effectively with employment challenges such as job insecurity through adopting a positive view, while low emotional intelligence employees resort to maladaptive coping mechanisms. This parallels recent findings by Tugade and Fredrickson that positive emotional states contribute to emotional resilience.

LEVEL 3: POSITIVE EMOTION AT THE INTERPERSONAL (DYADIC) LEVEL OF ANALYSIS

In discussing within-person differences in positive emotion (Level 1), we addressed the influence of positive emotions on the content of cognitive appraisals, and on information processing strategies. These effects of mood on cognition also have important consequences for interpersonal relationships. As proposed in AET and the AIM, positive affective events affect the content of situation appraisals and the way in which information is processed, which in turn influences people's behaviour in the workplace. That is, positive mood has a significant impact upon the way in which people interpret one another's behaviour, which has implications for subsequent interactions.

For example, Forgas et al. demonstrated that happy people perceive significantly more positive and skilled behaviours and fewer negative, unskilled behaviours both in themselves and in their partners than did sad people. In terms of the AIM, these effects occur because affect priming influences the kinds of interpretations, constructs, and associations that become available as people evaluate intrinsically complex and indeterminate social behaviours in the course of substantive, inferential processing. In the workplace, therefore, the same performance review between a manager and employee that is judged to be positive and constructive by a happy person may be perceived to be negative and critical by someone in a bad mood. A behaviour that is of particular relevance to workplace functioning is requesting. There are several workplace situations in which the ability to formulate a request confidently, in a manner which maximizes the likelihood of compliance, is of strategic importance to the achievement of workplace or personal goals.

For example, requesting help from colleagues may be critical to one's ability to complete a task, and the achievement of compliance in the request for a pay rise may significantly affect one's future job satisfaction and personal well-being. In terms of the AIM, happy people should adopt a more confident, direct processing style, as a result of the greater availability and use of positively valenced thoughts and associations in their minds as they assess the felicity conditions for their requests. Consequently, people in a positive mood are more likely to be granted their request, as their requests are less equivocal and demonstrate less hedging, leaving the person receiving the request little opportunity to avoid meeting the object of the request. Moreover, Forgas has also demonstrated that people respond to people's requests more positively when in a positive mood than when in a negative mood.

Negotiation is another interpersonal task that is critical to organizational outcomes. Particularly with regards to top management, the ability to negotiate or bargain for optimal organizational outcomes is of great importance. Again, Forgas has shown that happy people are more confident during the negotiation process, are more assertive and persistent in reaching their desired goals, behave more cooperatively, and are more willing to use integrative strategies and make reciprocal deals than were those in a negative mood. As such, positive mood produces better outcomes for happy people than for sad individuals.

LEVEL 4: POSITIVE EMOTION AT THE GROUP LEVEL OF ANALYSIS

Schermerhorn et al. define a group as 'a collection of two or more people who work with one another regularly to achieve common goals'. As such, group members interact on a dyadic and collective basis, and naturally encounter all of the perceptions and experiences that we have outlined earlier in reference to individuals and their interactions. Nonetheless, groups introduce additional dimensions of cohesiveness, collective values, and leadership that render an added level of complexity to the discussion of emotions in workplace settings. In this respect, De Dreu, et al. see group settings as a sort of 'emotional incubator', where the emotional states of the group members combine to produce an overall group-level emotional tenor that, in turn, affects all group members. Kelly and Barsade argue more specifically that teams possess an 'affective composition' or a group mood, which begins either with the emotional characteristics of team members, and then develops through a process of emotional contagion, or the emotional expression of the group leader, which evokes emotion in group members.

Emotional contagion

Emotion contagion is 'a process in which a person or group influences the emotions or behaviour of another person or group through the conscious or unconscious induction of emotion states and behavioural attitudes'. Emotions are 'caught' by group members when they are exposed to the emotional expressions of other group members. Hatfield et al. posited that the degree to which emotional contagion occurs is mediated by attentional processes, with greater emotional contagion occurring when more attention is allocated.

When the emotional expression is observed, an affective state of the same valence (positive or negative) is then experienced by the observer group members. The actual mechanisms by which emotions are transferred are subconscious, automatic and 'primitive'. Psychological researchers have found that this process involves automatic non-conscious mimicry, in which people spontaneously imitate each others' facial expressions and body language, speech patterns and vocal tones. The second step of this primitive contagion process comes from the affective feedback people receive from mimicking others' nonverbal behaviours and expressions. This is also an automatic process. Several studies have demonstrated that the mimicking of nonverbal expressions of emotion results in the experience of the emotion itself through physiological, visceral, and glandular feedback responses. While group members ultimately become aware of this feeling, the initial process of emotion contagion is subconscious and automatic.

Zurcher argues that displays of positive emotion in group situations constitute an essential ingredient necessary for establishment of group cohesion. Furthermore, Lawler posits that emotion is the essential social process in group formation and maintenance. This is because positive emotions strengthen feelings of control. As such, positive emotion is a necessary precursor of group cohesiveness. In the context of organizational work groups, George has shown also that positive affect is a key ingredient for group effectiveness and satisfaction. Barsade found that positive emotion contagion amongst group members affects individual-level attitudes and group processes. Group members who experienced positive emotional contagion demonstrated improved cooperation, decreased conflict, and increased perceived task performance.

Group leadership and emotion [sh]

The role of leadership in communicating, expressing, and managing emotions in groups is axiomatic. According to Pfeffer leadership is seen as a process of symbolic management, and involves creating and maintaining shared meanings among followers. Ashforth and Humphrey argue that this process depends intrinsically on evocation of emotion. Based on Ortner's model, they note that symbols generate interacting cognitive and emotional responses, and they conclude, 'symbolic management involves orchestrating summarizing and elaborating symbols to evoke emotion which can be generalized to organizational ends'. Thus, leaders engage in communication of symbols designed to make followers feel better about themselves, and to strengthen followers' commitment to the organization.

It follows therefore that leadership entails perception, recognition, and management of emotional cues by both the leader and the led, which we described earlier as emotional sensitivity. A leader's displayed emotion is a critical determinant of the quality of relationships with group members, and consequently of the leader's ability to communicate emotionally evocative symbols. Thus, facilitated by processes of emotional contagion, positive group affect energized by emotionally aware leaders, can enhance organizational creativity performance by facilitating group cohesion and positive affect.

LEVEL 5: POSITIVE EMOTION AT THE ORGANIZATIONAL LEVEL OF ANALYSIS

Finally, at Level 5, the conditions necessary for positive emotion at the other levels of the model must be built and sustained across the whole organization through a healthy emotional climate. Level 5 of Ashkanasy's multi-level model is qualitatively different from the other levels. At the lower levels, organizational policies and values are interpreted in the context of face-to-face interactions, where all the basic biological and neurophysiological and physiological mechanisms we have discussed up to this point are salient. Thus, at this level of organization, a manager can recognize cues of real or felt emotion, and identify the positive emotional indicators of employees who are genuinely motivated toward goal achievement and confident of achieving their goals. When dealing with the organization-wide or macro view, on the other hand, the situation is much less clear. Although some members of a large organization will have meetings with senior managers, these meetings are likely to be brief and infrequent, and are also likely to be constrained by power differences. Instead, it is necessary to deal with the more nebulous concept of emotional climate, defined by De Rivera as 'an objective group phenomenon that can be palpably sensed - as when one enters a party or a city and feels an attitude of gaiety or depression, openness or fear'.

In the context of work organizations, organizational climate has been studied for some time now, and constitutes the collective mood of organizational members toward their jobs, the organization, and management. The concept is distinct from organizational culture, in that climate is essentially an emotional phenomenon, while culture is more stable, and rooted in beliefs, values, and embedded assumptions. Nonetheless, Schein makes it clear that assumptions underlying organizational culture are associated with deeply felt feelings. More recently, Beyer and Niño demonstrated how culture and organizational members' emotional views and states are intimately and reciprocally related. As such, both organizational climate and organizational culture arguably have emotional underpinnings.

A number of writers in the organizational literature have noted the emotional basis of organizational culture, but primarily in the context of displayed emotional states, rather than felt emotion. This begs the question as to how to ascertain real emotional climate (or culture) in organizations. Although Härtel et al. measured emotional climate and reported a correlation with job satisfaction, most advocates of an ethnographic approach argue that only through active day-to-day involvement in organizations is it possible to sense real as opposed to displayed emotion. De Rivera notes, however, that emotional climate is an objective phenomenon and is therefore amenable to objective perception and interpretation, provided the observer knows what to look for. In effect, his point is that observers need to be sensitive to markers of felt rather than displayed emotion. In this case, however, the markers are not so much in the individual expressions of organizational members, but in the social structures and patterns of behaviour that are manifest in the organization. De Rivera argues further that people are sensitive to such cues, and shape their beliefs and behaviours accordingly. It follows that the arguments developed earlier in the present paper in respect of interpersonal relationships and small groups may be extendable to the organization as a whole, especially since organizational policies ultimately come down to the perceptions, understanding, and behaviour of individuals, interacting dyads, and groups.

Note: For further knowledge regarding this chapter, reader can visit site of Cooper Tire & Rubber Company. Cooper Tire & Rubber (Cooper Tire) is engaged in the designing, manufacturing and selling of tires for passenger cars, light trucks, medium trucks, and motorcycles and racing vehicles. The company primarily operates in the US. It is headquartered in Findlay, Ohio and employs 13,311 people. www.coopertire.com

7

Communication in Organizations

Communication is a core process in any organization and as such is an essential element of operations. As such it needs to be planned, monitored and adjusted like any other business process. While the intent of a given communication activity may vary - from sharing the strategic direction of the company and its associated goals and objectives to obtaining feedback and input from employees and customers - its purpose is singular: to boost productivity and company performance.

The second way of looking at it is regarding the role communication plays in day-to-day management of an organization and its people. If you are a manager, you are responsible for helping people understand the goals and objectives you are pursuing and for ensuring that your staff is taking appropriate action to achieve those goals. In other words, you play the role of interpreter for those you are managing. And to do this effectively, you must first of all understand communication as a process, and have the right set of skills to perform this role. From a process point of view, managers learn the basics of face-to-face communication as articulated by Roger D'Aprix. Essentially D'Aprix has identified through his research a communication model centered on six fundamental questions that employees need to have answered. These questions are:

- What's my job?
- How am I doing?
- Does anyone care?
- How are we doing?
- What's our vision, mission and values?
- How can I help?

By understanding each of these questions, and what is behind them, and then using them as your day-to-day management program, it is possible to maximize staff alignment to business goals and increase, among other things, performance. From a skills point of view, we believe that a - if not the most - critical component of communications is listening..

LISTENING

Making change happen means bringing about changes in people's behaviour - our own, other people's or usually both. However, our willingness and ability to bring about behavioural change is directly related to our ability to use the various interpersonal tools at our disposal wisely and well. This synopsis is intended to give you an overview of one critical aspect of interpersonal competency - a core skill for the world of work and in personal relationships: active listening.

Active listening is an interactive process for improving the degree of understanding between two or more people. Good listening is not a passive skill. It takes effort, attention and intervention.

CONTENT AND FEELING

Any message a person tries to get across has two components: the content and the feeling or attitude underlying this content. The total meaning consists of both feeling and idea. The listener, when he or she talks, conveys an understanding of what has just been said -- its total meaning. Often, he or she responds not by pushing his or her own idea, but simply reflecting or summarizing the meaning of what the person has just said. Because understanding another person is actually more difficult than it at first seems, it is important to consistently test your ability to see the world in the way that the speaker sees it. You can do this by reflecting in your own words what the speaker seems to mean. A good rule of thumb is to assume that you never really understand until you can communicate this understanding to the satisfaction of the other person.

When people are listened to well, they tend to listen to themselves with more care and make a greater attempt to express themselves so as to make clear exactly what they are feeling or thinking. Group members tend to listen more to each other, become less argumentative, more ready to incorporate other points of view. Listening reduces the threat of having ideas criticized. Active listening is an important way to bring about changes in people. As a matter of fact, some of the most successful forms of counselling and psychotherapy rely on listening skills. Despite the popular notion that listening is a passive approach, research evidence shows that sensitive listening is one of the most effective ways of achieving group development.

LISTENING

By consistently listening (actively) to someone, you are conveying the idea that you are interested in them as a person, you think what they feel is important; you respect their thoughts, even if you do not agree with them. You are communicating that you value their contribution, that you understand, that you think they are worth listening to and finally that you are the kind of person they can talk to (you are trustworthy). It is difficult to convince someone that you respect them simply by telling them so. However, by listening actively, you are behaving in a respectful way.

ELEMENTS OF ACTIVE LISTENING

Two critical elements of active listening are: clarifying, or understanding the content of the message, and responding with empathy, or acknowledging the emotional component of the message.

Clarifying

Reflective responses are often one of the most useful ways of clarifying content. For example:

- Repeating the statement: "You're feeling tired today."
- Paraphrasing the statement: "Let me see if I can put what you just said into my own words...."
- Summarizing the statement: "It seems that your two main complaints are...."
- Interpreting the statement: "So you're suggesting that ..."
- Identifying assumptions: "Hearing what you have to say, I guess you were assuming that someone else was going to take care of the problem."

Asking for an expansion of the idea is another useful response:

Asking:

- For an example: "Can you give me an example of the kind of situation that bothers you?"
- For a definition: "Maybe you could tell me what you mean by......?"
- For a summary: "It would be really helpful for me if you could

summarize the points you have just made."

- For additional explanation: "Can you explain about your ideas some more?"
- For assumptions be identified: "What did you assume would happen after your conversation?"
- About inconsistencies: "What you just said seems to contradict what you said this morning; how do these things fit together?"
- Where the idea came from: "When did you first start thinking this way?"
- How much the person cares about this: "Sounds like this is (not) really important to you."

Avoid responses that are not helpful in clarifying, such as:

- Agreeing with the person: "Yes, that person is a jerk."
- Non-verbal signs of agreement: nodding, gestures, facial expressions, etc.
- Disagreeing with the person: "How can you say that? She's so nice."
- Non-verbal signs of disagreement: head shaking, gestures, facial expressions, body position, etc.
- Leading the person to a particular response: "Sounds to me like you really want to get back at them."
- Manipulating the person to a particular response: "He needs to stop putting people down; so why don't you just yell back at him next time?"
- Using tone of voice to reveal bias
- Presenting your own point of view: "The reason its not working is because....."
- Arguing: "No it's not!"
- Distorting the statement: "You don't feel confident in your ability to confront her about the problem."

Responding With Empathy

Responses reflecting back content and feelings are the most effective:

- Accurately reflecting the main idea of the statement: "You are concerned about the way you work together."

- Accurately reflecting the surface (obvious) feelings: "You seem anxious today." "I guess you were pretty angry."
- Communicating to the person that their feelings have been acknowledged and that they have been accurately understood: "When she cuts you off in mid-sentence, you feel as though she isn't interested in hearing what you have to say."
- Adding a new meaning to the person's statement: "It sounds like you're also feeling some resentment toward him."
- Enabling the person to examine a new dimension of the statement: "When you say you feel left out, are there some other feelings you are experiencing as well?"

Unhelpful responses that show partial awareness of obvious feelings are:

- Denying the person's right to feel that way: "You shouldn't feel that way because....."
- Disallowing the person's feelings: "You're not upset, you just can't see things the same way I can."
- Moralizing, sermonizing: "You have only yourself to blame...." "When you have made a mistake you have to expect people to get mad."
- Giving advice; tells person what to do: "If I were you I'd give him a piece of my mind." "Next time you should....."
- Telling the person how he or she feels: "If that's how you see the situation you are feeling angry with me."
- Asking stupid questions: "What do you mean you felt put down?"
- Asking for more information: "So she tore a strip off you in front of the whole group. Who else was there and what did they say?"
- Trying to solve the problem: "Well, if they did the problem would be solved."
- Implying reasons for someone's behaviour: "You are upset with me because..."

Ignoring feelings is very unhelpful:

- Being insensitive to very obvious feelings
- Shifting the topic away from person's concerns

- Making an irrelevant response
- Criticizing or being judgmental
- Being hurtful, devaluing or rejecting

IMPROVING LISTENING SKILLS

Principles

In learning to reflect what you have heard, the following points should be observed:

- Restate the other person's expressed meaning in your own words rather than mimic or parrot them.
- At first, preface reflected remarks with "You feel...", "You think...", It seems to you that...", "It sounds like...", and so on. These may be dropped as skill is developed.
- Formulate reflected remarks as statements, not questions.
- Wait out pauses.
- When many feelings and thoughts are expressed, as in a long speech, only the last feeling area expressed should be reflected.
- Only meaning actually expressed should be reflected. Do not go beyond what the other person is willing to admit -- even 'though you may think you can see something deeper.
- When someone contradicts something they have said earlier in the meeting, reflect only the most recent comment. Such changes indicate progress and clarification of feeling.

Avoid indications of approval or disapproval if you are trying to help the person explore his or her own feelings and ideas. Particularly when you are listening to someone who may be very upset, refrain from questioning, proving, blaming, interpreting, giving advice, persuading, reassuring, and giving sympathy. What is important is that you acknowledge the feeling.

COMMUNICATION PLAN

It is often asked what you believe to be the most important elements underlying a good communication plan. The strong belief is that there are a few elements that must be considered and factored into each and every plan - and if they are, (regardless of any tactical problems you may encounter) you will emerge with a fairly positive end result. It has been outlined them below and urge you to keep them at the forefront of your mind, and at the heart of your plan as you proceed.

LISTEN

Listen before you communicate. Listen while you are communicating. And listen after you communicate. Through listening, you learn - and more importantly you communicate to your audiences something that is extremely important - RESPECT. And don't forget - the best way to show you are listening is to take action on what you have learned.

BE CLEAR

Get focussed - say what you need to say, and let people know what is expected of them. Forget the corporate speak and jargon - use words and phrases that make sense and are easily understood. The greater the degree of clarity you can establish - with your messages and in your delivery, the greater degree of success you will encounter. If you fail here, your chance of achieving success is virtually zero.

TREAT YOUR EMPLOYEES AS ADULTS

They deserve it, and will be thrilled. Don't hide the bad news - doing so only leads to mistrust, frustration and an extremely active rumor mill. What he failed to understand was that instead of only a few people who would be laid-off knowing what their fate would be, thousands began to speculate. The result of course was a rapid decline in productivity, 'a ruined Christmas' for many, many more and a significant decline in trust that continues to show its impact all these years later. Had employees been told exactly what was happening, the result would have been significantly better - both short and long-term.

BE TIMELY

When the morning paper serves as the company newsletter, you have failed. Go out of your way to get information to people in a timely manner, and they will go out of their way to help you through almost any situation. This is one of the biggest areas of frustration staff have and there is no reason for it to be that way. Make the commitment and make it happen. Nothing more needs to be said on this issue.

BE RELEVANT

If you do your analysis work well, do your listening as you should, making your communication relevant to your audiences is easily accomplished. Missing the relevant issues and failing to make the connection between what you are communicating and the audience, will lead to failure.

THINK PROCESS - NOT EVENT

Finally, don't forget that communication is a process and not an event. It has a starting point, an end point and a journey in between. And more often than not, route changes will be required. As you plan, think clearly about each stage of the process you need to work through - including ensuring staff have access to the information you are conveying, developing awareness, understanding, acceptance and getting a commitment to take action.

COMMITMENT AND JOB SATISFACTION

Work expectations are those things people consider likely to happen in their job situation, either now or in the future. Whether spoken or unspoken, met or unmet, expectations have a powerful impact on our thoughts, feelings, and behaviors, and play a key role in driving our attitudes. Research shows that people who have clearly defined, well-communicated expectations find more satisfaction and success in their work than people whose expectations go unspoken or unrealized. And companies that employ satisfied, people reap the rewards of increased productivity and reduced turnover.

KEY EXPECTATIONS

In a typical employment situation, certain expectations - such as salary, hours, and job duties - are clearly understood by both employer and employee. Other expectations, however, are so intimately linked to an individual's concept of work that they oftentimes go unspoken or unacknowledged.

"Managing Work Expectations & Transforming Attitudes" helps people explore 10 work expectations that impact today's employment relationships:

1. Recognition
2. Autonomy
3. Expression
4. Career Growth
5. Diversity
6. Teamwork

7. Structure
8. Environment
9. Balance
10. Stability

Easy-to-use Learning Guide Delivers Immediate Results

"Managing Work Expectations & Transforming Attitudes" utilizes a 36 page self-assessment designed to help individuals uncover and explore their expectations in a variety of employment situations, including:

- Working on a team
- Transitioning to a new position
- Experiencing organizational restructuring
- Creating meaningful performance reviews
- Making the most of the daily routine.

Open the door to mutual understanding

- Identify their expectations
- Discover which expectations they consider most important
- Learn how to communicate, initiate action, and adjust expectations
- Get feedback on managing their expectations
- Improve their outlook and enhance their attitude toward work
- Enjoy the benefits of increased job satisfaction and improved performance

Managing Expectation

Expectations are your client's vision of a future state or action, usually unstated but which is critical to your success: A client who "wants the project to be quick and dirty," or who "wants to be involved in all the details" or "not involved at all," or who expects that your project will result in "reducing his work force by 80%." Expectation management techniques are very valuable in client service work. It's partly for our client's benefit - to keep their eyes on the ball, to work towards the same goals, etc. We also do it for our own benefit because our project targets are sometimes less precise than we wish they were, our performance criteria are demanding and many activities, such as presentations or deliverables are frequent opportunities for clients to pass judgment on us.

EXPECTATIONS CUT TWO WAYS

1. They are a primary measure of your success. In your client's mind, satisfaction is how close you have come to their expectations. NOT how close you were to the wording of the contract or the scope of work or even the performance criteria, but to their expectations. It may not even be the actual results of the project but the process with which you arrive there.
2. Expectations drive all of your client's actions and decisions. It's not their everyday duties or their "assigned role" or your very rational explanations that drive them, but their expectations.

1. Setting Expectations

Expectations are set by all kinds of events. Something you said or did, or even the way you said it, something somebody else said or did, or something the client picked up from somewhere else. But it's important to know that expectations, rational or irrational, valid or invalid, are not developed in a vacuum.

2. Capturing / Monitoring Expectations

You can't know what the expectation setting is unless you actively search for it and continue monitoring it. You might even have to test it, to see how it's set. Think of a power switch that doesn't have "on" and "off" labels. You don't know whether it's in the on or off position, unless you switch it on and off a couple of times. You can test expectations by dropping hints and clues of your next steps and watching how they react.

The old management adage says: "You cannot manage what you don't measure." Common measurement tools are sales targets, league standings, satisfaction surveys, click-thru rates, and in project work, "percentage complete", "estimate to completion" etc. The same adage can be re-stated for project work: "You cannot manage expectations unless you monitor them." That requires listening to your clients. Better yet, hearing them and understanding them.

3. Influencing Expectations

Once you have pinpointed the expectation and you know the source, it's time to play the influence challenge. This is what our managers usually meant when they said "manage their expectations." Often they overlook the setting and monitoring components and expect you to "talk your way" out of anything. But it's so hard to talk your way out of anything unless you address the root causes. On the other hand, sometimes no influence is needed. Their expectations may be well founded, and we may be the one who needs to change our approach and style. Managed expectations drive your success. Everything else is secondary. The S-M-I principles should give you enough to be prepared for your current client and future projects.

MORE ON MONITORING

Monitoring expectations requires listening to our clients. Better yet, hearing them and understanding them: Whether they're talking to you or to someone else. You should eavesdrop on your clients, only that you need not tune them out just because you're not the intended target of the conversation. Sometimes, the way they describe their needs or the project to an outsider can tell you about the real expectations. Put two and two together. Listen to what they say and what they don't say. When they don't say what you wish they'd say, there may be a good reason behind that.

Listen to their favorite subjects, and those they try to avoid. The ones they avoid are more likely to haunt you when least expected. Listen to the context in which it is being said. Especially if they bring up certain subjects "out of the blue." You could ask yourself, "What frame of mind would one have to be in to say that?" And another tactic is to ask them to describe their expectations. You will occasionally get a true description and at other times, you'll have to dig deeper. And certainly look at what they do. Actions speak louder than words.

Once you understand the expectations, it's time to find out the source. If you are the source, it will be easier to deal with. The two most challenging sources are (a) the client's personal or professional background and preferences and (b) expectations set by someone else, in effect committing you to something you're not aware of. The only way to get the first (personal / professional background) is to spend more time with them. The longer the face time, the better your chances of picking up clues and understanding their motivation.

As for others setting expectations for you, it could be a fellow team member, or (a common complaint) your own salespeople or an ad demonstrating the "incredible benefits" to be had from a particular product or service. In this "third party scenario," it would be best to ask the third party if any such promises were made. "Is there anything I should know where our client has had expectations set?" If you suspect that some were set that you cannot satisfy, see if you can get the help of the person who did the "setting." Expectations don't stand still. Take the time to periodically check that the expectations haven't changed. A brief recap of your expectation perception may reveal that either you're on course, or the expectations have changed.

INFLUENCING TECHNIQUES

What did Michael Jordan say in his announcement to return to basketball? "I may not be 100% for the first few games." This was his attempt at lowering expectations. He followed by saying, "I have learned that winning championships is not the only thing in basketball", which was very smart. Influencing . . . a subject all its own. There are rational, emotional, ethical and less ethical methods. Here are some basic techniques from experience and research:

1. Establish trust. People are influenced only by those they trust. And trust is not awarded, acquired, carried over, bought or sold. It is earned.
2. Educate, educate, educate. The more your clients know, the better. Because then they understand the complexity of your work, the dependencies and the impact their expectations have on your work.
3. Explain why. "It worked on my last three projects." (Demonstrating experience), or "It would cost less." (Demonstrating partnership), etc.
4. Do it in private. It's less confronting. People don't like to change their minds in public or to admit their lack of knowledge.
5. Show them, and then sell them. This is the "free sample" strategy. Let them experience the benefits of what you're suggesting before you go and attempt at selling them on the idea.
6. Balance the give and take. See if you can identify one or two of your client's expectations that you haven't acted on and which are relatively easy to satisfy. And make sure they're satisfied. Then and only then, bring up any expectation that you'd like to change.
7. Sooner is better than later. Expectations get firmed up the longer they are left alone. Work on them as early as possible.

And one last thought: Turn the tables for a change: See what YOUR expectations are when you start a project, see how they change and see how they influence your actions and behavior during the project. Were they valid expectations? Did you change them based on the realities of the project? How did that come about? Did you stick to your expectations? Why? The answer to these questions will give you clues you can use in your work. Managed expectations drive your success. Everything else is secondary. The S-M-I principles should give you enough to be prepared for your current client and future projects.

MATURITY AT WORK

Think of any situation where you have purchased something, and, at the end of the purchase experience, things got nasty. Assumptions you had made at the beginning of the process turned out to be incorrect. Promises that the vendor made were broken, and the vendor was very reluctant to make it up to you. The enthusiasm you and the vendor had at the beginning of the process was gone, and in its place were raw nerves, legitimate concerns, and a lot of haggling over "what we must do, now that we know what we didn't know before."

This is, unfortunately, a very common state of affairs in any complex sale. It's also completely unnecessary. Most, if not all, of the typical end-of-sale-process disappointments can be eliminated altogether, if expectations are set properly up front, and reinforced as the purchasing process proceeds. But, there's a catch. It takes a healthy amount of maturity to make it work. You have to plan ahead. You have to face facts, and convey them realistically and honestly. You have to realize that the client would rather know the bad news at the beginning of the process.

They'll be just as concerned about the difficulties at the beginning as they will at the end, but at least they will appreciate your honesty when you tell them the bad news at the beginning. If you wait until the end, they will wonder what else you've been hiding. They will stop trusting you, and the situation will only deteriorate from there. Let's look at an example. Let's say you're selling something that involves a lot of customization. You know, from past experience, that after you deliver the product (or the project is considered "finished"), the customer will find things that they hadn't thought of, that neither of you had noticed, nor that they want to change. Instead of just ignoring this reality, and suffering the negative consequences, you should manage the client's expectations.

Managing your client's expectations is one of the most important aspects in any commercial relationship, and yet it is almost universally ignored in sales training - and sales management. If you were selling this type of complex product or project, early in the relationship you'd say, "It's been our experience that after we deliver the product, our customers may find things that escaped our notice, or things they want to change. It's just the reality in this type of complex situation. So we always build a 'post delivery fine-tuning" module into the estimate to cover this period. Usually about 5% of the total cost covers whatever we discover together during this period. If we don't need it all, we won't bill you for it. But by holding it in reserve, it will be available just in case."

Handling it this way is much, much better than trying to get an additional 5% after the client believes he is done paying for your services. It's better than running out of money to pay your workers at the end. It's better than you - and your workers - getting hurried and sloppy at the end because the money is running out. Psychologically, if everyone is prepared for this "end of project fine-tuning" period, their performance and interest won't peak too soon. When you manage expectations properly, you are setting up a situation where the client, your vendors, and your workers will behave in a way that works for everyone. Mature management is really "behavior management." It is the anticipation of how things could go wrong and how to head those problems off at the pass. Here are some basic guidelines to successfully managing expectations.

- The truth is your friend. Every time you run from the truth, the resulting negative consequences come after you, like a mangy junkyard dog, snarling at you and never leaving you alone. The truth is more like a golden retriever. Sure, goldens need food and care, and sometimes they can be a pain, but they more than return the favor. The payback is enormous. Similarly, truth has momentum. Workers and clients alike will tell others that you can be trusted. Being trusted is one of those "go/no-go" factors in any sale. If someone says, "He's a good guy - very honest," you will continue to pursue a working relationship. If someone says, "He's smart, but he can't be trusted," you will take your business elsewhere. It's that simple.
- Confess early and often. If something is going wrong, immediately tell the client. Sure, you can take a few minutes to think about the best solution to the problem, so you're properly prepared when you call, but call - right away. The longer you wait, the less the client will think you can be trusted.

Sure, the client will be upset. But nowhere near as upset if he finds out later on. And, rest assured - he WILL find out. Your own employees or vendors - or a competitor - will make sure of it. Your number of friends and allies shrinks as you run from the truth.

- Make a list of all the things you need a client to know ahead of time. How does this always work? How long does it take, how much does it cost? What kind of help will you need from the client? Who else may have to get involved? What's really important and what is less important? What must be done first? Will things get difficult at some point, and what's the best way to deal with it? What have others done, and what can be learned from what they've done? What have you learned about this process that the client should know? What will you do if there is a problem?
- Put it in writing. A simple email spelling out the contents of the list, or summarizing a phone conversation about it, is more than sufficient in most cases. Yes, there is usually a contract of some sort with these types of complex products and projects, but contracts are mostly to protect both parties from the consequences of things really going off the rails. The purpose of managing client expectations is to keep things on the rails, running on time.

In the most successful relationships, nothing ever gets too far out of hand. Even the little things are brought up in a courteous manner, and discussed. An agreement is reached about how to handle that situation in the future. There is no arguing and no hurt feelings. The problem is addressed and solved, and everyone goes back to what they should be doing.

When you manage client expectations, you are anticipating what could happen, and also explaining what should happen. You are helping the client understand "what's going to happen after I buy." You are in charge, and you are mature. You don't let things get out of hand. You tell the truth. You face reality head-on. Imagine what it would be like if all businesspeople behaved this way. There wouldn't be any more horror stories about "my disastrous remodeling job" - just a happy customer referring others to the vendor who was mature enough to successfully manage expectations.

PERFORMANCE APPRAISALS

New managers often view employee performance appraisals with fear and loathing. In a perfect world, all employees would be spectacular and would receive glowing reviews. It would be a pure pleasure to meet with staff members and share the good news about their performance. Unfortunately, not all employees are top achievers, and pointing out weaknesses or deficiencies can be difficult. Many organizations treat appraisals as an annual burden consisting of a quick meeting between supervisor and subordinate that produce a written review that's filed and forgotten.

However, appraisals-if done carefully and thoughtfully-can add considerable value to the supervisor/employee relationship and can help structure and clarify expectations for both parties. A variety of techniques and models are available for developing good performance appraisals. But rather than describe each approach, the intent here is to point out several things to keep in mind when conducting performance appraisals no matter what technique you use. View the performance appraisal as a process and not an event.

- Take the process seriously. Poorly planned and conducted performance appraisals can damage morale and serve as grounds for employee grievances.
- Develop work standards that can be evaluated objectively and use language that is concise and unambiguous. Also, be sensitive to your own biases that can creep into the appraisal process.
- Address the impact that incentive bonuses and pay increases can have on the appraisal process.

It is important to understand that measuring performance is a fluid and ongoing process, one that can reflect the trusting and honest relationships you want to build with your team. A general rule of thumb is that if the formal appraisal uncovers significant surprises for either the employee or supervisor, the process is unsuccessful. The appraisal process consists of formal meetings where the appraisal is developed and agreed on and where performance is discussed and critiqued. However, the process also involves informal feedback on a regular basis from the supervisor about the employee's performance. Critiquing performance as it occurs can be an important motivator and can help your staff members redirect negative behavior or actions before they become a major problem.

It is essential to acquaint yourself with the policies and procedures established by your organization's human resources department on developing and implementing performance appraisals. This can include the correct forms to be used, the method of documenting work standards, the percentages, or weights, placed on each work standard according to its importance to the overall work effort, and the required documentation and timelines that need to be followed.

You can easily compromise the appraisal process and management's position with employees by not following the established policies and procedures. It is also important to be sensitive to the impact an appraisal can have on an employee and the work effort of the entire team. Generally, most people take pride in their work and their contributions. Performance appraisals conducted in a cavalier or disrespectful manner can be damaging. An employee is more likely to accept a negative performance critique if it is done in a careful and calm manner with examples cited and ideas for improvement discussed.

BE AS OBJECTIVE AND FAIR AS POSSIBLE

Base work performance on standards that can be clearly measured and documented. This includes technical requirements of an employee's work, as well as interpersonal skills, such as customer service and teamwork. Try to avoid value judgments, such as "does not seem committed to his work" or "does not care about his coworkers." Instead, use specific examples of behaviors that highlight your concerns, such as "does not complete tasks on schedule" or "does not keep coworkers or supervisor informed of problems with the LAN."

You can also take various approaches to guard against biased appraisals. For instance, you can ask employees to conduct self-appraisals, in which they evaluate their own performances based on the work plans, or you can conduct peer reviews, which gives coworkers the opportunity to evaluate the performances of each other or the overall team. These approaches should not replace the appraisals you perform on your direct reports, but they can help you gather important information to make your appraisals more accurate.

ADDRESS THE IMPACT OF INCENTIVE BONUSES AND PAY INCREASES

Most organizations tie incentive bonuses or pay increases into the performance appraisal process. This is good news for employees who are outstanding performers, since they will probably receive some sort of reward for their efforts. However, monetary rewards can create a negative team environment and damage trust if employees perceive them to be unfair. The best way you can address this issue is to acknowledge any frustrations your staff members have about not receiving monetary rewards for their efforts and work with them to identify performance goals that will likely result in monetary rewards in the future.

SAMPLE SCENARIO

Let's look at a hypothetical situation that illustrates some of these points. Jane had recently been promoted to supervise a team of technicians working on a LAN system in a midsize organization. She felt up to the task with regard to her technical ability and knowledge and was comfortable working with people who used the LAN. However, evaluating the work of her staff was a concern. She approached her HR representative and spoke to her about where to begin. The HR representative guided her through the process of evaluating employees and explained the paperwork and timelines. She also showed Jane some examples of best practices within the organization and examples of creative approaches to performance appraisals.

Many of these examples involved finding interesting ways to include her employees in the appraisal process, such as having them perform self-appraisals and using peer appraisals. Jane decided to use the appraisal process as a way to build strong supervisor/employee relationships within her team. She had her staff members perform self-appraisals and also asked them to evaluate the performance of the overall team. She was surprised to find that many employees pointed out things about their performances that could be improved and were receptive to discussing ways the improvements might be accomplished. She also found the team appraisals helpful because they made the team members feel they were contributing to the effort, and they provided some good ideas about what to prioritize to improve team performance.

MEETING THE CHALLENGE

Performance appraisals are a significant challenge for most new managers. However, it is possible to create a positive environment for appraisals by viewing them as a long-term and evolving process and not an event that occurs once per year, developing standards that are clear and objective, and using them as a tool for communicating with your employees about your expectations.

Note: Hot Topic is a specialty retailer that sells music/ pop culture-licensed and music/pop culture-influenced apparel, accessories and music; the company also sells apparel for plus-size women. The company operates in the US and Puerto Rico. It is headquartered in the City of Industry, California. The company employs 2,500 people who work on a full-time basis. www.hottopic.com

8

Power and Politics in Organization

Organizations are made up of formal and informal rules that coordinate actions of different people. But how can organizations make sure that people-who have diverse backgrounds, particular interests, and different understandings- comply with these rules? Raising these questions means addressing the fine line between the exercise of power and ethics. Power is the concept that encompasses the mechanisms, processes, and dispositions that try, not always successfully, to ensure that people act according to the rules of the game. Hence, power is one of the central concepts in both management practice and theory. Ethics, on the other hand, is concerned with doing the right things in the right way. Of course, the whole issue of ethics depends in the first place on the ethicality of the business proposition that underlies the organization. Is it ethical, for example, to build a business on cheating? Researchers in organization theory and management in the era after World War II era had developed a set of expectations about the exercise of power in organizations that they had derived from the formal structure of bureaucratic authority. However, a number of case studies refuted these expectations. Surprisingly, these case studies discovered bases of power outside the formal structure of authority and described the games they sanctioned and the rules that made them possible.

More recently, interest in discussions of power has shifted to issues of resistance- how people in organizations resist formal organizational authorities. However, perhaps of more pressing concern is not the question of why people resist but why they might obey, particularly where there are ethical issues attached to what it is that they are obeying, issues that come into particular focus when considering examples of extreme organizations that are known as total institutions. Although we can learn a great deal from the concentration of power that occurs in total institutions, in fact, most organizational power is neither so total nor so hard edged. Instead of making people do what they wouldn't otherwise do, this power is subtler-it operates through modes of soft domination.

SETTING THE SCENE

We spend at least one third of our adult lives working in organizations. Another third disappears in sleep and replenishment, and a further third in things we choose to do. Therefore, for one third of our lives, we cede control to others and enter into complex relations of power that range from others getting us to do things we would not otherwise do, to us doing the same to others. We will spend that third of our lives in different organizations. At best, these will be warm, friendly, welcoming, open places in which we can do our jobs with pride, growth, and achievement. At worst, however, they may be akin to places of concentrated power that frames and shapes our hours there. As organization theorists began studying the empirical workings of organizations rather than simply constructing abstract models, they noticed that some members of organizations were able to exploit and use seemingly impersonal rules for their own ends. The prevalent conception of organization hierarchy identified it with legitimacy; thus, when actions were identified that seemed to subvert or bypass the official hierarchy of authority, they were labelled "illegitimate"-they were not authorized. In this way, power came to be seen as illegitimate, whereas authority was legitimate. Certain resources within organizations seemed to provide bases for illegitimate expressions of power.

At various times, several key resources have been promoted as the basis for expert power in organizations. The most pervasive basis for arguing a special relationship between power and a specific resource relate to the ability to control uncertainty in bureaucratic organizations. More recently, there has been a shift in focus from bureaucracy to consideration of more empowered alternatives. But, as we shall see, empowerment is not necessarily all it is cracked up to be-it can mean even tighter control.

The world of organization power is complex-full of shifting alliances, words that mean something other than they say, and actions that do more than they proclaim. It is impossible to escape power in organizations, if only because organization means yoking together people with multiple and complex interests whose search for satisfaction is structured through a set of organizational relations with people that one would not necessarily choose to spend time with. If you had a choice, would you spend eight hours a day with the passing parade of megalomaniacs, incompetents, and cruelly brutal gossips that people most offices and other organizations? When the boss tells you that he wants everyone to work as one happy family, look around. Would you choose any or all of these people as partners with whom to make a family? Power is more profound than just the push and pull of attraction and repulsion, command and control. It also involves the structuring of dispositions and capacities for action as well as action itself. We explore these themes in this chapter, looking at the good, the bad, and the ugly in power relations. We take care to concentrate not only on the negatives but also to accentuate the positives. After all, if power is inescapable, we might as well learn how to use it wisely.

CENTRAL APPROACHES AND MAIN THEORIES

SOURCES OF POWER

If an organization makes people do things they normally wouldn't do, power must be the central issue. Many potential sources or bases of power have been listed, including information; expertise; credibility; stature and prestige; uncertainty; access to top-level managers and the control of money, sanctions, and rewards; and control over resources. We consider some of the more important of these bases of power in this section.

LEGITIMACY

Power works best when it is seen least. Power as legitimation needs to do nothing to secure its will if people already want to do what is expected of them. If legitimacy can be created for individual actions, it greatly reduces the chance of opposition to them because it creates a meaningful context in which they can be accepted and justified.

Some of the main sources of legitimacy are symbolic. Images can represent a great deal of power in simple ways. For example, the law is often portrayed as an institution that impartially weighs justice in its scales. That the common symbol of this power is blindfolded while holding the scales of justice is meant to represent it as a legitimate authority; it shows that an impartial judiciary resides over a mass population that is weighed equally in the scales. One of the most potent sources of power and its symbolism are the many remnants of imperialism that dot the globe.

UNCERTAINTY

As we have seen, uncertainty and power are not strange bedfellows, and their proximity has been much explored in organization theory. The view for the last fifty years has been that when an organization experiences uncertainty in areas of organizational action, if a person has organizational skills that can reduce that uncertainty, he or she will derive power from such expertise. In other words, this view states that despite formal hierarchies, prescribed organizational communications, and the relations that they specify, people will be able to exercise power when they control or have the necessary knowledge to master uncertain zones in the organizational arena

STRATEGIC CONTINGENCY THEORY

Hickson et al. sought to measure power in organizations. One of their theoretical innovations was to use a formal model. The organization was conceptualized as being composed of four functional subsystems or subunits. The subunits were seen as interdependent. Some were more or less dependent and produced more or less uncertainty for other subunits. What connected them was the major task of the organization, coping with uncertainty. The theory ascribes the differing power of subunits to imbalances in the way in which these interdependent subunits cope with and handle uncertainty. The most powerful are the least dependent subunits that cope with the greatest systemic uncertainty, although there are certain qualifications-namely, that the subunit is not easily substitutable with any other subunit and that it is central to the organization system. Note the absence of a vertical dimension and the assumption that each subunit is quite contained and unitary. To conceptualize an organization as composed of subunits is to flatten out the normal hierarchical representation of it as a "structure of dominancy," to use Weber's terms. This perspective views the organization on a horizontal rather than vertical axis. To view organizations as more horizontal than vertical is to make a number of assumptions about the unitary and functionally cohesive nature of subunits. In reality, each subunit is typically a hierarchy with a more or less problematic culture of consent or dissent. For it to be treated as if it were unitary, there needs to exist some internal mechanisms of power that allow for such a representation. In other words, there must be a hierarchy of order that is effectively reinforced through everyday organizational actions.

Strategic contingencies theory assumes that management's definitions prevail. Indeed, sometimes they do, in which case management has exercised power. When they do not, management is outmaneuvered. Being outmaneuvered is a fate that most managers are familiar with. Thus, the strategic contingencies theory of power unfortunately explains very little that is important in understanding hierarchical power. Indeed, it refrains from such an explanation, given its tacit assumptions. And these tacit assumptions mean that it explains very little that is useful because it is assumed that the organizational configuration will be simply bureaucratic. Indeed, in the later empirical analysis conducted using the framework, the researchers deliberately sought out a simple and tightly regulated bureaucracy to test the theory. It worked.

RESOURCES

Similar to strategic contingencies theory is the resource dependency view, derived from the work of social psychologists such as Emerson and related work by French and Raven. All resource dependence theorists view a certain resource as key in organizations, but they differ in which resource is regarded as key. Pfeffer and Salancik argued that power could be both vertical and horizontal in organizations, and their focus, like Hickson et al.'s, was on subunit power. They hypothesized that power would be used in organizations to try to influence decisions about the allocation of resources. Subunits may be thought of as departments in the organization. To the extent that subunits contributed critical resources, including knowledge, that the organization needs, other subunits submitted to their demands and ceded power to them. The similarities to strategic contingencies theory are striking. Using archival data on university decision making in the University of Illinois, they confirmed their hypotheses, suggesting that power is a positive-sum game for those that have control of critical resources-using the power these resources bestow, they can acquire yet more resources, to leverage more power. Those that have resources attract more resources and thus more power. From this perspective, power is often conceptualized as if it were a zero-sum game in which, rather like being on a seesaw, more resources on the part of one party outweigh those of another party because they can be gained only at the expense of the other party. It is assumed that there is a fixed amount of power to go around.

Crozier subsequently revisited the links between power and uncertainty as a critical resource. Members of an organization meet each other in spaces that offer relatively open opportunities for control of rules and resources. People do not adapt passively to the circumstances that they meet; they use these circumstances creatively to enhance the scope of their own discretion, through shaping and bending rules and colonizing resources. Power is still seen in terms of the control of uncertainty as it is played out in daily struggles over the rules of an uncertain game.

CONTEXTS FOR POWER GAMES

There is no doubt that uncertainty-as well as the other contenders for strategic resource status-can be a source of power, but not in a context independent way. What counts as a resource can be made to count only in specific contexts. For instance, box cutters, which are used for cutting paper and cardboard, are not usually thought of as powerful resources-or at least they were not until September 11, 2001. Then, in the hands of determined terrorists, they were responsible for what has now passed into history as 9/11. So, if information, uncertainty- or box cutters-are to count as resources for power, they will do so only in specific contexts. To the extent that specific resources are related to power in a general way, without regard for context, they are not very helpful. Anything can be a resource in the right context-the context is what is important. Thus, possessing scarce resources is not enough to deliver power over and above that formally authorized; one also needs to have an explicit knowledge of context and how to use resources accordingly.

POLITICS

The process of mobilizing power is the process of politics. Given the stress on authority and formal organization in the literature, politics are what happens when members of organizations behave in ways that are potentially authoritatively illegitimate. Pettigrew sees the mobilization of power as what happens when either individuals or subgroupings within organizations make a claim against the extant resource-sharing system of the organization. As Pettigrew suggests, power is central to the strategy process in organizations because decisions about what strategy to maintain or innovate will always be political. Such decisions are likely to threaten the existing distribution of organizational resources as represented in salaries, in promoting opportunities, and in control of tasks, people, information, and new areas of business. These politics are generated by the following:

- Structural cleavages in the organization between different component elements and identities, and the different values, affective, cognitive and discursive styles associated with these.

- The complexity and the degree of uncertainty attached to the dilemma.
- The salience of the issues for different actors and identities in the organization.
- The external pressure coming from stakeholders or other actors or organizations in the environment.
- The history of past politics in the organizations in question.

Consequently, power and organizational politics are absolutely central to a great deal of what normally goes on in organizations. This would have to be the case because, according to Pettigrew, organization politics fundamentally concern the management of meaning, as protagonists in these politics seek to legitimate the ideas, values, and demands that they espouse while simultaneously denying or decrying those that they seek to oppose. Hence, power ultimately is deployed in games of organizational symbolism, wrapped up in myths, beliefs, language, and legend-the stuff of organizational culture. As we will see later, whenever discussion switches to organization culture, organizational politics are not far behind. The most crucial issue, as Lord Acton noted at the outset of the chapter, is the potential for power to corrupt those who have it. Another way of addressing this issue is to ask, "Who controls the controllers?" These are not just academic issues; in many countries around the world, the ethicality and controllability of major and politically important public sector organizations is very much at issue.

ORGANIZATIONS AS POLITICAL ARENAS

In Mintzberg's terms, the organization is a political arena, one in which the system of politics comes into play whenever the systems of authority, ideology, or expertise may be contested in various political games-that is to say, almost always. Mintzberg identifies various commonly occurring political games, including the following:

- Insurgency games: Played by lower-status participants against the dominant elites.
- Counter-insurgency games: Played by the dominant elites against the insurgents.
- Sponsorship games: Played by patrons and clients.
- Alliance-building games: Played among peers who implicitly seek reciprocal support.

- Empire-building games: A political actor or subsystem seeks to capture others and enroll them as subordinate to its interests.
- Budgeting games: The objective is to secure resources.
- Expertise games: The games of strategic contingency.
- Lording games: Relatively powerless players seek to "lord it" through using their legitimate power over those supplicant or lower in status.
- Line vs. staff games: Each side uses legitimate power in illegitimate ways in games of rivalry.
- Rival camps games: Alliance or empire-building games develop into rival blocks that face each other in zero-sum games.
- Strategic candidate games: Those in power seek to ensure the succession of preferred candidates as vacancies arise.
- Whistle-blowing games: Participants, usually lower-status ones, seek to expose malfeasance or illegitimacy outside the organization to effect internal policy or strategy changes.
- Young Turks games: Organizational authority is preserved, but a coup unseats its present incumbents to institute a regime change

In organizations, politics are normal and serve many orderly functions. They can be the harbinger of a need for realignment, the midwife to change, the source of refreshing innovation or, sometimes, the instrument of death. Thus, political games are to be expected-they are neither aberrant nor deviant. The types that Mintzberg specifies are not mutually exclusive, of course, and may often overlap and interlink, but they typically find expression in four major forms in the political arena:

- Confrontation: Characterized by intense, confined, and unstable conflict, as in a takeover or merger
- Shaky alliances: Characterized by conflict that is moderate, confined, and relatively stable, as in professional organizations subject to public accountability, such as public hospital or education systems
- Politicized organizations: Characterized by conflict that is moderate, pervasive, and relatively stable, such as large public sector bodies or regulatory agencies
- Complex political arenas: Characterized by intense, pervasive,

and brief unstable conflict, such as organizations riven by major fault lines of factional and doctrinal division, both internally and in terms of external alliances and relations.

Social democratic political parties with strong external sponsors, such as the union movement, are examples of complex political arenas. Traditionally, these parties represented organized labour. However, in many countries the labour movement is considerably less significant than it used to be, with most employees not being union members except in a few sectors. For those parties that had once relied on union-friendly policies, a new recipe for success needed to be found. Only very large organizations or those with no competition can survive sustained complex politics for long.

POWER AND THE POLITICS OF RESISTANCE

Resistance is a term that has long been a part of the vocabulary of students of organization. Coch and French noted that resistance to change is normal. Because power in organizations rarely if ever flows effortlessly as pure authority-because its legitimacy is often contested-power is typically not free of friction. And where there is friction, there must be resistance. To use these metaphors betrays the origins of the terms-they derive, of course, from physics. They are rather mechanical terms, as is so much of the vocabulary in organization and management theory. However, resistance need not be simply a question of physics-it can be more organic and dialectical. Dialectics refers to the contradiction between two conflicting forces, where each shapes the other, often against the pressure that is being exerted. A picture says more than a thousand words.

Resistance is "a reactive process" whereby people embedded in power relations actively oppose initiatives enacted by others. Often, resistance has been researched in terms of industrial relations conflicts at work between management and workers, especially where the latter are collectively organized in unions. More recently, researchers have focused on subjectivities of resistance as these are constituted through memories of a fairer time or better work, perhaps, or through social organization, such as familial or local community networks, or solidaristic organization, such as trade unions.

CRITICAL ISSUES: DOMINATION AND HEGEMONY

Hardy and Clegg suggest that "organizational structures and systems are not neutral or apolitical but structurally sedimented phenomena. There is a history of struggles already embedded in the organization." The paradox of power seems to be that you have power only if you are in a superior position in the organization and are opposed in what you want to do by others who are at the same or a lower level; when you want to do something against the resistance of these others, it is termed authority. When they want to do something against superordinate will, it is considered resistance. Authority is seen as legitimate; resistance is seen as illegitimate. Organizational politics become defined as the unsanctioned or illegitimate use of power to achieve unsanctioned or illegitimate ends, as Mintzberg, Mayes and Allen, Gandz and Murray, and Enz all argue. From this perspective, organizational life reduces to a morality play about efficiency: Either members do what they are scripted to do in their formal organization roles in the terms that authorities determine for them, or, if they do not, they are behaving illegitimately. Being moral and being efficient become coterminous in a well-designed system.

Organizations should never be seen just as systems, as engineering that is more efficient when there is less resistance, in the analogies of physics. Organizations always have vested within them traces of the past, as something recurrent, shifting, taking on new meanings, shaping the future. In Weber's terms, organizations already incorporate a "structure of dominancy" in their functioning. The relations that they encompass are invariably saturated and imbued with power. It is distilled deep in the structure, culture, and history of the organization, which often "normalizes" power relations so that they hardly seem like power at all. One of the major strategies of normalization is to practice empowerment. Thus, much recent management theory has been written in praise of teamwork and against bureaucratic hierarchies, because it is believed that this is the way to minimize the expression of power. In the next section, we show that neither the presence of teams nor the absence of hierarchy means an end to power. First, we look at power structured through soft domination, where hierarchies seem to be blurred by project teams, and then consider the role power plays in teams.

SOFT DOMINATION

The central tension in organizations, when viewed through a power lens, is between resistance and obedience. On the whole, from the perspective of management control, the latter is a far more productive result of policies than the former. Excessive use of coercion and force invites resistance; therefore, power as a hard instrumentality, a presence as unsubtle as a billiard ball ricocheting around the table, will, on the whole, be declined in favour of more subtle mechanisms. One theorist who has explored such methods is Steven Lukes, who built on debates in political science to analyze power not only in terms of its mechanics but also its underlying dimensions. The main insight was that power could be used to prevent conflict by shaping perceptions, cognitions, and preferences in such a way that [people] accept their role in the existing order of things, either because they can see or imagine no alternative to it, or because they view it as natural and unchangeable, or because they value it as divinely ordained and beneficial. Power is able to achieve these effects to the extent that it is effectively subsumed through legitimation within an integrated system of cultural and normative assumptions. Given the integrated system of cultural and normative assumptions and an efficient organizational apparatus, goals can be achieved. Hence, analysis of power in organizations needs also to focus on the subtle mechanisms through which obedience is produced-soft domination. Soft domination is characterized by the administration of rules that give managerial discretion to managers while reinforcing the strength of centralized authorities, because those who are delegates know that their obligation is to act creatively within the systems of authority. Authorities create legitimated rules reinforced by clear and credible threats to career, rewards, status, employment, and so on.

What sustains senior management and limits organizational members, ultimately, is the political concentration of the power of control over the deployment of human resources in the hands of a minority combined with the regular use of credible sticks (e.g., formal warnings) and carrots (e.g., performance-related pay) deployed within clear rules. Soft domination is based on the appearance of equality in the organization among peers and the reality of a pervasive system of controls, chief among which are instrumentally legitimate techniques used by the entire management community, such as human resource management, audit, and holding managers accountable to plans. These are modern modes of making people responsible, of rendering them surveyable, and of exercising surveillance over them. More often than not, these forms of accountability and surveillance become the basis for the games people play at work. People conceive of the workplace as a game in which they are "survivors." There are many things to survive-for example, a performance appraisal, not losing face over a policy or procedural conflict, not being downsized and made redundant, and not getting a promotion. Above all, these people are skilled game players- they know the rites and the rules of the games inside out and constantly use the spaces that they can create from these to exercise whatever discretion they can produce and to rationalize that which they cannot.

ELECTRONIC SURVEILLANCE

A number of writers, including Poster, Lyon, Bogard, and Sewell, see modern electronic forms of surveillance as replacing the apparatus of power labouriously constructed by bureaucracy. Extended electronic surveillance has been seen as the hallmark of high modernity, of a world in which surveillance is insidious, making the majority of people increasingly transparent to others who may not be transparent to them.

Zuboff introduced the "Information Panopticon" as a key term. The Information Panopticon privileges organizational elites by making it possible to consolidate various sources of electronic information about the many who serve the organization. Sewell argues that electronic surveillance supplements, rather than replaces, earlier forms of surveillance. Its basic thrust is to make people in organizations more accountable and less autonomous. However, it is often used in conjunction with policies whose avowed purpose is quite opposite to these intentions. Sewell concentrates on teamwork. Teams operate with two dimensions of surveillance: vertical and horizontal. Vertical surveillance focuses on the aberrant: aberrant waste, time, quality, and so on. To define the aberrant, you must first define the normal, which is usually done by establishing performance norms on a statistical basis that enables the aberrant to be immediately transparent-it stands out as a deviation from the norm of time taken, quality produced, or waste accumulated. Electronic forms of monitoring of performance make the norms more transparent and are supported by peer review through horizontal surveillance. Although electronic and traditional forms of surveillance reinforce the vertical dimension, which seeks to make the subject of surveillance his or her own monitor, the horizontal dimension causes us to monitor each other. Panopticism explains only some vertical aspects of this group scrutiny.

EMPOWERMENT

Teamwork is not usually thought of as a mechanism of power, but recent theory has suggested that it is. Indeed, as Sewell notes, teamwork is usually associated with the rhetoric of empowerment, trust, and enhanced discretion. Sometimes it is even referred to as "giving away" power. There is a flood of popular management books whose message is cast in terms of this normative rhetoric, as analysis by Barley and Kunda demonstrates. These books often espouse single-answer solutions for harried managers; TQM (total quality management), organizational learning, lean production, and BPR (business process reengineering) are among the recipes that Sewell notes. What all of these methods have in common, he suggests, is a reversal of the highly individualistic approach to the employee that earlier perspectives such as scientific management had championed. Rather than isolate, observe, and individually measure the times taken by individuals for doing standardized tasks and discouraging them from communicating with others while doing so, the new approach encourages communication and sociability. No longer are employees to be set competitively against each other; instead, they work together as members of teams that have been designed to cope better with more flexible manufacturing methods and to provide opportunities for more intelligent organization of work, where there is greater distributed intelligence of systems and discretion. However, teamwork does not abolish politics but relies on what Barker terms "concertive control" as its horizontal mode of surveillance. The forms of power at work help create the types of subjects that work there.

BARKER ON CONCERTIVE CONTROL

Barker begins his account with a brief snatch of interview data with an employee called Ronald, who is reported as saying that he is more closely watched under a new team-based work design than when he was closely supervised by a manager. The team is a stricter supervisor than his supervisor had been! Barker calls this situation one of "concertive control," something that occurs where there is "a substantial consensus about values, high-level coordination, and a degree of self-management by members or workers in an organization."

Concertive control, argues Barker, is what occurs when organizations become post-bureaucratic, when they adopt decentralized, participative and more democratic designs, a strategy that has long been promoted by more liberal management theorists such as Follett and Lewin. Recently, the trickle of liberal management writing has become a flood as theorists increasingly have sought an alternative to bureaucratic models. What characterizes these arguments is a stress on a new age of post-bureaucratic liberation, in which control by formal rules and hierarchy is abandoned in favour of consensual and values-based action by organization members. Popular writers such as Kanter, Peters, and Drucker promote the benefits of "unimpeded, agile authority structures that grow out of a company's consensual, normative ideology, not from its system of formal rules."

The argument is that "cutting out bureaucratic offices and rules" will "flatten hierarchies, cut costs, boost productivity, and increase the speed with which they respond to the changing business worlds." Employees collaborate to develop the means of their own control. The Panopticon sought to make each worker the governor of what they did at work, aware as they were of the supervisory gaze, and concertive control reinforces this awareness through the discipline of teams. Under the new forms of concertive control and soft domination, power is refined into ever more subtle techniques using instrumental means to make employees accountable and transparent. For example, there may be a vision statement that states, "We are a principled organization that values teamwork." On this basis, team members agree that being principled means that they all arrive at work on time-and they ensure that they do, using norms that they have enacted from the agreed-upon value statement to structure the systems of their own control. Authority shifts from the hierarchy and formal rules to the team and socially created and generated rules.

One arena in which teamwork can be seen to great effect is in collaborations between national defense forces in peacekeeping and related operations. Here the normal relations of command and hierarchy, which flow within the national military, have to be combined with collaboration across organizations, between different national defense forces. Teamwork is now seen to have a much wider utility. It is not just a means of producing collaboration between distinct organizational units; it is also a way to enhance the effectiveness of members of the same organizational unit.

Empowered organizations not only provide new means for control, as Barker suggests, but also make opportunities for the everyday negotiations and games of power more difficult. It is more difficult to negotiate when the people that you work with, rather than a supervisor, impose the limits. It is much easier to steal some time from a supervisor or manager with whom you do not share any obvious interest, other than a necessity to work, than it is from colleagues. You all depend on each other-and that is the subtlety of concertive control. Everyone is empowered to speak-but with the same agreed-upon voice.

ORGANIZATIONAL HEGEMONY IN THE INTERNATIONAL MONETARY FUND

Organizational hegemony occurs when one point of view is predominant. It is marked by a strong organizational culture and an absence of countervailing points of view, because almost everyone has come to accept the dominant views. The best way to guard against hegemony in organizations is to develop polyphony-exposure to and tolerance of many voices. Polyphonic organizations, theoretically, are incipiently democratic and deconstructive. In this section, we consider a case in which the absence of polyphony has been crucial for a very significant global organization. Joseph Stiglitz provides an account of the International Monetary Fund (IMF). The IMF is an organization that was established in the late stages of World War II with the express purpose of minimizing the harm from-and, if possible, preventing-global depressions. Its mandate was to maintain international liquidity through loans to economically distressed countries that had insufficient economic resources to stimulate aggregate economic demand domestically. It is a global organization funded by taxpayers around the world. Yet it is not responsible to them, nor does it have their views represented to it. Instead, it hears, represents, and reflects the views of national finance ministries and central bankers, over which one country-the United States-has effective veto in its deliberations. Its contemporary policies champion "market supremacy with ideological fervour . . . the IMF typically provides funds only if countries engage in policies like cutting deficits, raising taxes or raising interest rates that lead to a contraction of the economy."

These policy positions were the outcome of a hard-fought battle in the IMF that occurred in the early 1980s, when it became dominated by freemarket economists who were under the thrall of the fashionable prescriptions associated with the governments of President Reagan in the United States and Prime Minister Thatcher in the United Kingdom. Stiglitz argues that the IMF has functioned in what is sometimes called, after a medical metaphor, an "iatrogenic" manner-its policies have exacerbated the very problems that they were supposed to solve, rather as a surgical procedure might complicate an underlying condition it was designed to cure. Rather than contributing to global stability, they have made the international economy less stable, more crisis-ridden, and indebted countries poorer. Why and how has that been possible? Central to the argument is the absence of polyphony and the presence of homogeneity. Stiglitz sees two main factors contributing to the absence of polyphonic reason (debate between opposing viewpoints): first, a problem of governance, and second, a problem of representation. Governance addresses the question of who decides. Commercial and financial interests from the wealthiest countries in the world dominate the IMF.

Its policies reflect these interests-hence the market emphasis-because why would the suppliers of capital let the state do something that they believe markets cannot only do better but certainly more profitably? These suppliers are the dominant commercial and financial interests in the wealthiest countries. Institutions such as the IMF, as well as the World Bank and the World Trade Organization, intervene in the economic management of poorer countries. But those intervening are always representatives of the most developed countries, are chosen by those developed countries behind closed doors, and do not necessarily have any experience of the developing world. As Stiglitz says of these institutions, they are "not representative of the nations they serve."

Raising the problem of representation addresses the issue of who speaks for the countries in need of assistance. The answer is simple: "At the IMF it is the finance ministers and the central bank governors" who "typically are closely tied to the financial community; they come from financial firms, and after their period of government service, that is where they return." Such people "naturally see the world through the eyes of the financial community" in the advanced economies. It is not surprising that the IMF policies have been addressed more to the interests of commercial and financial power rather than those of poor peasants or hard-pressed local businessmen trying to pay off the taxes that the IMF imposes. Taxation without representation is what Stiglitz calls it.

Classic political sociology suggests that when people are taxed without political representation, they resist through nonrepresentational means-they take to the streets, riot, and rebel. Ever since the WTO met in Seattle in 1999, the rebellions in the developing world have been echoed in the heartlands of the global institutions, as idealistic and impassioned opponents of the dominant consensus about globalization have rioted to try and have their alternative views broadcast. In organizations designed to be more polyphonic through more inclusive governance and representation, there would be less need for illegitimate means of resistance.

THE EXTREMES OF POWER

We can bring polyphonic organization into sharper relief if we contrast it with its antithesis-organizations that are total institutions, those in which hegemony is reinforced by the totality of the organization's everyday practices. There are two extremes to power, which we can characterize as negative and positive. Whereas negative power is constraining, positive power is enabling. First, we take a look at some extremes of negative power and consider some of the ethical questions they raise. Then, we return to the question of polyphonic, positive power and of how you, as a manager, might manage in such an environment.

TOTAL INSTITUTIONS

Organizations always place constraints on freedom of action, which people sometimes resist. However, a more important question about power in organizations is not why people sometimes resist but why, much of the time, they do not. Obedience, in fact, is a far more fundamental question than resistance. One way of researching the mechanism of obedience is to look at some extreme cases. The rationale for doing this is that in extreme cases, the normal tendencies of everyday organizational life are more obvious because they are more concentrated. The Canadian sociologist Erving Goffman used anthropological research to investigate how authority was configured in extreme contexts. He chose extremes because the everyday mechanisms of authority and power were much more evident there than in the world of the corporate "organization man." Goffman initiated the discussion of extreme organizations when he coined the term "total institution."

Total institutions are organizations that contain the totality of the lives of those who are their members. As such, people within them are cut off from any wider society for a relatively long time, leading an enclosed and formally administered existence. In such contexts, the organization has more or less monopoly control of its members' everyday life. Goffman's argument is that total institutions demonstrate in heightened and condensed form the underlying organizational processes that can be found, albeit in much less extreme cases, in more normal organizations. Total institutions are often parts of a broader apparatus, such as a prison or detention centre. Total institutions do not just include organizations that make people inmates against their will, however. They can also include organizations founded on membership contracted on voluntary inclusion-for instance, a professional army, a boarding school, a residential college, or a religious retreat, such as a monastery or nunnery. Several types of organization can be a total institution:

- Places to put people that the state deems incapable of looking after themselves (these people, who vary historically and comparatively, have included the "feeble," the "lunatic," or the "disabled")
- Restrictive organizations that institutionalize people who pose a threat to others, such as people with communicable diseases of contagion who are legislatively contained in sanitaria for the duration of their disease
- Punitive organizations, such as prisons, gulags, concentration

camps, reform schools, prisoner-of-war camps, or detention centers for asylum seekers

- Organizations dedicated to a specific work task, such as boarding schools, military barracks, and vessels at sea, or remote company towns
- Retreats from the world, such as monasteries, abbeys, convents, or growth and learning centers What do these very different types of organizations have in common that make them total institutions?
- Each member's daily life is carried out in the immediate presence of a large number of others.
- The members are very visible; there is no place to hide from the surveillance of others.
- The members tend to be strictly regimented.
- Life in a total institution is governed by strict, formal rational planning of time. (Think of school bells for lesson endings and beginnings, factory whistles, timetables, schedules, and so on.)
- People are not free to choose how they spend their time; instead, it is strictly prescribed for them.
- Members lose a degree of autonomy because of an all-encompassing demand for conformity to the authoritative interpretation of rules.

TECHNIQUES OF POWER

When we master a technique, our skill has its own charm, aesthetics, and beauty, and we can take sheer delight in using it, irrespective of its moral effects: Technical responsibility differs from moral responsibility in that it forgets that the action is a means to something other than itself . . . the result is the irrelevance of moral standards for the technical success of the bureaucratic operation.

When technique is paramount, action becomes purely a question of technical power-the use of means to achieve given ends. For instance, as a master of logistics, Eichmann was enormously proud of his achievements in the complex scheduling of trains, camps, and death. Organizational power that makes you technically accountable and responsible for results expressed in a purely quantitative form has two profound effects. First, it makes you utterly transparent-you either achieve your targets or you do not. Second, it relieves you of moral indeterminacy-if you are authorized to do something and given targets to achieve by superordinates guiding strategies and plans, obedience surely is appropriate, and authority should be served.

Organization work is a ceaseless round of activity. Most organizational members are in the middle of organizational chains whose links are not always clear. People are not always aware of the consequences of what they do and do not do-after all, most of the time, they are just doing what they are told (shred those files, write those checks, dispatch those troops, maintain those train schedules). Divisions of labour in the complex chains enable us to keep a distance from effects; we can represent them in terms of intermediary forms of data (kill rates, efficiency statistics, and so on). Our labour moves minute cogs in a bureaucratic machine necessarily intermeshed with so many others that we are just one small element in the overall scheme of things. We don't even have to try to understand the totality.

The system of which we are a part is responsible, not us. Especially when actions are performed at a distance on people defined as administrative categories, the people are effectively dehumanized. The more dehumanized they are, the easier becomes the application of pure technique to their cases. When whatever is being worked on can be represented quantitatively, as a bottom-line calculation, it is so much easier to make rational decisions (cut costs, trim fat, speed throughput, increase efficiency, defeat the competition) without concern for the human, environmental, or social effects of these decisions.

MANAGING WITH POSITIVE POWER

One consequence of the insight that power is a normal feature of organizations is that managers must learn how to manage with power on a daily basis in ways that are enabling, genuinely empowering, and positive rather than merely constraining, smart but unethical, and largely negative. To be a good manager means knowing how and when to use what kind of power wisely to manage polyphony so that it is neither anarchic nor stifled. Modifying Pfeffer somewhat, we can note that there are seven steps to the effective use of power:

- Decide what your goals should be and what you are trying to accomplish in consultation with direct stakeholders in your organization.
- Diagnose patterns of dependence and interdependence; which

individuals both inside and outside the organization are influential and important to achieving these goals?

- What are the points of view of the important people likely to be? How will they feel about what you are trying to do?
- What are the power bases of the important people? Which of them is the most influential in the decision?
- What are your bases of power and influence? What bases of influence can you develop to gain more positive control over the situation?
- Which of the various strategies and tactics for exercising power seem most appropriate and are likely to be effective, given the situation you confront?
- Based on Steps 1 through 6, choose an ethical course of action to get something done.

When using power to manage others, always remember that those you are seeking to manage probably also will be trying to manage you with power, so the old adage "do unto others as you would have others do unto you" is worth recalling. Although you may think of their response as resistance, to do so presumes a value legitimacy that may not be justified on your part. They are trying to manage your management of power through their management of the power that they can enact in the situations in which they find themselves or that they can create. Power is nothing if not creative. Crucially, your managing with power means achieving common definition, a genuine accord, on which to base strategies, tactics, and actions. Positive uses of power make things happen that wouldn't otherwise have happened-not by stopping some things from occurring, but by bringing new things into creation, involving less force and more listening, working with, rather than against, others. Managing with power does not always mean seeking to impose a specific meaning on an uncertain context because it entails arbitrary structuring of others realities. In contrast, the alternative model is often seen as one where people advocate bottom-up decision making, seeking to listen to what others in the organization have to say. From empowerment (the giving of voice to those frequently unheard), organizations that use this model seek to enhance the overall systemic powers of the organization, to mobilize resources, and to get things done. This use of power frequently means giving way in the organization conversation, not claiming a special privilege because of title or experience, and not being selectively inattentive to others, but listening and attending to them. The challenge for future power theory, as Pfeffer suggests, is "to manage with power," where you recognize, diagnose, and respect the diversity of interests and seek to translate and enroll members within organizational courses of action, while at the same time listening to what others are saying, modifying your position accordingly, and choosing the appropriate strategies and tactics to accomplish whatever is chosen. Sometimes, after taking all that into consideration, it still means making others do what they would not otherwise have done, against their resistance. Power can be like that. Yet, it does not have to be so. Coercive power should be the refuge of last resort for the diplomatically challenged and structurally secure, not the hallmark of management's right to manage.

Organizations may listen or may not, may work with the creativity and diversity of people's identities or work against them. The politics of power can be based on active listening rather than assertive denial through the instrumentality and ritual of established power. To build such organizations-ones that seek to extend the organization conversation rather than to exploit its lapses-would seem to be one of the more pressing aspects of the agenda for future managers.

SUMMARY

The pervasiveness of power is the most central aspect of organizational life. Much of the time, it is wrapped up in the velvet glove of authority, but inside that velvet glove is an iron fist. This fist has control of the levers of power that authority confers-the power, essentially, to determine policies and practices within the organization, most fundamentally expressed as whom the organization chooses to employ and whom it chooses not to employ. Many organizations shape whether we work and how we are employed if we do; thus, these types of organizations have power over most of our life chances as wage earners. For this reason, it is important to understand the limits of power and authority, resistance and obedience. In organizations, we have to put up with people and situations while doing the work we have to do or choose to do. It is important that our choices in how we equip these duties can be defended ethically. Fundamentally, power is shaped by what we know and how we know what to do. Organizationally, it is easy for this knowledge to be applied questionably, which is why it is important that organizations always be polyphonic rather than totalitarian spaces. Being able to articulate organizational dissent should be a normal and essential bulwark of civil liberty.

Note: For detailed information related to this chapter reader can visit site of United Technologies. United Technologies (UTC) provides technology products and services to the building systems and aerospace industries. The company provides helicopters, elevators, air conditioning equipment, hydrogen fuel cells, life support systems, aerospace products and aftermarket services, and fire and security protection services. The company primarily operates in the US. It is headquartered in Hartford, Connecticut and employs 223,100 people. utc.com

9

Conflict Management

Conflict may be defined as a struggle or contest between people with opposing needs, ideas, beliefs, values, or goals. Conflict on teams is inevitable; however, the results of conflict are not predetermined. Conflict might escalate and lead to nonproductive results, or conflict can be beneficially resolved and lead to quality final products. Therefore, learning to manage conflict is integral to a high-performance team. Although very few people go looking for conflict, more often than not, conflict results because of miscommunication between people with regard to their needs, ideas, beliefs, goals, or values. Conflict management is the principle that all conflicts cannot necessarily be resolved, but learning how to manage conflicts can decrease the odds of nonproductive escalation. Conflict management involves acquiring skills related to conflict resolution, self-awareness about conflict modes, conflict communication skills, and establishing a structure for management of conflict in your environment.

INTRODUCTION

Research into behaviour in organizations can be divided into two categories: normative and descriptive. Normative research is concerned with how things should be, whereas descriptive research addresses itself to what is - rather than what could or should be. This dual perspective is most apparent in approaches to the issues of conflict and conflict management in organizations. Normative approaches reflect attitudes and beliefs which identify all conflicts as destructive and promote conflict-elimination as the formula for organizational success. Descriptive approaches accept conflict as inevitable and consider its proper management the primary responsibility of all administrators. This paper pertains to the descriptive mode of inquiry in presenting a framework for the study of conflict in organizations. But it goes beyond this domain in suggesting that administrators must take the offensive and seek to manage conflict, and also in advocating that traditional methods of dealing with conflict be replaced by a new and more sophisticated approach.

CONFLICT: TOWARDS A DEFINITION

Conflict is endemic to all social life. It is an inevitable part of living because it is related to situations of scarce resources, division of functions, power relations and role-differentiation. Because of its ubiquity and pervasive nature, the concept has acquired a multitude of meanings and connotations presenting us with nothing short of a semantic jungle. Like other terms, conflict generates considerable ambivalence and leaves many scholars and administrators quite uncertain about:

1. Its meaning and relevance and
2. How best to cope with it.

The normative conception of conflict, strongly influenced by a preoccupation with stability and equilibrium in organizational design, links conflict to violence, destruction, inefficiency and irrationality.

This form of intellectual myopia was especially invidious in suggesting that administrators have the responsibility of avoiding, controlling or eliminating conflict. Descriptive approaches challenge the whole basis and rationale of these assumptions. They permit us to depart from an outmoded paradigm by suggesting that any social interaction in which the parties (however they may be structured or defined) compete for scarce resources or values has the potential for conflict. Using the term in a broad sense we suggest that conflict refers to all kinds of antagonistic interactions. More specifically, it can be defined as a situation in which two or more parties have incompatible objectives and in which their perceptions and behaviour are commensurate with that incompatability.

This definition is purposely broad. It suggests that conflict is a social phenomemon that is found in personal, group or organizational interactions. As such it comprises several dimensions. Fink distinguishes between (1) antagonistic-psychological relations and (2) antagonistic behaviour, whereas Pondy observes that conflict is made up of (1) antecedent conditions, (2) affective conditions, (3) cognitive conditions and (4) behavioural conditions. We advance a conception of conflict which emphasizes its three, interrelated dimensions, namely: (1) conflict situation (the basic incompatibility), (2) conflict attitudes (range of psychological factors) and (3) conflict behaviour (set of related behaviour).

Conflict refers to more than just overt behaviour. Concentrating only upon its behavioural manifestation is an extremely limiting exercise. The three-dimensional conception of conflict emphasizes the need to consider the situation in which parties (individuals, groups or organizations) come to possess incompatible goals, their structure of interaction and the nature of their goals. We have to consider emotional (e.g. distrust) and cognitive (e.g. stereotyping) orientations that accompany a conflict situation as well as the range of action undertaken by any party in a situation of conflict.

Administrators often feel that discussions of fundamental terms are merely academic. This is not always the case. Effective action and sensible responses depend upon clear thinking and systematic analysis. Understanding must precede action. If administrators consider the problem of conflict and understand that conflicts stem from ineradicable human qualities and are related to situations of interdependence, scarce resources and perceptions of incompatibility, they might readily accept conflict and recognize its values - provided, that is, they are properly aware of "conflict management" and the need to find a solution. Both conflict management and a satisfactory solution are easier to attain when it is accepted that what we normally call conflict is a complex, multidimensional phenomenon. It is not caused by "inadequate" structures, nor is it undesirable. It is natural and inevitable and, properly managed, it is productive, relevant and creative.

CONFLICT IN ORGANIZATIONS

Organizations are living systems consisting of interacting units performing a task in a mutually dependent manner within a structure of scarce resources. It seems commonplace to suggest that conflicts would be present in such a setting. The parties in an organization may have a conflict about the distribution of resources, or they may have a more fundamental conflict about the very structure of their organization and the basic nature of their interaction. Once the parties are in a situation of goal incompatibility, their conflict develops in a dynamic fashion, initiating valuable and much-needed constructive changes or leading to escalating strategies and destructive consequences.

As there is nothing pre-determined about its course or development, it seems erroneous to view conflict from a negative perspective only - as destructive or dysfunctional. It is true that conflict may be uncomfortable, it may even be a source of problems, but it is absolutely necessary if change is to occur, if organizations are to survive and adapt. Organizational change and innovation does not just happen, it requires a stimulant. That stimulant is conflict.

Administrators must accept the need to influence the developmental dynamics of a conflict, so that the parties' attitudes and actions will lead to better coordination and a more appropriate interdependence. They must not seek to stifle or eliminate organizational conflict - for that is hardly a realistic goal. As Rico has noted, an organization devoid of conflict "... may indicate autocracy, uniformity, stagnation and mental fixity." It would also be protecting only the vested interests of the status quo. Administrators must accept and indeed occasionally encourage conflict, because change and other desirable consequences are products of conflict. The challenge administrators face is to utilize such conflict management techniques that would ensure that as a conflict passes from a latent to a manifest phase, it proceeds towards its potential and realizes its constructive values.

ANALYZING ORGANIZATIONAL CONFLICT

Three distinct criteria define the role of an administrator in an organization: planning, resource allocation and conflict management. There is no doubt that managing conflict permeates every aspect of the administrative role. Awareness of the various forms of conflict management that can be employed at different stages of the development of a conflict is vital, if administrators are to organize efforts towards influencing the conflict situation, the parties' attitudes or their behaviour. In addition to that, effective conflict management requires a recognition of the sources that generate a conflict. What, then, are the sources or bases of organizational conflicts?

Sources of Conflict. Organizational conflict appears in a variety of forms and has varying causes. These can generally be separated into several categories. Katz identifies three sources of conflict. These are:

1. Structural conflict (conflict arising out of the need to manage the interdependence between different organizational sub-units),
2. Role conflict (conflict arising from sets of prescribed behaviour) and
3. Resources conflict (conflict stemming from interest groups competing for organizational resources).

Robbins identifies three sources of organizational conflict and indicates that an understanding of the source of a conflict improves the probability of effective conflict management. The main factors which serve as sources of conflict are identified as:

1. Communicational (conflicts arising from misunderstandings etc.),
2. Structural (conflicts related to organizational roles), and
3. Personal (conflicts stemming from individual differences).

Methods of conflict management which are appropriate in one case may not necessarily be appropriate when applied to a conflict generated from another source. Here we wish to suggest a different perspective which traces the source of organizational conflict to the unit of analysis involved. Units of analysis are the parties to a conflict. They perceive, initiate and sustain a conflict. Their characteristics specify the conditions which affect the course of a conflict and determine the mode of its management. Thus, we have conflicts that originate in the individual person, conflicts that have their basis in the relationship between individuals, and conflicts that occur as a result of interactions between groups. These may be described as:

1. Intrapersonal conflict,
2. Interpersonal conflict, and
3. Interdepartmental conflict.

Each of these categories raises different questions about the three interrelated components of conflict and each emphasizes different aspects of conflict management.

Intrapersonal Conflict. Intrapersonal conflict is internal to the individual (though its effects can profoundly influence organizational functioning) and is perhaps the most difficult form of conflict to analyze and manage. Intrapersonal conflict is basically a conflict between two incompatible tendencies. It arises when a stimulus evokes two different and incompatible tendencies and the individual is required to discriminate between these tendencies. In such a situation it is common for individuals to experience frustrations and to allow their conflict situation to be expressed in a range of behavioural strategies ranging from apathy and boredom to absenteeism, excessive drinking or destructive behaviour. If such behavioural consequences are to be avoided, then it is essential to diagnose individual perception and utilize some techniques that would reduce anxiety-eliciting stimuli and increase consonance between individual behaviour and organizational requirements.

Interpersonal Conflict. Interpersonal conflict emphasizes the interaction of human factors in an organization. Here we are concerned with these factors as they appear in a dyadic relationship. We can broadly suggest two classes of factors as conflict sources. These are:

1. Personal. Individuals are not identical, constant or consistent. When two individuals are brought together and kept together, each with his own qualities, needs and skills, a conflict may ensue if their attributes are not meshed together in a coordinated way. Interaction between individuals with different attitudes, values and needs can produce conflict behaviour and affect organizational performance.
2. Functional. Individuals in organizations have roles which are expected sets of behaviour associated with their position. In theory, individuals are not expected to engage in any discretionary behaviour. Such specification would be consistent with organizational preferences for consistency and predictability. In practice, however, role specifications tend to be ambiguous and incomplete, and in their interaction with others, some individuals often feel dissatisfied with their role or position, or they may feel that their aspirations for higher positions are being frustrated. Interpersonal conflict can be accounted for, to a great extent, in terms of the incumbents' roles and their expectations in particular situations.

Interdepartmental Conflict. The third major cause of organizational conflict is structural. Organizations are designed around product lines, regions or technical specialities. These activities are assigned to departments that often have mutually exclusive structured interests and goals and that interact within a framework of scarce resources and task dependence. When resources are relatively fixed and when one department's gain is at the expense of another, conflict should be expected. If two sub-units in an organizational system have differentiated goals and are functionally interdependent, conditions exist for conflict. Interdependence produces the need for collaboration, but it also presents occasions for conflict.

Other contextual factors which affect the interaction structure between departments and create the conditions for interdepartmental conflict include: different attitudes between line and staff units, organizational size (directly related to level of conflict) and standardization (inversely related to conflict), physical or communicational barriers between departments, unequal access to authority, rewards or organizational resources and ambiguity or uncertainty in assigning tasks or rewards to different departments.

These, then, are the sources of conflict situations in organizations. How a conflict situation will change over time, how its interrelated components will alter and the environment in which it occurs will respond, is dependent upon the administrator's efforts to manage or influence it. This, in turn, is related to one's understanding of the source of a specific conflict situation.

CONFLICT MANAGEMENT

Ways of managing organizational conflict are as varied as its causes, origins and contexts. The purpose of conflict management, whether undertaken by the parties in conflict or whether involving the intervention of an outside party, is to affect the entire structure of a conflict situation so as to contain the destructive components in the conflict process (e.g. hostility, use of violence) and help the parties possessing incompatible goals to find some solution to their conflict. Effective conflict management succeeds in (1) minimizing disruption stemming from the existence of a conflict, and (2) providing a solution that is satisfactory and acceptable. We describe efforts directed towards containing or limiting some aspects of behaviour as strategies of conflict settlement and efforts directed towards the parties' attitudes, situations as well as behaviour as strategies of conflict resolution. Skilled administrators are aware of these methods and techniques and know how to utilize them effectively. All organizations, however simple or complex, possess a range of mechanisms or procedures for managing conflict. These are built into the organizational structure and are consciously employed by administrators to influence the course and development of a conflict. The success or effectiveness of such procedures can be gauged by the extent to which they limit conflict behaviour and the extent to which they help to achieve a satisfactory solution. It is the contention of this article that strategies of conflict avoidance, conflict prevention or institutionalization of conflict will change or replace coercive behaviour, but that only the injection of a behavioural social scientist, acting in a facilitative, non-directive and nonevaluative fashion, will achieve a resolution with respect to the basic issues, attitudes and structure of interaction. If administrators care for optimal methods of conflict management, they should give their strongest support to a strategy that can end a conflict in a satisfactory and selfperpetuating manner.

All this is not to contend, however, that conflict resolution is the immediate outcome of any intervention. The outcome of a conflict depends upon many aspects of the conflict process prior to the efforts to manage it (e.g. issues in conflict, relative power of actors, degree of proximity etc.). What we are suggesting is that if four basic conflict outcomes may be distinguished - namely (1) withdrawal, (2) imposition or dominance, (3) compromise and a (4) creative, problem-solving resolution - then the most likely mode by which outcome (5) may be reached pertains to the voluntary intervention of an outside consultant acting as a professional helper. Let us then present a model of conflict management which can describe the relationship between modalities of conflict management and conflict outcomes and give some directions for managing organizational conflict.

MANAGING INTRAPERSONAL CONFLICT

Intrapersonal conflict is predicated upon an incongruity between individual needs and organizational requirements. Intrapersonal conflict unfolds over time and manifests itself in a complex and multiform range of attitudinal and behavioural consequences. These may vary from psychosomatic consequences (e.g. frustration, emotional instability) to physical consequences (e.g. absenteeism, destructive behaviour). As such consequences are obviously correlated with decreased performance and work-motivation, managing intrapersonal conflict will help the individual to promote his capacity for adaptation and attain an equilibrium in his relationship with the organization.

Personal existence is, inevitably, punctuated by conflicts and other emotionally charged experiences. When a person experiences an inner conflict and feels that he can not master his situation, or change his environment, a number of methods of conflict management can be employed. These are conveniently divided into (1) cognitive strategies and (2) behavioural strategies. Cognitive strategies, often called defence mechanisms, help an individual to falsify, distort or deny a particular conflict. Cognitive strategies represent an attempt to control or manage negative and disturbing feelings associated with conflict and to allow an individual to carry on with his normal activities. Cognitive strategies include repression (an attempt to push conflict out of existence), rationalization (hiding the truth from oneself), fantasy or even denial of reality. Behavioural strategies for coping with intrapersonal conflict include escape, withdrawal and aggression (especially against convenient targets). These strategies can not resolve intrapersonal conflict in any permanent way. They can be successful in the short-run. They can help an individual to reduce his level of anxiety and diminish his tension. They can prevent or avoid disruptive behaviour, but they can not generate a solution. This can come about through the involvement of an expert consultant, acting in an accepting manner and encouraging the individual to evaluate his situation rationally and decide upon more effective responses. Interventions in intrapersonal conflicts entail consideration of substantive issues, discussions and self-observations, helping an individual to unload his burdensome thoughts and reactions and reorienting his thinking towards a more benevolent and self-maintaining pattern of behaviour.

The strength of this approach to conflict management is that it helps an individual to concentrate on his situation and on ways to evaluate alternatives that may have gone unnoticed. The consultant remains detached from an individual, but his intervention, listening, probing, interviewing and explicit confrontation of the conflict issues, sets the basis for self-diagnosis and improved performance. It eliminates distortion and increases self-knowledge. It is a method which seeks not merely an amelioration of the surface symptoms, but a successful change in the situational (e.g. reevaluating a conflict situation), attitudinal (e.g. reduced anxiety, increased self-esteem) and behavioural (e.g. stimulate productive behaviour) components of a conflict.

Consultants may be internal to an organization, or they may be introduced by an administrator when circumstances require it. They have several roles to play, all intended to aid a person to be more effective in his organization. What characterizes all these roles is that they are enacted in an informal and flexible fashion and in a facilitative and diagnostic manner. Techniques which are congruent with implementing the consultant's role include:

1. Facilitative techniques (e.g. facilitating individual exploration and self-observation, giving information, advice, reassurance and encouragement),
2. Behavioural modification techniques (e.g. establish, through negative or positive reinforcement, contingencies of behaviour that should be decreased) and
3. Cognitive techniques (e.g. learn to undo old values and acquire a new perception of the self).

When organizations experience difficulties as a result of intrapersonal conflicts, administrators would be well-advised to manage such conflicts by leading their organization to seek professional help from persons who are trained to fulfill the role of organizational consultants. Successful organizational change does, after all, depend upon a strong commitment to conflict resolution.

MANAGING INTERPERSONAL CONFLICT

Interpersonal interactions are extraordinarily complex. Individuals are brought together and kept together because of personal attraction or complementary needs. A great deal of individual behaviour takes place in organizations (university, hospital, factory) in which they occupy various positions. Such positions are interlocked or interdependent so that the attitudes and behaviour of one individual affect the attitudes and behaviour of another. Indeed, we may describe organizations as networks of repetitive, reciprocal and predictable interactions between individuals. Although persons in an organization interact in a relatively consistent way along a stable-cooperative dimension (organizations develop norms to ensure stable interactions), interpersonal conflict is an essential aspect of organizational life. The causes of interpersonal conflict in organizations can be ascribed to personal differences (interaction between dissimilar people maximizes conflict potential), perceptual differences (individuals perceive an unfair allocation of organizational resources) and functional differences (conflicts arising from incompatible role requirements). On the whole interpersonal conflict generates new ideas and work patterns, but when it is augmented by personal distrust, misperception and competition, it can very easily be transformed into destructive and costly behaviour. To avoid detrimental effects on individual as well as organizational functioning, administrators need to identify the causes of interpersonal conflict and take appropriate action to deal with it.

Following Blake and Mouton, we can suggest five possible modes of conflict management: withdrawal, smoothing, compromise, forcing and problem-solving. Withdrawal is an attempt to manage interpersonal conflict by avoidance. Smoothing involves emphasis of common, organizational interests and yielding by one or both parties. Compromise is an attempt to manage conflict by expecting each person to give up something. Forcing occurs when interpersonal conflict is managed in a fashion which compels one person to acquiesce. Problem-solving is an attempt to achieve close collaboration and integrative decision-making between individuals. Under the prevailing influence of behaviourism, interpersonal conflict management has been directed mainly towards the behavioural components of a conflict situation. Attitudes and perceptions have been considered beyond the realm of conflict management. As a result of this, conflict management has tended to force individuals to choose between fixed and simplified behavioural alternatives, defined in terms of two rigid behavioural goals, winning or losing. The choices and incentives associated with this orientation of victory versus defeat were strongly constrained, forcing individuals into relatively primitive modes of interaction and providing administrators with an untrustworthy vehicle for potential conflict management.

Of the five methods of managing interpersonal conflict it appears that problem-solving is the only method that is directed towards the attitudinal, situational and behavioural components of conflict. It is the only method that does not focus on relatively automatic, unthinking responses. It is the only method which seeks to utilize higher mental processes to achieve a high-quality, integrative and satisfying outcome. Empirical support for the notion that problem-solving is the most effective method for dealing with the underlying problem and feelings of interpersonal conflict and generating a sound resolution may be obtained from a number of studies. Lawrence and Lorsch examined the use of the various conflict management methods in six organizations and concluded that the highest performing organizations used problem-solving to a greater extent than other organizations. Burke asked seventy-four administrators to describe the way they dealt with conflicts and, in comparing scores of constructive conflict management, found that the most effective administrators used problem-solving methods (followed by smoothing and compromise). In a second study he compared fifty-three descriptions of effective conflict management with fifty-three descriptions of ineffective conflict management from fifty-seven administrators and found that 58.5 per cent of statements about effective conflict management related to problem-solving (followed by 24.5 per cent for forcing and 11.3 per cent for compromise). Organizations that can increase the use of problem-solving in interpersonal conflict can offer a better working experience, more constructive consequences and a more creative conflict resolution.

Problem-solving as a method of conflict management is not a common experience. A number of elements or conditions have to be present if problem-solving is to be realized. These conditions appear to be as follows: Situational requirements (e.g. informality and flexibility of interactions, absence of time pressures, power symmetry etc.). Attitudinal requirements (e.g. trust and confidence in each other, belief in conflict resolution rather than conflict avoidance etc.). Perceptual requirements (e.g. individuals do not perceive threats or need to win or dominate the other) and Behavioural requirements (e.g. free information, definition of issues, discussion of alternatives, exhaustive search for solutions etc.). On the whole these requirements are absent in dyadic conflict management where individuals' responses are as likely to escalate as to reduce conflict. The implication of this is that parties outside the dyad must intervene to alter the fundamental parameters of individual interactions in organizations and to introduce the conditions which are suitable to problem-solving.

The intervention of a behavioural consultant - either from within or outside the organization - can achieve this goal. Consultation-based approaches to interpersonal conflict focus on understanding the psychological and operational environment of an individual, utilizing behavioural scientists in a supportive-facilitative way and promoting the establishment of problem-solving. Interventions by behavioural consultants may take the form of offering theoretical inputs (e.g. providing individuals with conceptions about conflict), offering content observation (e.g. suggesting various outcome interpretations) and offering process observations (e.g. increasing productive interactions through openness, synchronization of efforts etc.). They give individuals the freedom, opportunity and motivation to move away from rigid behaviour or from reiterating their positions as prescribed by organizational norms. They address themselves to the attitudinal and behavioural dimensions of interactions and in combining task and socio-emotional activities, they exemplify and help to establish the conditions of problem-solving.

In constrast to other methods of conflict management, the intervention of a behavioural consultant accentuates the positive and highlights commonly held views of the actors. Applications of this approach in the interpersonal sphere rest upon the following assumptions:

1. Deficiencies in perception are the main cause of interpersonal conflict.
2. Barriers to improved information prolong and aggravate a conflict.
3. Inadequate interactions between individuals prevent them from management their conflict constructively.

Techniques of intervention in interpersonal conflict are closely related to these assumptions and include perceptual, informational and interactional procedures. Perceptual procedures involve:

1. Identifying conflict issues,
2. Defining alternative issues, and
3. "Reality-lesting".

Informational procedures involve:

1. Clarifying issues.
2. Encouraging and gathering information (through interviews, meetings or other instruments).
3. Increasing frequency, openness and accuracy of communication.

Interactional procedures entail:

1. Regulating the pace of interaction,
2. Offering "process" observations to help individuals see how to be more effective,
3. Injection inputs in the form of concepts, models or principles which might be useful in understanding a conflict and
4. Helping in the design of implementation steps through which conflict resolution would be possible.

Through his interventions a behavioural consultant becomes the information-gathering instrument and a "resource person". Administrators who are concerned about organizational change and more productive results would be well advised to be aware of the strengths - as well as limitations - of this approach to interpersonal conflict management.

MANAGING INTERDEPARTMENTAL CONFLICT

Conflict between departments is a natural consequence of organizational activities. As organizations move towards greater differentiation and complexity, as they change or adapt to new circumstances, the stage is set for incompatibility of goals or competition for scarce resources. The resulting conflict between departments may have ambivalent consequences for an organization. On the one hand it may have a dysfunctional and counterproductive effect on the organization, and on the other hand it can be highly functional and stimulate intra-organizational creativity. For conflict to be a vehicle for organizational growth and creativity, there must exist an appropriate method of conflict management between departments. An administrator should know when he is faced with interdepartmental conflict and be informed of the processes for coping with it or resolving it. Before exploring the methods and techniques for managing interdepartmental conflict, it is pertinent to examine briefly the attitudes and behaviours which characterize interdepartmental conflict. These can be described in terms of the following categories:

1. Effects within each department. When departments are in conflict, individual members tend to bury their differences and display greater loyalty to their department. Departments become more cohesive, more formal in their behaviour and more insistent upon individual conformity and accomplishment of prescribed tasks.
2. Effects between departments. Each department begins to experience perceptual distortions and to develop a strong self-image and a negative stereotype of the other.

With the rise of prejudicial attitudes between departments there is an increase in hostility and a decrease in communication. Each department strives to enhance its own image and performance and to downgrade the other's. Under such conditions a conflict becomes a matter of victory or defeat, winning or losing. The fundamental significance of a win-lose dynamic is that it is, to some degree, intrinsic to any complex and stratified organization, but that feelings of in-group versus out-group are especially strong in conflict situations. The attitudinal characteristics of such a pattern include a competitive orientation, the evaluative characteristics include antagonistic feelings and the behavioural characteristics include circumscribed interaction and distorted communication. The structural attributes of a conflict relationship must be taken into account in proposing a strategy of conflict management.

Traditional approaches to managing interdepartmental conflict emphasized such methods as:

1. Conflict avoidance (separating departments by relocating them physically).
2. Regulating a conflict by introducing new rules and procedures.
3. Seeking a form of "legalistic" solution (by appealing to higher organizational authorities).
4. Using departmental representatives to reach a compromise agreement.
5. Seeking mediation or arbitration from an outside body.

Such conflict management methods may indeed produce an agreement. They may reduce the level of conflict behaviour between departments and even legitimize new levels of performance. They can not, though, achieve a genuine conflict resolution because they merely reflect, perpetuate and occasionally aggravate a win-lose pattern of interactions. Separation, withdrawal, institutionalization, bargaining or legal approaches are essentially forms of a win-lose confrontation. They all start with a polarized, adversary orientation, in which each department tries to attain as much as possible by outsmarting the other. They bury a conflict, ignore it, produce power-based decisions or allow departments to withdraw from it. They do not stimulate a search for conflict resolution.

A range of new approaches to managing interdepartmental conflict may be suggested. These approaches acquire new significance because they become integral parts of an interaction process between departments, because they move away from win-lose type of strategies and because they can meet the need for conflict resolution more effectively. They are best summarized in terms of the social psychologists out of whose experiments these approaches evolved:

I. Sherif et al.: Sherif and his associates suggest two broad strategies which are designed to increase cooperation between departments, facilitate mutual communication of needs and minimize the effects of hostility and negative attitudes. Both strategies are broad in their scope. Their target of change is the organizational structure, but changes in individual attitudes and improvement in interpersonal competence may also be involved.

1. Locating a common enemy. When departments are engaged in a conflict, their incentive structure (i.e. conflict of interest) may be changed and a mutual understanding as well as favourable attitudes may be promoted if they perceive a threat from a competing organization. Shifting the level of interdepartmental conflict to the higher level of interorganizational conflict will produce a new structural relationship within each organization, a relationship that would harness departmental efforts and help them to compete more successfully against another organization. The perception of an external threat or the identification of a common enemy supersedes any conflict that departments within an organization may have. As a

strategy of conflict management within an organization, it operates on two levels. First, it affects individual attitudes, perceptions and feelings of trust and distrust. Second, it influences organizational role structure. It transforms interactions which are characterized predominantly by differentiation to accommodative interactions of a collaborative and integrated orientation.

2. Locating a superordinate goal. Superordinate goals are goals which are greatly desired by several departments and can only be achieved by combining the energies and resources of all involved. The introduction of a superordinate goal (e.g. developing a new product-line which would attract great customer demand) will create a cooperative context in which departments may interact on problems of joint interests, develop favourable attitudes and seek to achieve solutions that are mutually satisfactory. The introduction of a superordinate goal converts a conflict between departments to friendly interactions. The logic of introducing a superordinate goal is related to the very definition of a conflict. If conflict develops from the perception of incompatible goals, then cooperation would be promoted from common goals. To be successful in resolving interdepartmental conflict, a superordinate goal must be of such importance that departments can forget their differences and work together. It must involve several episodes taking into account the time dimension and it must be introduced by a third party. The cumulative efforts of developing cooperative activities are an important determinant of successful conflict management between departments.

II. Blake and Mouton: Blake and Mouton accept that the most important aspect of a successful conflict management strategy is the attempt to shift the behavioural and attitudinal components of a relationship from a competitive to a cooperative orientation. They do, however, suggest that both the common enemy and the superordinate goal approaches fall short of the need to achieve a genuine conflict resolution. This is because both can be seen as (1) being mainly temporary in character, (2) both are primarily defensive and (3) both strategies may widen a conflict by externalizing it. They offer an approach which emphasizes consultation-based interventions, openness of communication, greater participation in decision-making and problem-solving interactions.

Blake and Mouton accept that traditional conflict management strategies can only deal with the behavioural component in conflict and bring about a patchwork solution. They suggest an approach to conflict management which involves interventions by organizational consultants (usually applied behavioural scientists), who have no vested interest in the conflict itself, but who have the competence and experience to generate a productive mode of conflict management. They avoid the pitfalls of adjudicating or evaluating which department is "right" or "wong" (so often the hallmark of traditional conflict management). Nor do they seek to impose a solution. They intervene in order to generate creative thinking and to establish a problem-solving attitude.

Consultation-based approaches to interdepartmental conflict accept conflict situations as inevitable and see them as useful occasions which permit departments to disagree and to work out the disagreements and ultimately to understand each other better. The general functions of a consultant usually consist of (1) avoiding power-based outcomes, (2) providing knowledge and skills regarding conflict processes, (3) inducing an emotional-cognitive change as a prelude to collaborative interactions and (4) providing a supportive, informal and learning environment well-suited to creating the requirements conducive to problem-solving. The technologies of consultation consist of educational activities and techniques, laboratory training observations, survey-feedbacks, questionnaires and interviews. The structure of consultation activities is so designed as to engage individuals as whole persons, not merely as segmented individuals striving to cope with their role demands.

Conflict management - and indeed all forms of organizational behaviour - is determined by the interaction of (1) information, (2) skills, (3) values and (4) situation. Each of these factors acts as a precursor of some consultation-based activities. Behavioural consultants provide parties in conflict with more information and an understanding of the complexities of conflict interactions. They promote social interaction skills (which should be recognized as important as technical skills). They promote values of cooperation and help to create a situation in which people can interact freely and feel that they are as important to an organization as are its resources or products.

The sequence of consultation activities commences with upgrading individual skills and abilities, moves on to team-building activities and then to restructuring intergroup and interdepartmental activities. The institutionalization of these activities consists of four steps. The first step - bringing in the consultant - represents an administrative response to a felt need for effective conflict management. The second step - entry - is associated with various information-giving activities. The third step is aimed at attitudinal change through data-feedback, team-training, sensitivity and T-Group training or Grid development. The final step involves a structural change in the relationship between departments and a move towards integrative interactions and conflict resolution. Effective conflict management is quite a major undertaking. There are not too many guideposts to indicate where we are or how to move towards conflict resolution. It is, therefore, a task which demands attention to attitudinal and behavioural elements, to outcome and emotional needs and to interpersonal as well as interdepartmental requirements. The intervention strategies of a behavioural consultant can, we have argued, move us towards that direction. We can not be certain that the intended effects will always be achieved. We can suggest, with some certainty, that such interventions move us forward in the direction of effective conflict management and success in problem-solving. With this consideration in mind, administrators should encourage such interventions and help to produce more effective programmes.

CONCLUSION

Organizations are social entities segmented into hierarchies of departments and individuals. The basic realities of organizational life can not but stimulate comparisons, competitions and conflicts between departments and individuals. Conflict is an omnipresent feature at each of these organizational levels. Since conflict may have functional as well as dysfunctional consequences, it is essential that administrators explore various methods and techniques of conflict management. Effective conflict management is indispensable if coordinated efforts and productive achievements are to result. We have suggested above that the planned intervention by behavioural scientists represents the most effective method since it can produce organizational change and a sense of personal accomplishment. A wide range of intervention activities may be utilized to deal with conflicts at various organizational levels. It is beyond the scope of this article to provide a manual that can possibly foresee all the contingencies or to evaluate the effectiveness of different types of intervention.

This chapter purported to view conflict management as an integral part of the administrative process. Administrators should be able to ascertain the presence of a conflict, its basic sources, the level at which it manifests itself, its degree of intensity and the ways of furthering the objectives of conflict resolution. From a pragmatic viewpoint administrators should direct their attention to four issues: Is there a conflict? Where is the conflict? Does it require to be managed? How best to implement an effective conflict management strategy? With these issues in mind, the main features of this article may be summarized by developing a conceptual framework for conflict management in organizations. Conflict and conflict in organizations has only recently begun to receive the attention it deserves. In this chapter we have sought to address ourselves to the two most important issues in this field, namely, the determinants of conflict and the effectiveness of different methods of conflict management. Working from a conceptual basis this article represents only an initial step in the direction of systemizing our understanding of conflict and conflict management. Our task lies in stimulating a more thorough analysis to fill the gap between our knowledge and the realities of organizational life. The administrators' task lies in accepting conflict evaluation as part of their role and in developing the creative abilities that are necessary to deal with it.

Note: Reader can visit Benchmark Electronics company's site www.bench.com for a detailed study connected to this chapter. Benchmark Electronics (Benchmark) manufactures electronics and provides services to original equipment manufacturers (OEMs) of telecommunication equipment. The company also provides to OEMs of computers and related products for business enterprises, medical devices, industrial control equipment, and testing and instrumentation products. It is headquartered in Angleton, Texas and employs 10,522 people.

10

Stress Management

INTRODUCTION

Stress is an exceedingly complex concept that does not lend itself to a simple definition. It can best be understood in terms of the internal and external conditions necessary for its arousal and the symptoms by which it is identified. Its identifiable symptoms are both psychological and physiological. Stress carries a negative connotation for some people, as though it were something to be avoided. This is unfortunate, because stress is a great asset in managing legitimate emergencies and achieving peak performance.

MEANING & DEFINITION OF STRESS

Some definitions of stress are given below:

According to J. C. Quick and J.D Quick, "Stress, or the stress response, is the unconscious preparation to fight or flee a person experiences when faced with any demand". According to Mikhail A., "Stress refers to a psychological and physiological state that results when certain features of an individual's environment challenge that person, creating an actual or perceived imbalance between demand and capability to adjust that results in a non-specific response".

THE GENERAL ADAPTATION SYNDROME (GAS)

Hans Selye, the world's foremost authority on stress, was the first to describe systematically the changes through which the body passes to deal with a perceived threat. He described what he called the General Adaptation Syndrome (GAS), an adaptive response; that occurs in three phases: A, an alarm reaction; B, the stage of resistance; and C, the stage of exhaustion. GAS has 3 stages.

Alarm Stage: According to this model, the general adaptation syndrome begins when a person in encounters a stressor and enters the alarm stage. A person in this stage wonders how to cope and feels anxiety, even panic. The person breathes faster, blood pressure rises, pupils dilate and muscles tense. At this stage, the person is coping ineffectively.

Resistance: Assuming the person can summon the resources to cope with the stressor, he or she begin to feel more confident and to think of how to respond. During the second stage of the general adaptation syndrome, "resistance", the person channels his or her energy and uses it to resist the stressor's negative effects. The person tackles the problem, delegates the challenge, or adjusts to the change. Resistance to the stressor is high, but the person's resistance to other stressors may be low because the body's resources are being used up. Evidence shows that a person's immune system function tends to decline during periods of stress.

Exhaustion: Many stressors are short term - the person can solve the problem, or the situation ends on its own. In such cases, the general adaptation syndrome ends during resistance stage. But occasionally a stressor persists. In situations where stressors persist, the person may enter the third stage: exhaustion. In this stage, the symptoms of the alarm stage return and the person eventually uses up his or her adaptive energy.

APPROACHES TO STRESS

We will review four different approaches to defining stress:

- Homeostatic / Medical Approach.
- Cognitive Appraisal Approach.
- Person-environment fit Approach.
- Psychoanalytic Approach.

These four approaches to stress will give you a more complete understanding of what stress really is.

THE HOMEOSTATIC / MEDICAL APPROACH

Walter B Cannon Was the medical psychologist who originally discovered stress and called it "the emergency response" or "the militaristic response", arguing that it was rooted in "the fighting emotions". According to Cannon, stress resulted when an external environmental demand upset the person's natural steady-state balance referred to as "homeostasis". He called the stress response the fight-or flight response. Cannon believed the body was designed with natural defence mechanisms to keep it in homeostasis.

THE COGNITIVE APPRAISAL APPROACH

According to Richard Lazarus (1977), "stress is a situation that someone regards as threatening and as possibly exceeding his or her resources". Lazarus pointed out, that the stress evoked by an event depends on how people interpret the event and what they can do about it. For example, pregnancy may be much more stressful for a 16 year old unmarried schoolgirl than it is for a 25 year old married woman.

Lazarus saw stress as a result of a person-environment interaction, and he emphasized the person's cognitive appraisal in classifying persons or events as stressful or not. Individual differ in their appraisal of events and people. What is stressful for one person may not be stressful for another. Perception and cognitive appraisal are important processes in determining what is stressful, and a person's organizational position can shape such perception.

To the extent that stress is related to our interpretation of an event, not simply to the event itself, people can learn to cope with potentially stressful events. They can learn to deal with events actively instead of feeling threatened by them. Therefore, stress would have to include not only the unpleasant events (hassles) that we have to deal with but also the pleasant events (uplifts) that brighten our day and help to cancel out the unpleasant events. Thus, Lazarus introduced problem-focused and emotion-focused coping. Problem-focused coping emphasizes managing the stressor, and emotion-focused coping emphasizes managing your response.

THE PERSON-ENVIRONMENT FIT APPROACH

Robert Kahn's approach emphasized how confusing and conflicting expectations of a person in a social role create stress for the person. A good person-environment fit occurs when a person's skills and abilities match a clearly defined, consistent set of roles expectations. Stress occurs when the role expectations are confusing and conflicting or Stress when a person's skills and abilities are not able to meet the demands of the social role. Thus, Kahn was concerned with the social psychology of stress.

THE PSYCHOANALYTIC APPROACH

Harry Leveson believes that two elements of the personality interact to cause stress:-

i. Ego Ideal: is the first element, the embodiment of a person's perfect self.

ii. Self-Image: is the second element - how the person really sees himself or herself, both positively and negatively.

Stress results from the discrepancy between the idealized self (ego ideal) and the real self-image; the greater the discrepancy, the more stress a person experiences- Psychoanalytic theory helps us understand the role of unconscious personality factors as causes of stress within a person.

THE CAUSES OF STRESS

The causes of stress are found within the environment, the individual, and the interaction between the two. The stress experienced by a given individual is seldom traceable to a single source. Stress has become increasingly common in organizations, largely because individuals experience increased job complexity and increased economic pressures. In exploring the causes of stress it is important that a clear distinction be made between stress and the stressor (the source of the stress). It is confusing and technically incorrect to speak of a "stressful situation" as though anyone placed in that situation would experience stress. For purposes of analysis and understanding, stressors are divided into two classes:

i. Those that lie within the individual, and

ii. Those that are a part of the external environment.

INTERNAL STIMULI FOR STRESS

The internal sources of stress are complex and difficult to isolate. There are three internal sources of stress. Each of these internal influences on stress is considered separately, although they function in continual interaction.

1. Inner Conflicts: For many people stress is a constant companion regardless of how favourable or unfavourable external conditions may be. Non-specific fears, anxiety and guilt feelings maintain the body in a state of readiness for emergency action on a continuing basis.

2. Perceptual Influences: Perception is influenced by a number of internal factors. Certainly people with inner conflicts sufficient to cause stress are more likely than self-confident

people to perceive environmental conditions as threatening. Because the environment is presumed to be full of danger, evidences of danger are perceived everywhere. They are selectively perceived in exaggerated form.

3. Thresholds of Stress: The threshold of stress is not independent of the two factors just discussed. People who have few internal conflicts and a minimum of perceptual distortion can withstand external conflict and pressure that weaken personalities would find intolerable. People who have high thresholds for stress have high levels of resistance to it.
4. Motivational Level: People who are ambitious and highly motivated to achieve are more likely to experience stress than are those who are content with their career status. Persons whose self-expectations exceed their abilities and opportunities are especially stress prone.

ENVIRONMENTAL STRESSORS

Environmental and internal conditions that lie beyond an individual's control are called environmental stressors. Such stressors can have a considerable impact on work performance and adjustment. We can organize environmental stressors into the following categories:

1. Task Demands: Task demands are factors related to a person's job. They include the design of the individual's job, working conditions, and the physical work layout. Changes and lack of control are two of the most stressful demands people face at work. Change leads to uncertainty, a lack of predictability in a person's daily tasks and activities and may be caused by job insecurity related to difficult economic times. Technology and technological innovation also create change and uncertainty for many employees, requiring adjustments in training, education and skill development. Lack of control is a second major source of stress, especially in work environments that are difficult and psychologically demanding. The lack of control may be caused by inability to influence the timing of tasks and activities, to select tools or methods for accomplishing the work, to make decisions that influence work outcomes, or to exercise direct action to affect the work outcomes.
2. Role Demands: The social-psychological demands of the work environment may be every bit as stressful as task demands at

work. Role demands relate to pressures placed on a person as a function of the particular role he or she plays in the organization. Role conflicts create expectations that may be hard to reconcile or satisfy. Role conflict results from inconsistent or incompatible expectations communicated to a person. The conflict may be an inter-role, intra-role or person-role conflict.

a. Inter-role Conflict: is caused by conflicting expectations related to two separate roles, such as employee and parent. For example, the employee with a major sales presentation on Monday and a sick child at home is likely to experience inter-role conflict.
b. Intra-role Conflict: is caused by conflicting expectations related to a single role, such as employee. For example, the manager who presses employees for both vary fast work and high-quality work may be viewed at some point as creating a conflict for employees.
c. Person-role Conflict: Ethics violations are likely to cause person-role conflicts. Employees expected to behave in ways that violate personal values, beliefs or principles experience conflict.

The second major cause of role stress is role ambiguity. Role ambiguity is created when role expectations are not clearly understood and the employee is not sure what he or she is to do. Role ambiguity is the confusion a person experiences related to the expectations of others. Role ambiguity may be caused by not understanding what is expected, not knowing how to do it, or not knowing the result of failure to do it.

3. Inter-personal Demands: These are pressures created by other employees. Lack Stress of social support from colleagues and poor interpersonal relationships can cause considerable stress, especially among employees with a high social need. Abrasive personalities, sexual harassment and the leadership style in the organization are interpersonal demands for people at work.

   a. The Abrasive Person: May be an able and talented employee, but one who creates emotional waves that others at work must accommodate.
   b. Sexual Harassment: The vast majority of sexual harassment is directed at women in the workplace, creating a stressful working environment for the person

being harassed, as well as for others.

c. Leadership Styles: Whether authoritarian or participative, create stress for different personality types. Employees who feel secure with firm, directive leadership may be anxious with an open, participative style. Those comfortable with participative leadership may feel restrained by a directive style.

4. Physical Demands: Non-work demands create stress for people, which carry over into the work environment or vice versa. Workers subject to family demands related to marriage, child rearing and parental care may create role conflicts or overloads that are difficult to manage. In addition to family demands, people have personal demands related to non-work organizational commitments such as churches and public service organizations. These demands become more or less stressful, depending on their compatibility with the person's work and family life and their capacity to provide alternative satisfactions for the person.

INDIVIDUAL RESPONSE TO STRESS (INFLUENCE OF PERSONALITY)

The same stressful events may lead to distress and strain for one person and to excitement and healthy results for another. Even when all employees agree that a source of stress is negative, some will cope better than others. Individual differences play a central role in the stress-strain relationship. Several factors that help explain these individual differences are:

1. Life Events: Some employees are affected by workplace stress because they experience life events requiring change outside of work. The stress of coping with the changes away from the workplace leaves these employees less able to cope with work-related stressors. Dr. Thomas H Holmes and his colleagues have developed a stress scale measured in life change units (LUC), and have predicted that people whose LCU points exceed 300 run the risk of becoming seriously ill within the next two years. If, in the course of a year, a person experiences life events whose points total 150 to 300, that person has a 50% chance of a serious health problem in the following year. The risk rises to at least 70% among people

whose total points exceed 300. In other words, life events requiring readjustment appear to be a source of stress.

2. Type A Behaviour Pattern: Type A behaviour pattern is a complex of personality and behavioural characteristics, including competitiveness, time urgency, social status insecurity, aggression hostility and a quest for achievements. Type A people set high standards, push themselves to achieve and worry about time pressure. They try to get more and more done in less and less time. According to M Friedman and R. H Rosenman, Type A individual is "aggressively involved Stress in a chronic, incessant struggle to achieve more and more in less and less time, and if required to do so, against the opposing efforts of other things or other persons". These characteristics tend to be highly prized and positively associated with ambition and the successful acquisition of material goods. The medical advice to hard-working Type As is to slow down and learns to relax. Organizations face ethical and practical challenges in managing these individuals. The need to accomplish work and the Type A person's need to achieve might suggest that managers should assign Type A employees to difficult projects. Type A behaviour has been linked to high performance in academic settings, but the evidence for such a link in other settings has been mixed. So far, the research literature does not provide firm conclusions to help managers resolve this ethical dilemma. Other things being equal, it might be best to select Type A employees for the less complex jobs or at least to notify them of the risks.

3. Type B Behaviour Pattern: The alternative to the type A behaviour pattern is the Type B behaviour pattern. According to M Friedman and R. H Rosenman, Type B's are "rarely harried by the desire to obtain a wildly increasing number of things or participate in an endless growing series of events in an ever decreasing amount of time". Type B's behaviour pattern is

   - Never suffer from a sense of time urgency with its accompanying impatience;
   - Feel no need to display or discuss either their achievements or accomplishments unless such exposure is demanded by the situation;

- Play for fun and relaxation, rather than to exhibit their superiority at any cost; and
- Can relax without guilt.

Type B people are less coronary prone, but if they do have a heart attack, they do not appear to recover as well as those with type A personalities. Organizations can also be characterized as Type A or Type B organizations. Type A individuals in Type B organizations and Type B individuals in Type A organizations experience stress related to a misfit between their personality type and the predominant type of the organization. However, preliminary evidence suggests that Type A individuals in Type A organizations are most at risk of health disorders.

4. Personality Hardiness: Instead of looking for what makes people susceptible to the effects of stress, some psychologists have focused on identifying and describing people. Who resist illness when exposed to stressors. This view considers people's appraisal to stressors as well as the stressors themselves. People who have personality hardiness resist strain reactions when subjected to stressful events more effectively than do people who are not hardy. The components of personality hardiness are

- Commitment (versus alienation)
- Control (versus powerlessness) and
- Challenge (versus threat).

Commitment: Commitment is a curiosity and engagement with one's environment that leads to the experience of activities as interesting and enjoyable. Commitment therefore refers to a person's belief in the truth, importance and interest value of self and work.

Control: Control is a person's belief that he or she can influence events, coupled with the tendency to act accordingly. Control therefore is an ability to influence the process and outcomes of events that lead to the experience of activities as personal choices.

Challenge: Challenge is the belief that people seek change rather than routine and stability.

The hardy personality appears to use these three components actively to engage in transformational coping is actively changing an event into something less subjectively stressful by viewing it in a broader life perspective, by altering the course and outcome of the event through action and / or by achieving greater understanding of the process. The alternative to transformational coping is regressive coping, a much less healthy form of coping with stressful events characterized by a passive avoidance of events by decreasing interaction with the environment. Regressive coping may lead to short-term stress reduction at the cost of long-term healthy life adjustment. People experiencing significant stressors are less likely to become mentally or physically ill if they have a high level of hardiness. These people are likely to use such coping strategies as keeping the stressors in perspective, knowing that they have the resources to cope, and seeing stressors as opportunities rather than threats.

5. Negative Affectivity: A person who is high in negative affectivity has a mood state characterized by anger, fear and depression. This type of person tends to focus on the negative side of life, including the bad traits of self and others. People with negative affectivity tend to perceive themselves as being under stress and in poor health. Organizational attempts to alleviate stress may have relatively little impact on employees with negative affectivity.

6. Self-Reliance: Self-reliance is a personality attribute related to how people form and maintain supportive attachments with others. Self-reliance is a healthy secure, interdependent pattern of behaviour. It may appear paradoxical because a person appears independent while maintaining a host of supportive attachments.

   - Self-reliant people respond to stressful, threatening situations by reaching out to others appropriately.
   - Self-reliance is a flexible, responsive strategy of forming and maintaining multiple, diverse relationships.
   - Self-reliant people are confident, enthusiastic and persistent in facing challenges.

     Self-reliance results in a secure pattern of attachment and interdependent behaviour. The two insecure patterns of attachment are counter dependence and over dependence.
   - Counter dependence: Counter dependence is an unhealthy, insecure pattern of behaviour Stress that leads to separation in relationships with other people. Counter dependence may be characterized as a rigid, dismissing, denial of the need for other people in difficult and stressful times. Counter dependent people exhibit a fearless, aggressive and actively powerful response to challenges.

- Over dependence: Over dependence is also an unhealthy, insecure pattern of behaviour. Over dependence may be characterized as a desperate, preoccupied attempt to achieve a sense of security through relationships. Over dependence prevents a person from being able to organize and maintain healthy relationships and thus creates much distress.

7. Social Support: Social support system is the circle of people who care about the individual. A person's resistance to stress also may be strengthened by his or her social support system. A strong social support system provides a place to share problems and put them in perspective. To make the social support system effective, the person must perceive that the support system enhances self-esteem, is available when needed and provides relationships that are satisfying. A person's social support system includes spouse, relatives and friends.

CONSEQUENCES OF STRESS

An individual who is experiencing a high level of stress may develop high blood pressure, ulcers, loss of appetite etc. Stress shows itself in a number of ways. All the consequences need not be negative. The consequences of healthy, normal stress (called eustress, for "euphoria + stress") include a number of performance and health benefits to be added to the more commonly known costs of stress listed above known as distress. The three consequences of stress are explained below:

1. Performance and Health benefits of stress: The stress response is not inherently bad or destructive. Performance and health benefits of stress indicate that stress leads to improved performance up to an optimum point. Beyond the optimum point, further stress and arousal have a detrimental effect on performance. Therefore, healthy amounts of stress are desirable to improve performance by arousing a person to action. The stress response does provide momentary strength and physical force for brief periods, thus providing a basis for peak performance. The various individual and organizational forms of distress often associated with the word stress are the result of prolonged activation of the stress response, mismanagement of the energy induced by the response, or unique vulnerabilities in a person.

2. Individual Distress: In general, individual distress usually takes one of the three basic forms -
   a. Physiological Symptoms: A number of medical illnesses have a stress-related component. The most significant medical illnesses of this form are heart disease and strokes, backaches, peptic ulcers, and headaches. Most of the early concern with stress was directed at physiological symptoms. This was primarily because specialists in the health and medical sciences researched the topic. The link between stress and particular physiological symptoms is not clear. There is no clear evidence that stress is a direct causal agent. However, stress may play an indirect role in the progression of disease. For example, an extreme preoccupation with work may result in acute individual distress, such as the unique Japanese phenomenon of "Karoshi" (death by overwork).
   b. Psychological Symptoms: The most common types of psychological distress are depression, burnout, and psychogenic disorders. In the early stages, depression and burnout result in decline in efficiency; diminished interest in work; fatigue; and an exhausted run-down feeling. Psychogenic disorders are physical disorders with a genesis (beginning) in the psyche (mind). For example, the intense stress of public speaking may result in a psychogenic speech disorder; that is, the person is under so much stress that the mind literally will not allow speech to occur.
   c. Behavioural Symptoms: Behavioural problems are the third form of individual distress. These problems include violence, substance abuse of various kinds and accidents. Behaviourally related stress symptoms include changes in productivity, absence and turnover as well as changes in eating habits, increased smoking or consumption of alcohol, rapid speech, fidgeting and sleep disorders. Accidents, both on and off the job, are another behavioural form of distress that can sometimes be traced to work-related stressors. For example, an unresolved problem at work may continue to preoccupy or distract an employee driving home and result in the employee

having an automobile accident. These three forms of individual distress cause a burden of personal suffering.

3. Organizational Distress: The University of Michigan studies on organizational stress identified a variety of indirect costs of mismanaged stress for the organization, such as low morale, dissatisfaction, breakdowns in communication and disruption of working relationships. The problems caused by organizational distress are:

   - Participation problems: Participation problems are the costs associated with absenteeism, tardiness, strikes and work stoppages and turnover.
   - Performance decrements: Performance decrements are the costs resulting from poor quality or low quality of production, grievances and unscheduled machine downtime and repair.
   - Compensation awards: Compensation awards are a third organizational cost resulting from court awards for job distress.

MANAGING STRESS

Stress is an inevitable feature of work and personal life. As organizations and their employees have come to perceive the consequences of stress as serious, they have tried to manage it. Some of these efforts have sought to limit the amount of stress employees experience; most are directed at improving employees' coping ability. Both kinds of Stress efforts may be conducted at the individual level and at the organizational level.

1. Individual Level: An employee can take personal responsibility for reducing his or her stress level. At the individual level stress management usually focuses on becoming more able to cope with stress. Individual strategies that have proven effective include implementing time-management techniques, increasing physical exercise, relaxation training and expanding the social support network.

A. Time Management: A practical way to manage stress is to better control your use of time. Many people manage their time poorly. The well-organized employee, can often accomplish twice as much as the person who is poorly organized. The basic principle beyond time management is to decide what tasks are most important, then do those things first. So an understanding and utilization of basic time-management principles can help individuals better cope with tensions created by job demands. A few of the more well-known time-management principles are: -

- Make daily or weekly lists of activities to be accomplished.
- Prioritising activities by importance and urgency. Therefore you must rate them A (must be performed) B (should be performed) or C (optional).
- Scheduling activities according to the priorities set. You then structure your time to ensure you do the A-level items. If time remains, you devote it to the B-level items and then the C-level items.
- Knowing your daily cycle and handling the most demanding parts of your job during the high part of your cycle when you are most alert and productive.

To be truly effective, time management should include making sure you are clear about what is expected of you and saying no to activities that are not required or that you feel you cannot fit into your schedule. This requires being realistic about making promises. Improving time management skills can give people a greater sense of control. Furthermore, because time management emphasizes focusing on the most important task, it provides the satisfaction of accomplishing worthwhile goals.

B. Non-Competitive Physical Exercise: Employees can seek to improve their physical health by exercising regularly. Non-competitive physical exercise such as aerobics, walking, jogging, swimming and riding a bicycle have long been recommended by physicians as a way to deal with excessive stress levels. When people exercise regularly, they improve their physical health. In addition, they tend to feel more confident, more optimistic and less stressed. These forms of physical exercise increase heart capacity, lower at-rest, provide a mental diversion from work pressures, and offer a means to let off steam.

C. Relaxation and Biofeedback: Individuals can teach themselves to reduce tension through relaxation techniques such as meditation, hypnosis, and biofeedback. People can also benefit from a variety of tactics that helps them slow down.

- Relaxation decreases muscle tension, lowers heart rate and blood pressure and slows breathing. The objective is to reach a state of deep relaxation, where one feels physically relaxed, somewhat detached from the immediate environment and detached from body sensations. 15 to 20 minutes a day of deep relaxation releases tension and provides a person with a pronounced sense of peacefulness.
- Meditation provides the conditions for relaxation: a quite environment, closed eyes, comfortable posture, and a word or phrase to repeat silently or aloud.
- Simply taking regular vacations is a basic but important part of relaxation.
- Biofeedback or monitoring physiological responses such as brain waves, heart rate, muscle tension, and blood pressure, then using the information to control those responses. In this way, biofeedback helps people relax. It also helps with stress management by showing people they have some control over their bodies.

D. Development of Social Support Systems: Having friends, family or work colleagues to talk to provide an outlet when stress levels become excessive. Developing a social support system to help with the routine stress of organizational life requires committing time to family and friends. Regularly laughing, crying or discussing problems, help people blow off steam before problems become intolerable. Research also demonstrates that social support moderates the stress-burnout relationship. That is, high support reduces the likelihood that heavy work stress will result in job burnout.

E. Adjustment of Perceptions: Effective stress management may require conscious adjustment of your thinking because perceptions of a stressor play a role in the way the stressor is experienced. A basic type of looking at the stressor is to view yourself as facing challenges rather than problems.

F. Learned Optimism: Optimism and pessimism are two different thinking styles people use to explain the good and bad events in their lives to themselves. Pessimism is an explanatory style leading to depression, physical health problems and low levels of achievement. Optimism is an alternative explanatory style that enhances physical health and achievement and averts susceptibility to depression. Optimistic people avoid distress by understanding the bad events and difficult times in their lives as temporary, limited and caused by something other than themselves. Learned optimism begins with identifying pessimistic thoughts and them distracting oneself from these thoughts or disputing them with evidence and alternative thoughts. These explanatory styles are habits of thinking learned over time, not inborn attributes. Learned optimism is nonnegative thinking.

G. Leisure Time Activities: Leisure time activities provide employees an opportunity for rest and recovery from strenuous activities either at home or at work. Leisure is increasingly a luxury among working people. The key to the effective use of leisure time is enjoyment. Leisure time can be used for spontaneity, joy and connection with others in our lives.

H. Diet: Diet may play an indirect role in stress and stress management. Good dietary practises contribute to a person's overall health, making the person less vulnerable to distress.

I. Opening Up: Everyone experiences a traumatic stressful or painful event in life at one time or another. One of the most therapeutic, curative responses to such an event is to confide in another person. Confession need not be through personal relationship with friends. It may occur through a private diary. For example, a person might write each evening about all of his or her most troubling thoughts, feelings and emotions during the course of the day. Confession and opening up may occur through professional helping relationships. The process of opening up and confessing appears to counter the detrimental effects of stress.

2. Organizational Level: Management controls several of the factors that cause Stress stress -particularly task and role demands, and organization structure. As such, they can be modified or changed. In some cases, organizations recognize that they can improve performance by reducing the amount of work-related stress employees' experience. Ways to do this include improving the work environment and clarifying roles. In addition, the organization can support employees' efforts to cope with stress by offering wellness programmes and it can

foster a supportive organizational culture.

A. Job Redesigning: Redesigning jobs to give employees more responsibility, more meaningful work, more autonomy, and increased feedback can reduce stress because these factors give the employee greater control over work activities and lessen dependence on others. Job redesign to increase worker control is one strategy of preventive stress management. It can be accomplished in a number of ways, the most common being to increase job decision latitude. Increased job decision latitude might include greater decision authority over the sequencing of work activities, the timing of work schedules, the selection and sequencing of work tools, or the selection of work teams. A second objective of job redesign should be to reduce uncertainty and increase predictability in the workplace. Uncertainty is a major stressor.

B. Goal Setting: Organizational preventive stress management can also be achieved through goal-setting activities. These activities are designed to increase task motivation, while reducing the degree of role conflict and ambiguity to which people at work are subject.

C. Role Negotiation: Role negotiation begins with the definition of a specific role, called the focal role, within its organizational context. The person in the focal role then identifies the expectations understood for that role, and key organizational members specify their expectations of the person in the focal role. The actual negotiation follows from the comparison of the role incumbent's expectations and key members' expectations. The point of confusion and conflict are opportunities for clarification and resolution. The final result of the role negotiation process should be a clear well-defined focal role with which the incumbent and organizational members are both comfortable.

D. Organizational Communication: Increasing formal organizational communication with employees reduces uncertainty by lessening role ambiguity and role conflict. Given the importance that perception play in moderating the stress-response relationship, management can also use effective communications as a means to shape employee perceptions.

E. Employee Wellness Programmes: Organizations may sponsor

wellness programmes, which are designed to promote employee health and well-being. Evidence suggests that wellness programme make economic sense. Employees have access to exercise equipment and may participate in educational programmes. An ethical issue with regard to wellness programmes is whether the employer has the right to have input in what employees eat, whether they smoke and how much they exercise. Often, some employees are not receptive to involvement in wellness programme. This implies that employees who could most benefit from a wellness programme are least likely to benefit from it.

F. Social Support System at the Work Place: Team building, is one way to develop supportive social relationship in the work place. However, team building is primarily task oriented, not socio-emotional in nature. Although employees may receive much of their socio-emotional support form personal relationships outside the workplace, some socio-emotional support within the workplace is also necessary for psychological well-being. Social support system can be enhanced through the work environment in a number of ways. These relations provide emotional caring, information, evaluative feedback, modelling and instrumental support.

G. Organizational Culture: The organization's culture can help employees manage stress by limiting stress, strengthening coping skills and providing shared values and beliefs. Such a culture recognizes that employees are human beings in need of rest, social support, and a good laugh once in a while.

EMPLOYEE STRESS ISN'T A MANAGEMENT PROBLEM

The recent attention given to employee stress by behavioural scientists has blown totally out of proportion. Undoubtedly, a small proportion of the working population suffers from stress. These people have ongoing headaches, ulcers, high blood pressure and the like. They may even turn to alcohol and drugs as an outlet to deal with their stress. But if there is a problem, it's a medical one. It's not a management problem. In support of this position, we argue that:

a. Stress is not that important because human beings are highly adaptive;

b. Most stress that employees experience is of the positive type;

and

c. Even if the first two points were't relevant, a good portion of what causes excessive work stress tends to be uncontrollable by management anyway.

Those who seem to be so concerned about employee stress forget that people are more adaptable than we traditionally give them credit for. Individuals are amazingly resilient. Most successfully adjust to illnesses, misfortune, and other changes in their lives. All through their school years, they adapted to the demands that dozens of teachers put on them. They survived the trials of puberty, dating, beginning and ending relationships, and leaving home - to name a few of the more potentially stressful times we have all gone thrrough. By the time individuals enter the work force, they have experienced many difficult situations and, for the most part, they have adjusted to each. There is no reason to believe this ability to adapt to changing or uncomfortable conditions breaks down once people begin their working careers. Stress, like conflict, has a positive as well as a negative side. But that positive side tends to be overshadowed by concern with the negative. A life without stress is a life without challenge, stimulation, or change. Many positive and exciting life events - marriage, the birth of a child, inheriting a large sum of money, buying a new home, a job promotion, vacations - have been found to create stress. Does that mean these positive events should be avoided?

The answer is obviously "No". Unfortunately, when most people talk about stress and the need to reduce it, they tend to overlook its positive side. Finally, there is the reality that many sources of employee stress are outside the control of management. Management can't control environmental factors. If stress is due to an inherent personality characteristic, here again, the source lies outside management's control. Most other individual factors, too, are outside management's influence. Even if stresses created by such individual factors as family and economic problems can be influenced by managerial actions, there remains the ethical question: Does management have the right to interfere in an employee's personal life? Undoubtedly, a good portion of any employee's total stress level is created by factors that are uncontrollable by management - martial problems, divorce, children who get into trouble, poor personal financial management, uncertainty over the economy, societal norms to achieve and acquire material symbols of success, pressures of living in a fast-paced, urban world, and the like. The actions of management didn't create these stressors. Most are just part of modern living. More importantly, employers can do little to lessen these stressors without extending their influence beyond the organization and into the employee's personal life. That's something most of us would agree is outside the province of the employer-employee relationship.

FRAMEWORK FOR PREVENTIVE STRESS MANAGEMENT

Stress is an inevitable feature of work and personal life. Individual and organizational distress are not inevitable. Primary Prevention: Primary prevention is intended to reduce, modify or eliminate the demand or stressor causing stress. True organizational stress prevention is largely primary in nature, because it changes and shapes the demands the organization places on people at work. Secondary Prevention: Secondary prevention is intended to alter or modify the individual's response to a demand or stressor. People must learn to manage the inevitable. Tertiary Prevention: Tertiary prevention is intended to heal the individual of symptoms of distress and strain. Tertiary prevention is therapeutic, aimed at arresting distress and healing the individual.

MANAGERIAL IMPLICATIONS OF STRESS

Stress is an inevitable result of work and personal life. Managers must learn how to create healthy stress for employees to facilitate performance and well being without distress. They should be sensitive to early signs of distress at work, such as employee fatigue or changes in work habits, in order to avoid serious forms of distress. Distress is important to the organization because of the costs associated with turnover and absenteeism, as well as poor-quality production. Managers can use the principles and methods of preventive stress management to create healthier work environments. They can practice several forms of individual stress prevention to create healthier lifestyles for themselves, and they can encourage employees to do the same.

Stress carries a negative connotation for some people, as though it were something to be avoided. This is unfortunate, because stress is a great asset in managing legitimate emergencies and achieving peak performance. The causes of stress are found within the environment, the individual, and the interaction between the two. Hans Selye described the General Adaptation Syndrome (GAS), an adaptive response that occurs in three phases: A, an alarm reaction. B, the stage of resistance; and C, the stage of exhaustion. Stress is an inevitable feature of work and personal life. As organizations and their employees have come to perceive the consequences of stress as serious, they have tried to manage it. Some of these efforts have sought to limit the amount of stress employees experience; most are directed at improving employees' coping ability. Managers can use the principles and methods of preventive stress management to create healthier work environments. They can practice several forms of individual stress prevention to create healthier lifestyles for themselves, and they can encourage employees to do the same.

Note: For a case study visit company's site of Ryder System, Inc. www.ryder.com. Ryder System (Ryder) is engaged in the provision of transportation, logistics and supply chain management solutions worldwide. It also undertakes maintenance of commercial trucks, tractors and trailers. The company primarily operates in the US. It is headquartered in Miami, Florida and employs 28,000 people.

11

Crisis Management

Corporate leaders must ensure that the company, its stakeholders and the community are protected to the greatest degree possible.

SCOPE

A Crisis Management Process can apply to any size company. It describes a series of interrelated processes and activities that will assist in creating, testing, and maintaining an organization-wide plan for use in the event of a crisis that threatens the viability and continuity of the organization. Emergency planning is a continuous cyclical process starting with prevention and including preparedness, response and recovery. The learnings from each incident and training scenario are used to continually improve the process. When initiating a response, it is important to insure that the goals protect the following interests in order of their priority:

- Save lives and reduce chances of further injuries/deaths
- Protect the environment
- Protect assets
- Restore critical business processes and systems
- Reduce the length of the interruption of business
- Minimize reputation damage
- Maintain customer relations

MODELS AND THEORIES ASSOCIATED WITH CRISIS MANAGEMENT

Crisis Management Model: Successfully diffusing a crisis requires an understanding of how to handle a crisis - before it occurs. Gonzalez-Herrero and Pratt created a four-phase crisis management model process that includes: issues management, planning-prevention, the crisis, and post-crisis.

Management Crisis Planning: No corporation looks forward to facing a situation that causes a significant disruption to their business, especially one that stimulates extensive media coverage. Public scrutiny can result in a negative financial, political, legal and government impact. Crisis management planning deals with providing the best response to a crisis.

Contingency Planning: Preparing contingency plans in advance, as part of a crisis management plan, is the first step to ensuring an organization is appropriately prepared for a crisis. Crisis management teams can rehearse a crisis plan by developing a simulated scenario to use as a drill. The plan should clearly stipulate that the only people to speak publicly about the crisis are the designated persons, such as the company spokesperson or crisis team members. The first hours after a crisis breaks are the most crucial, so working with speed and efficiency is important, and the plan should indicate how quickly each function should be performed. When preparing to offer a statement externally as well as internally, information should be accurate. Providing incorrect or manipulated information has a tendency to backfire and will greatly exacerbate the situation. The contingency plan should contain information and guidance that will help decision makers to consider not only the short-term consequences, but the long-term effects of every decision.

Business Continuity Planning: When a crisis will undoubtedly cause a significant disruption to an organization, a business continuity plan can help minimize the disruption. First, one must identify the critical functions and processes that are necessary to keep the organization running. Then each critical function and or/process must have its own contingency plan in the event that one of the functions/processes ceases or fails. Testing these contingency plans by rehearsing the required actions in a simulation will allow for all involved to become more sensitive and aware of the possibility of a crisis. As a result, in the event of an actual crisis, the team members will act more quickly and effectively.

Structural-Functional Systems Theory: Providing information to an organization in a time of crisis is critical to effective crisis management. Structural-functional systems theory addresses the intricacies of information networks and levels of command making up organizational communication. The structural-functional theory identifies information flow in organizations as "networks" made up of members and "links". Information in organizations flow in patterns called networks.

Diffusion of Innovation Theory: Another theory that can be applied to the sharing of information is Diffusion of Innovation Theory. Developed by Everett Rogers, the theory describes how innovation is disseminated and communicated through certain channels over a period of time. Diffusion of innovation in communication occurs when an individual communicates a new idea to one or several others. At its most elementary form, the process involves:

- An innovation,
- An individual or other unit of adoption that has knowledge of or experience with using the innovation,
- Another individual or other unit that does not yet have knowledge of the innovation, and
- A communication channel connecting the two units. A communication channel is the means by which messages get from one individual to another.

PLANNING PROCESS

PREVENTION

Process Safety Management / Risk Management

The best response plan is one that is never used, but emergency response and crisis planning is needed because accidental or intentionally caused incidents are part of history. Frequency can be reduced by applying Process Safety Management. Process Safety Management / Risk Management (PSM / RMP) is the application of management principles and systems to the identification, understanding and control of process hazards to prevent process related injuries and accidents.

Successful risk management is a blend of sound organizational practices and the use of basic safety related technology. Risk management in process industries handling hazardous materials has tended toward using a multilayered approach for protective systems. Should the inner layers of safety protection fail to prevent or sufficiently mitigate the incident's effects, both on-site and off-site, then emergency response may be necessary.

SECURITY ENHANCEMENT

The primary focus of facilities that manufacture, store, use or handle hazardous chemicals has been the prevention of unintentional events.

After the terrorists attacks on the United States on September 11, 2001, the possibility of an intentional release with catastrophic consequences must be part of the prevention program. To address intentional acts, a security vulnerability assessment process using a risk-based approach to managing chemical plant security should be employed. Security assessment should include overall warning signs and detection measures. Examples of a crisis that can have warning signs include:

- Workplace violence (erratic or threatening employee behaviour)
- Activism, protests, riots
- Product contamination
- Terrorism
- Natural disasters (hurricanes, blizzards, certain floods, wild-fires, etc.)

PREPARATION

Foundation

Develop a policy that specifies the role of corporate organizations in managing an incident, such as: providing field support resources to the site, role of executives (informed and decision makers but probably not on the team), providing a buffer for the site so they can address the emergency; site reporting requirements, etc. Policy parameters should be established in advance, including potential pre-approval by the insurance provider of any response related contractors. Where possible, the amount of funds to help support the response team should be determined in the planning process.

A written plan with procedures to be followed when an internal or external disaster occurs should address at least the following emergency situations:

- An incident with extreme danger to life, property, and the environment.
- An incident that goes beyond the site property and can impact public health, safety, and the environment and requires large scale protective action.
- Requires resources beyond those available at the incident scene, including local fire services, industrial mutual aid units, and public safety resources.
- Requires resources and expertise of corporate, regional, state,

federal or private organizations, especially in a kidnapping, serving of a search warrant or an incident where terrorism is suspected.

- An incident likely to generate significant questions from the media or government agencies outside the local community.

Each site in the in the company should have an emergency response plan that is compatible with the corporate plan, including team assignments, procedures and a command centre.

Notification Procedure

The notification process for initially contacting internal and external resources should be easy to use and efficient in establishing the degree of the emergency, the corporate response and alert to the corporate team. Some form of automated phone system to contact the team and provide information is desirable. A hierarchy of contact should be developed for use in case personnel cannot be reached. The facilities need an easy to remember central number to notify the corporate team leader. When assembly of the corporate crisis management team is appropriate, the system should allow the team leader to notify the team with a description of the incident and instructions. The team should always have a leader in place. If necessary, an interim leader should be identified until the designated leader arrives.

Corporate Crisis Management Team

It is important that an appropriate administrative structure be in place to effectively manage a crisis. Clear definitions must exist for a management structure, authority for decisions, and responsibility for implementation. Most senior managers are not trained and typically do not have the resources to simultaneously manage a crisis and carry out normal business duties. Senior managers who are not members of the crisis management team should carry on with their normal business unless requested by the team leader.

Following the Incident Management System (IMS) should be considered to correspond to typical plant site organization and function. The corporate team should be comprised of such functions as human resources, operations, security, legal, communications/media relations, EH&S, and distribution. The Crisis Management Team may be assisted by as many internal Support Teams as appropriate, taking into account such factors as organization size and type, number of employees, location, incident type, etc. Depending on the nature of the incident, certain functions are critical for adequate support. If a person representing a critical function is not available, these duties need to be assumed by one or more team members.

The core Corporate Crisis Management Team (CMT) should include:

- Team Leader: The team leader, or its designate, is responsible for managing the CMT, and is the primary contact with the site or incident scene team leader. The Team Leader also communicates with the appropriate company executives and is usually the person that declares the emergency a corporate crisis and assembles the corporate team. The team leader assures that all team functions are covered and initiates the plan to address the emergency. Ideally, the team leader should be a strong senior executive or manager who is trusted and decisive, but not impulsive and who has the authority to act without fear of being second-guessed. The manager needs a long-term perspective and should be freed from other responsibilities to lead the crisis management team until the crisis ends.
- Environmental, Health and Safety (EH&S): Coordinates the EH&S response from the corporate level with the EH&S contact at the site. Should have a broad range of EH&S and product integrity experience or be able to contact appropriate experts. Arranges for dispersion modelling, provides technical advice to medical, environmental and other responders, provides data from or interpretation of MSDS, provides advice on proper protective equipment, provides disposal information, notifies government agencies and liaison with governmental agencies as those contacts are being made, etc.
- Public Relations: Assures accurate and timely public response is being made and is proficient in developing press releases and interfacing with the media. Coordinates media response with the site's public relations member, incorporating legal advice in communications, prepares updates for executives, arrange executive travel to the incident scene and advises the incident scene in media relations.
- Human Resources: Assures human relations issues are being addressed and coordinates these with the site's human resources member. Should have a broad range of HR expertise or be able to contact appropriate experts. Provides for crisis

counselling, access to employee database, support in contacting family members, assembly of necessary internal and external HR resources, etc.

- Legal: Provides legal counsel to the team. Coordinates with the legal coordinator at the incident scene and arranges for external legal support as needed. Participates in communication preparation and provides advice on securing incident scene for subsequent investigation.
- Security: Advisor to site or incident scene team and liaison with the various agencies and security contractor(s). Provide investigative support to determine if the incident is accidental or intentional. Has a lead role in government interaction if the incident was a result of terrorism.

Team Coordinator: This person or persons (could rotate this position but it is always filled) stays in the crisis centre and assures the members are working with the most current information. Appointed by and assists the Team Leader in managing the crisis team activities including:

- Records information and comments from the team.
- Makes team leader aware of new information.
- Records chronological events.
- Updates team members as they arrive or return to the command centre.
- Records questions from team members that can be used as prompts for communication between the corporate and incident scene team leader or follow-up by the team.
- Assists team leader in managing CMT activities.
- Tracks/documents key phone numbers, contacts, etc. that may not be predetermined prior to the crisis (e.g., hotel where site crisis team is operating during a hurricane).

Team Resource (Admin Position)

If not a specific individual, these duties need to be assumed by one or more team members

- Provides computer support to access data and procedures.
- Operates and relays fax(s).
- Provides copies of documents, such as of MSDS.

- Provides weather conditions from the internet.
- Gathers information that may be needed - e.g. trucking company, disaster contractor, access crisis calendar, etc. Helps to set up the room.
- Makes sure phones are ready to use.

Document Control/Security Coordinator: (could be part of the Team Resource position)

This position coordinates the many requests for corporate documents (from government agencies, media, etc) and works closely with legal to facilitate distribution and protection of company assets. Should decide as part of the planning process, who will be allowed to receive specific documents.

Note: The purpose of flip charts and other notes taken during a crisis is to assist the team in managing the crisis. These notes are drafts only and are not intended to memorialize the event for any future purpose. Given how rapidly information must be processed during a crisis and how quickly information can change, it is recommended that, at the end of the crisis, all notes be condensed into a final report (reviewed by the legal department for accuracy and completeness) which will become the official record of the team response. Having done so, the draft notes should then be destroyed.

Ad Hoc / Support Team Members: The Crisis Management Team may be assisted by as many internal Support Teams as appropriate. Support Teams should be reassigned from existing organizations in the company and able to respond to various aspects of potential crises, such as technical support, damage assessment, site restoration, payroll, financial, and administrative support. The following are examples of additional support for the Core Team:

- Corporate Services: Provide support for such issues as travel arrangements, secretarial help for the Corporate Crisis Team, or communications and audio-visual support.
- Engineering: Support could include assessing site damage, assisting with the planning and management of repair activities, developing options for temporary facilities and plume dispersion modelling.
- Financial: Provide information as needed and coordinate activities. Information Technology: Assess system damage and

activate appropriate backup systems and disaster recovery plans.

- Medical: Assist in assessing the human health consequences of an event. Secure and interface with appropriate medical providers.
- Supply Chain: Provide administrative, logistical, and other support regarding the supply of essential materials.
- Technology: Provide technical information such as toxicology. Identifies and collaborates with consultants and others with specialized knowledge of specific chemistries and exposure/ contamination situations.

Protocols - Team Operating Procedure

A good planning process at the beginning of an incident will go a long way to provide the needed support to the incident scene team as the incident unfolds. During the initial contact with the incident scene, the team leader should:

- Establish dedicated phone numbers in the Corporate Command Centre and at the incident scene; a full-time open line should be considered
- Establish maximum time between contacts and who will make the contact
- Authorize contact between other members of the corporate and incident scene team.
- The initial phase of the incident after assembling the team, the leader should:
- Ensure all the appropriate roles are filled based on the type of incident and:
- Assign a team coordinator and team resource
- Account for the appropriate functions
- Make reassignments to fill gaps
- Make plans for relief if the incident could be long term
- Make sure everyone in the command centre has the latest information
- Determine how to contact anyone that leaves the command centre

- Ask each function to list possible action plan based on the information available - avoid duplication
- List questions for the incident scene

Crisis Command Centre [sh]

The command centre and an alternate command centre should be equipped to provide for any contingency. It is best to have a dedicated room and an alternate site. If the room has multiuse, it must be available when needed. Ideally the command centre should be on a UPS/backup power system. Typical equipment in the command centre includes:

- Phones - A primary line and at least one additional line is needed. More than 3 phones could result in a situation where there is too much noise in the command centre. More phones in the vicinity of the command centre are desirable. Ideally, phones should be set up to rollover automatically to an open line in the command centre if the main line is busy
- Cell Phone - at least one cell phone is desirable. It could also be used to locate team members that leave the command centre.
- Satellite Phone - Early in an incident land lines and cell phones may experience heavy use and become jammed. Each site and the corporate centre should have at least one satellite phone.

NOTE: Satellite phones generally do not work inside - need line of sight to satellite.

- Teleconferencing Equipment - may be needed early in an incident if the team is not immediately able to assemble or to allow multiple participation in discussions
- Dedicated computer with internet and intranet access - The crisis plan and critical information for specific sites or an anticipated crisis should be on the computer hard drive and / or a web site. Maps, weather, etc could be obtained from internet sites. Record the sites as favourites for quick access.
- Laptop connection(s) - to a printer, the internet, etc.
- Printer - connected to a desktop and accessible to laptops
- Video teleconferencing - useful for follow-up site communication, but probably not during the emergency
- Fax machine - connected to a dedicated phone line
- Photocopier - easily accessible to the command centre

- TV with satellite connection - provides ability to monitor the news
- Key office supplies - pens, markers, flip charts, paper, etc
- LED Projector
- Status Board
- Clock - multiple if more than one time zone is involved
- Sign in/out board - track location of team members

Other considerations:

- A conference table to facilitate team meetings and for review of large maps, drawings.
- Assigned work stations for each key function, plus at least one "ad hoc" station for supplemental members.
- Hardcopy backups of key site or reference information. Although potentially out of date, such hardcopy documents often are more readily accessible in the incipient stages of crisis response.

IMPLEMENTATION - MANAGING THE CRISIS

INITIAL RESPONSE TO A CRISIS

As soon as a major emergency has been declared or identified, rapid communications is critical to mitigate the incident. The notification process must work quickly and efficiently and the initial information must be accurate and complete as possible. The call from an offsite location should come to a location that has hour coverage. At a minimum the initial information collected must include the callers name, return phone number and basic facts concerning the nature of the emergency. The receiver of the call must be able to make contact with the leader of the crisis team (primary or backup) within minutes of receiving the call. The call-back to the location of the incident should obtain information that includes:

- What happened?
- Has a cause been identified, e.g. accidental or intentional?
- Who is affected and what is known about those affected?
- What response is underway and who is involved in the response?

The answers to these questions will allow the corporate team leader to assess the degree of involvement of the corporate team and the initial focus required of the corporate team. The next step is to provide this information to the full or selected members of the corporate team and to develop an action plan. The contact procedure for the corporate team must allow both an alert to an incident and a method to provide the initial information that the leader obtained. The corporate team leader should prepare a short message for the crisis team and then notify the call centre to immediately contact the team. The message to the team can be transmitted either by the call centre or through a voice mail system. The key to an effective response requires contacting the team leader and assembling the team in "automatic" mode. The process needs to be instinctive, which only comes with practice.

A list of backups should be developed in the planning phase to insure all functions can be covered. Another approach is to assemble all primary and backup team members to assure coverage and then dismiss the backups if the function is covered. If it is likely the incident will extend beyond the current shift, the backups could be assigned relief roles.

MANAGING THE RESPONSE

In the midst of an emergency it is difficult to get all the facts, especially since the incident may be changing every minute. The situation is likely to be chaotic and fluid with rapidly changing information that is difficult to ascertain and possibly unreliable. By the time corporate is notified, there may be a myriad of Local, State and Federal agencies involved. It is important to follow the policies and procedures established in the CMP since normal company policies and procedures may hurt rather than help at first.

If there is a question about what was reported, repeat information for clarity, but try to separate fact from conjecture and opinion. This would be a good time to ask some questions even if the information isn't available. It could direct the caller to think about next steps and where help might be needed. Questions such as: "has there been any notification to government agencies?, what notification has been given to plant personnel?, what are the weather conditions?, or what is your most immediate need?" Before ending the call, arrange for the next communication and set who will make the call and the phone numbers to use.

The next steps flow from this initial information which is used in the initial communication to the team. Based on this information, the team can begin to develop some plans that would support the incident scene such as preparation to run a dispersion model, alert hospitals, begin to develop a press release, response to government information requests, etc.

Prior to September 11, 2001, it would have been assumed that the cause of an incident was accidental. Now it is important to determine if the incident was intentional and if it cannot be determined, then proceed with the possibility that the incident scene may be a crime scene and that additional attacks at the site could occur.

It may not be possible to determine who has been affected by the incident but this needs to be a priority in early communication with the incident scene. The extent of injuries and the extent of the damage determine the business and legal issues and the communication needed. The effected parties will determine the type and priority of communication:

- If employees are being transported to local hospitals then a request for chemical effects should be anticipated.
- If there is a threat to the community then local officials must be notified.
- In environmental cases, the appropriate agencies must be notified within established time-frames.
- It is critical that all external constituents such as the general public, neighbors, customers, regulators, suppliers, vendors and contractors as well as internal constituents such as employees, shareholders and insurers be identified early in the incident. Each may require a separate but factually consistent communication. Identification of these constituents prior to an incident would significantly improve the response time.

OUTSIDE INVOLVEMENT IN THE RESPONSE

As early as possible determine which federal, state and local agencies and responders are involved or are likely to become involved. Local contacts are best left to the site or incident scene team, but it may be helpful for corporate to begin to establish communications with the federal and state agencies. This could go a long way in freeing up site personnel to handle the emergency. If possible, all responding agencies should be directed to an identified assembly location for daily briefings.

Develop a Plan

Each incident will require its own set of response procedures, but getting organized has some basic steps. As the team is assembling, it is important to maintain continuity of communications between the team and with the incident scene. Until the team is assembled, the primary contact is between the corporate and site or incident scene team leaders. Unless the corporate team leader is within minutes of the command centre it may be necessary to turn over leadership to the first team member that reaches the command centre. If some critical functions on the corporate team cannot assemble in the command centre it may be necessary to connect them to the command centre by web or teleconference.

Once a core team has assembled, the team leader (or acting team lead) should make sure the functions critical for this specific incident is available and the team has the latest information. Each team member should announce their plan of action followed by a brief discussion to find any gaps and / or duplication. This discussion may also raise many questions for the incident scene which should be recorded and addressed in the next call to the incident scene. As new information is obtained from the incident scene, each function can adjust their plan.

One or more team members should be assigned to maintain a chronology of the event, questions raised and answers obtained from the incident scene. This person needs to act as the eyes and ears for the team leader and a source of up to date information for team members as they arrive or return to the command centre In certain crises (e.g., a severe hurricane), a site crisis management team may be unable to provide effective coordination and communication for a period of time due to local infrastructure damage and access restrictions (e.g., curfews, emergency teams only, etc.). In these situations, the corporate crisis management team may need to assume a more direct response and decision role regarding site-specific issues.

Communications

If there is a critical aspect to the management of a crisis for both immediate support of the site or incident scene team and long-term recovery for the company, it is communications. The audience is varied and may require slightly different focus and timing, but in no case should the information be "sugar coated" or minimized. Only report what you know and don't speculate. You can say you don't know and will get back to them, but make sure you do get back. Your audience may be one or all of the following:

- Employees and their families
- Customers/Clients

- Contractors/Vendors
- Boards of Directors
- Media
- Onsite Contractors/Vendors
- Government and Regulatory Agencies
- Local law enforcement
- Emergency responders
- Investors/Shareholders
- Insurance Companies
- Surrounding communities

The media is likely to be your first and most persistent audience. They will react quickly, en masse and relentlessly. The incident scene should designate a single primary spokesperson, with back-ups identified, who will manage/disseminate crisis communications to the media, responding government agencies, and others. This individual should be trained in media relations prior to a crisis. All information should be funneled through a single source to assure that the messages being delivered are consistent. The spokesperson must be available to the media and it is important that the same person continue the contacts in order to establish an ongoing relationship and continuity. A spokesperson from the site will generally understand the community and its issues and will be more likely to have credibility versus a representative from Corporate. Be aware that company history will be fair game including any government actions, the environmental record at any site and activist allegations. It is possible, especially for an incident off-site, that the official spokesperson will not be a company representative. All communication should be cleared through or made by the official spokesperson.

It is important that the company spokesperson at the scene coordinate with corporate communications. Support from corporate in preparing the press release is critical to avoid misstatement, especially for the initial release. The CMT may have knowledge of issues or concerns unknown to the scene person. This will also give the Legal Department a chance to review the release. Early in an event there is limited information so the questions can be collected and used for a later report.

Some hints in your communication plan:

- The initial release should be developed and distributed quickly.

Consider using the internet and intranet. Communications should be timely and honest.

- Regular, detailed situation update information sharing is critical. Let the audience know the timing of the next update
- Responsiveness to regulatory agencies and government officials is critical
- Help agencies or officials communicate to media and public:
- Set up daily briefings at a designated location
- Consider joint news releases or media interview opportunities
- Consider community meetings
- Exert control over the story, guide media on story angles
- When possible, provide information before being asked
- Do what it takes to be responsive
- Speak directly to the public whenever possible
- Let them vent their anger, fear and frustration. This is painful, but necessary
- Assume no event at a plant is a small story
- Don't underestimate the level of interest about the plant
- You can't hide anything, so don't try
- Relationships built during earlier phases of the incident pay dividends
- To the extent possible, an audience should hear news from the organization first
- Communications should provide objective and factual assessments without conjecture.
- All employees should be informed at approximately the same time.
- Drafts of message templates, scripts, and statements can be prepared in advance in generic terms.
- Provide technical resources for the Public Relations representative to assist then in answering technical questions.
- Communicate in a manner appropriate to circumstances:
  - Face-to-face meetings (individual and group)
  - News conferences

— Voice mail/email
— Toll-free hotline
— Special newsletter
— Announcements using local/national media.

Immediate Aftermath & Recovery

In situations where the CMT had to assume a more direct leadership role for site issues (e.g., the hurricane example), site-specific decisions typically are returned to the site crisis team during this phase.

The assessment and business recovery begins as soon as the emergency is stabilized. If the emergency is considered a crime scene, legal advice is essential to maintain the integrity of the investigation. As the investigation proceeds, the information flow will improve and more and more reliable information will become available. Communication of new or revised information should be discussed with the Corporate Crisis Team before it is released to both confirm the information and avoid confusion. It is likely that rumors, blame and false reports will already be circulating, making the timing and content of communication of the revised information critical.

In the days and weeks following the incident the long term effects will become more obvious and details and fact will emerge. Blame will likely come from many sources and effective, not reactionary communication, will be critical. The audience for subsequent communications will be as broad as initial communication, including company personnel, the community and authorities. Appropriate members of the Corporate Crisis Team will likely be involved in the communication effort many days and possibly weeks following conclusion of the incident

TRAINING & MAINTENANCE

TRAINING

The Crisis Management Teams should be educated about their responsibilities and duties. Checklists of critical actions and information to be gathered are valuable tools in the education and response processes. CMT members should be trained at least annually and new members should be trained when they join. To extent practicable, the team leader should receive additional training in appropriate emergency and crisis response, such as HAZWOPER incident command. Training should include testing and practice. The scope of testing should be designed to assess the level of understanding of the participants. Also, training should be reinforced through practice drills of various sizes and complexities up to a full-scale activation of the CMP, including external participation by public safety and emergency responders. Initially, tests should start out relatively simple, becoming increasingly complex as the test process evolves. Early tests could include checklists, simple exercises, and small components of the CMP.

MAINTENANCE

A plan is only effective if it is current and practiced. Keeping a plan current is an ongoing task that needs constant attention. Obviously phone numbers require the most vigilance and could be tied to a database for easier maintenance, but there is other information that must be tracked. Contact information for external contacts and procedures are likely to change. An effective method of providing current information is to apply ISO type document control procedures. Each list and procedure is assigned to a team member or their representative and a regular review cycle is established.

Access to the information is also important. The team information could be stored on a server or accessed from an Intranet web site. In either case someone must be responsible for keeping the information current. Since access to the information is critical, the information should be available from a remote location.

Note: For a very good case study regarding this topic, reader can visit company's website of Ford Motor Company www.ford.com. Ford Motor (Ford) is one of the largest automotive manufacturers in the world. It manufactures and distributes automobiles across six continents. The company's automotive vehicle brands include Ford, Lincoln, Mercury and Volvo. The company primarily operates in the US and Europe. It is headquartered in Dearborn, Michigan, and employed 213,000 people.

12

Organizational Change

INTRODUCTION

There is nothing permanent except change. It has become an inescapable fact of life; a fundamental aspect of historical evolution. Change is inevitable in a progressive culture. Change in fact, is accelerating in our society. Revolutions are taking place in political, scientific, technological and institutional areas. Organizations cannot completely buffer themselves from this environmental instability. Change is induced by the internal and external forces. Meeting this challenge of change is the primary responsibility of management. An organization lacking adaptability to change has no future. Adaptability to change is a necessary quality of good management. Modern managers have the responsibility to device the management practices to meet the new challenges and make use of the opportunities for the growth of the organization.

MANAGING CHANGE IN THE ORGANIZATIONAL CONTEXT

The topic of managing change is one that comes closest to describe the totality of a manager's job. Practically everything a manager does is in some way concerned with implementing change.

- Hiring a new employee - Changing the work group
- Purchasing a new piece of equipment - Changing work methods
- Rearranging work station - Changing work flows

All require knowledge of how to manage change effectively. Organizational change refers to a modification or transformation of the organization's structure, processes or goods. Flexibility requires that organizations be open to change in all areas, including the structure of the organization itself. In a flexible organization, employees can't think of their roles in terms of a job description. They often have to change the tasks they perform and learn new skills. The most flexible organizations have a culture that values change and managers who know how to implement changes effectively.

FORCES FOR CHANGE IN ORGANIZATION

More and more organizations today face a dynamic and changing environment that, in turn requires these organizations to adapt. Change has become the norm in most organizations. Plant closing, business failures, mergers and acquisitions, and downsizing have become common experiences for most organizations. Adaptiveness, flexibility and responsiveness are terms used to describe the organizations that will succeed in meeting the competitive challenges that businesses face. In the past, organizations could succeed by claiming excellence in one area - quality, reliability or cost. But this is not the case today. The current environment demands excellence in all areas.

IMPORTANCE OF ORGANIZATIONAL CHANGE

From outside and inside the organization a variety of forces press for change. "We live in the midst of constant change" has become a well-worn but relevant cliché. Pressures for change are created from both inside and outside the organization. Organization must forge ahead on these forces to survive. Some of these are external, arising from outside the company, whereas others are internal arising from sources within the organization.

1. External Forces: When the organization's general or task environment changes, the organization's success often rides on its ability and willingness to change as well. Modern manager is change-conscious and operating in the constantly changing environment. Many external changes bombard the modern organizations and make change inevitable. The general environment has social, economic, legal and political and technological dimensions. Any of these can introduce the need for change. In recent years, far-reaching forces for change have included developments in information technology, the globalization of competition, and demands that organizations take greater responsibility for their impact on the environment.

These forces are discussed below:

a. Technological Change: Rapid technological innovation is a major force for change in organizations, and those who fail to keep pace can quickly fall behind. It is perhaps the greatest factor that organizations reckon with. According to C. Handy "the rate of technological changes is greater today than any time in the past and technological changes are responsible for changing the nature of jobs performed at all levels in the organization". For example, the substitution of computer control for direct supervision is resulting in wider spans of control for managers and flatter organizations. Technological innovations bring about profound change because they are not just changes in the way work is performed. Instead, the innovation process promotes associated changes in work relationships and organizational structures. Sophisticated information technology is also making organizations more responsive. The team approach adopted by many organizations, leads to flatter structures, decentralized decision making and more open communication between leaders and team members.

b. Globalization: The global economy means competitors are likely to come from across the ocean. The power players in the global market are the multinational and trans-national organizations. This has led companies to think globally. There are no mental distinctions between domestic and foreign operations. Globalization, for an organization, means rethinking the most efficient ways to use resources, disseminate and gather information and develop people. It requires not only structural changes but also changes in the minds of employees. Successful organizations will be the ones that can change in response to the competition. They will be fast on their feet, capable of developing new products rapidly and getting them to market quickly.

c. Social and Political Changes: A firm's fate is also influenced by such environmental pressures as social and political changes. Many new legal provisions in the corporate sector get introduced every time that affects the organizations.

d. Workforce Diversity: Related to globalization is the challenge of workforce diversity. Workforce diversity is a powerful force for change in organization. The demographic trends contributing to workforce diversity are

- The workforce will see increased participation form females, as the majority of new workers will be female.
- The workforce will be more culturally diverse than ever (part of this is attributable to globalization).
- The workforce is aging. There will be fewer young workers and more middle aged working.

2. Managing Ethical Behaviour: Employees face ethical dilemmas in their daily work lives. The need to manage ethical behaviour has brought about several changes in organizations. Most centre on the idea that an organization must create a culture that encourages ethical behaviour. Society expects organizations to maintain ethical behaviour both internally and in relationships with other organizations. Ethical behaviour is expected in relationships with customers, environment and society. These expectations may be informal or they may come in the form of increased legal requirements. These challenges are forces that place pressures to change on organizations. Organizations cannot afford to be rigid and inflexible in the wake of environmental pressures, they must be rather dynamic and viable so that they survive.

3. Internal Forces: Besides reacting to or anticipating changes on the outside, an organization may change because someone on the inside thinks a new way of doing things will be beneficial or even necessary. Pressures for change that originate inside the organization are generally recognizable in the form of signals indicating that something needs to be altered. These internal forces are discussed below:

   a. Changes in Managerial Personnel: One of the most frequent reasons for major changes in an organization is the change of executives at the top. No two managers have the same styles, skills or managerial philosophies. Managerial behaviour is always selective so that a newly appointed manager might favour different organizational design, objectives procedures and policies than a predecessor. Changes in the managerial personnel are thus a constant pressure for change.

b. Declining Effectiveness: Declining effectiveness is a pressure to change. A company that experiences losses is undoubtedly motivated to do something about it. Some companies react by instituting layoffs and massive cost cutting programmes, whereas others view the loss as symptomatic of an underlying problem, and seek out the cause of the problem.

c. Changes in Work Climate: Changes in the work climate at an organization can also stimulate change. A workforce that seems lethargic, unmotivated, and dissatisfied is a symptom that must be addressed. This symptom is common in organizations that have experienced layoffs. Workers who have escaped a layoff may find it hard to continue to be productive. They may fear that they will be laid off as well and may feel insecure in their jobs.

d. Deficiencies in the Existing System: Another internal pressure for organizational change is the loopholes in the system. These loopholes may be unmanageable spans of control, lack of coordination between departments, lack of uniformity in politics, non-cooperation between line and staff etc.

e. Crisis: A crisis may also stimulate change in an organization. Strikes or walkouts may lead management to change the wage structure. The resignation of a key decision maker is one crisis that causes the company to rethink the composition of its management team and its role in the organization.

f. Employees, Expectations: Changes in employees expectations can also trigger change in organizations. These forces may be:-

1. Employees' desire to share in decision-making.
2. Employees' demand for effective organizational mechanism.
3. Higher employees' expectation for satisfying jobs and work environment.
4. Employees' desire for higher wage payment.

All these forces necessitate change in organizations. Besides these forces, a company that hires a group of young newcomers may be met with a set of expectations very different from those expressed by older workers. Although organizational changes are important, managers should try to institute changes only when they make strategic sense. A major change or two every year can be overwhelming to employees and create confusion about priorities. A logical conclusion is that managers should evaluate internal forces for change with as much care as they evaluate external forces.

FORMS OF CHANGE

Change has become the norm in most organizations. Adaptiveness, flexibility and responsiveness are terms used to describe the organizations that will succeed in two basic forms of change in organizations that will succeed in meeting the competitive challenges that businesses face. There are two basic forms of change in organizations: Planned change and unplanned change.

- Planned Change: Planned change is a change resulting from a deliberate decision to alter the organization. It is an intentional, goal-oriented activity. The goals of planned change are: l First it seeks to improve the ability of the organization to adapt to changes in its environment.
- Second, it seeks to change the behaviour of its employees.
- Unplanned Change: Not all change is planned. Unplanned change is imposed on the organization and is often unforeseen. Responsiveness to unplanned change requires tremendous flexibility and adaptability on the part of organizations. Examples of unplanned changes are changes in government regulations and changes in the economy.

THE ROLE OF CHANGE AGENTS

Change in organizations is inevitable, but change is a process that can be managed. The individual or group who undertakes the task of introducing and managing a change in an organization is known as a change agent. Change agents can be of two types:

a. Internal Change Agents: Change agents can be internal such as managers or employees who are appointed to oversee the change process.

   Internal change agents have certain advantages in managing the change process. They are:

- They know the organization's past history, its political system, and its culture.
- Internal change agents are likely to be very careful about managing change because they must live with the results of their change efforts.
- There are also disadvantages of using internal change agents. They are:
- They may be associated with certain factions within the organization and may easily be accused of favouritism.
- Internal change agents may be too close to the situation to have an objective view of what needs to be done.

b. External Change Agents: Change agents can also be external, such as outside consultants. They bring an outsider's objective view to the organization. External change agents have certain advantages:

- They may be preferred by employees because of their impartiality.
- They have more power in directing changes if employees perceive the change agents as being trustworthy, possessing important expertise, having a track record that establishes credibility.
- There are also disadvantages of using external change agents. They are:
- External change agents face certain problems, including their limited knowledge of the organization's history.
- They may be viewed with suspicion by organization members.

RESISTANCE TO CHANGE

As the manager contemplates and initiates change in the organization one phenomenon that is quite likely to emerge anytime in the change process is the resistance to change. People often resist change in a rational response based on self-interest. Resistance to change doesn't necessarily surface in standardized ways. Resistance can be overt, implicit, immediate, or deferred. It is easiest for management to deal with resistance when it is overt and immediate. The greater challenge is managing resistance that is implicit or deferred. The sources of resistance to change can be categorized into two sources: individual and organizational.

1. Individual Resistance: One aspect of mankind that has remained more or less constant is his innate resistance to change. Individuals resist change because they attach great preference to maintain status quo. Individual sources of resistance to change reside in basic human characteristics such as perceptions, personalities and needs. The following are the reasons:-
   a. Economic Reasons: The economic reasons to fear change usually focus on one or more of the following:
      i. Fear of technological unemployment.
      ii. Fear of reduced work hours and consequently less pay.
      iii. Fear of demotion and thus reduced wages.
      iv. Fear of speed-up and reduced incentive wages.
      v. Changes in job tasks or established work routines can also arouse economic fears if people are concerned they won't be able to perform the new tasks or routines to their previous standards, especially when pay is closely tied to productivity.
   b. Fear of the Unknown: Change often bring with it substantial uncertainty.
      - Employees facing a technological change, such as the introduction of a new
      - computer system, may resist the change simply because it introduces ambiguity
      - into what was once a comfortable situation for them. This is especially a problem when there has been a lack of communication about the change.
   c. Fear of Loss: When a change is impending, some employees may fear losing their jobs, particularly when an advanced technology is introduced. Employees may also fear losing their status because of a change. Another common fear is that changes may diminish the positive qualities the individual enjoys in the job. For example, computerizing the customer service positions, threaten the autonomy that sales representatives previously enjoyed.
   d. Security: People with a high need for security are likely to resist change because it threatens their feeling of safety.
   e. Status quo: Perhaps the biggest and most sound reason

for the resistance to change is the status quo. As human beings, we are creatures of habit. Change may pose disturbance to the existing comforts of status quo. When confronted with change, this tendency to respond in our accustomed ways becomes a source of resistance. Change means they will have to find new ways of managing them and their environment - the ways that might not be successful as those currently used.

f. Peer Pressure: Individual employees may be prepared to accept change but refuse to accept it for the sake of the group. Whenever change is unwilling to the peers, they force the individuals who want to accept change to resist change.

g. Disruption of Interpersonal Relationships: Employees may resist change that threatens to limit meaningful interpersonal relationships on the job.

h. Social Displacement: Introduction of change often results in disturbance of the existing social relationships. Change may also result in breaking up of work groups. Thus when social relationships develop, people try to maintain them and fight social displacement by resisting change.

2. Organizational Resistance: Organizations, by their very nature are conservative. They actively resist change. Some of the organizational resistances are explained below:

a. Resource Constraints: Resources are major constraints for many organizations. The necessary financial, material and human resources may not be available to the organization to make the needed changes. Further, those groups in organization that control sizable resources often see change as a threat. They tend to be content with the way things are.

b. Structural Inertia: Some organizational structures have in-built mechanism for resistance to change. For example, in a bureaucratic structure where jobs are narrowly defined, lines of authority are clearly spelled out change would be difficult. This is so because formalization provides job descriptions, rules, and procedures for employees to follow. The people who are hired into an organization are chose for fit; they are then shaped and directed to behave in certain ways. When an organization is confronted with change, this structural inertia acts as a counterbalance to sustain stability.

c. Sunk Costs: Some organizations invest a huge amount of capital in fixed assets. If an organization wishes to introduce change then difficulty arises because of these sunk costs.
d. Politics: Organizational change may also shift the existing balance of power in organization. Individuals or groups who hold power under the current arrangement may be threatened with losing these political advantages in the advent of change.
e. Threat to established power relationships: Any redistribution of decision-making authority can threaten long established power relationships within the organization. Managers may therefore resist change that introduces participative decision making because they feel threatened.
f. Threat to expertise: Change in organizational pattern may threaten the expertise of specialized groups. Therefore specialist usually resists change.
g. Group Inertia: Even if individuals want to change their behaviour, group norms may act as a constraint. For example, if union norms dictate resistance any unilateral change made by management, an individual member of the union who may otherwise be willing to accept the changes may resist it.

MANAGING RESISTANCE TO CHANGE

Although resistance to change is a common phenomenon in organizations, it must be noted that not all changes are resisted. In fact, if we look at any organization closely we would probably find that far more changes are accepted than resisted. The traditional view of resistance to change treated it as something to be overcome, and many organizational attempts to reduce the resistance have only served to intensify it. The contemporary view holds that resistance is simply a form of feedback and that this feedback can be sued very productively to manage the change process. One key to managing resistance is to plan for it and to be ready with a variety of strategies for using the resistance as feedback and helping employees negotiate the transition. Some tactics have been suggested for sue in dealing with resistance to change.

a. Education and Communication: Communication about impending change is essential if employees are to adjust effectively. The details of the change should be provided, but equally important is the rationale behind the change. Employees A B C want to know why change is needed. If there is no good reason for it, why should they favour the change? Providing accurate and timely information about the change can help prevent unfounded fears and potentially damaging rumours from developing. It is also beneficial to inform people about the potential consequences of the change. Educating employees on new work procedures is often helpful.

b. Participation: It is difficult for individuals to resist a change decision in which they participated. Prior to making a change, those opposed can be brought into the decision process. When employees are allowed to participate, they are more committed to the change.

c. Empathy and Support: Another strategy for managing resistance is providing empathy and support to employees who have trouble dealing with the change. Active listening is an excellent tool for identifying the reasons behind resistance and for uncovering fears. An expression of concerns about the change can provide important feedback that managers can use to improve the change process.

d. Negotiation: Another way to deal with potential resistance to change is to exchange something of value for a lessening of the resistance. Where some persons in a group clearly lose out in a change, and where groups have considerable power to resist, negotiation and agreements are helpful. It becomes relatively easy to avoid major resistance through negotiation. Negotiation as a tactic may be necessary when resistance comes from a powerful source.

e. Manipulation and cooperation: Manipulation refers to covert influence attempts. Twisting and distorting facts to make them appear more attractive, withholding undesirable information and creating false rumours to get employees to accept a change are all examples of manipulation. It involves giving individuals a desirable role in design or implementation of change.

f. Coercion: Coercion is the application of direct threats or force on the resisters. They essentially force people to accept a change by explicitly or implicitly threatening them with the loss of their jobs, promotion possibilities and transferring them. Coercion is mostly applied where speed is essential in implementing change and the change initiator possesses considerable power.

CONCLUSION

Change in fact, is accelerating in our society. Meeting this challenge of change is the primary responsibility of management. An organization lacking adaptability to change has no future. Adaptability to change is a necessary quality of good management. Practically everything a manager does is in some way concerned with implementing change. Although organizational changes are important, managers should try to institute changes only when they make strategic sense. Adaptability to change is a necessary quality of good management practice.

Note: For a very good study of this chapter see St. Jude Medical, Inc. website. St. Jude Medical is engaged in developing, manufacturing and distributing cardiovascular medical devices for the global cardiac rhythm management, cardiology, cardiac surgery and atrial fibrillation therapy areas. The company also makes implantable neurostimulation medical devices for the management of chronic pain. The company markets its products in about 100 countries across the world. It primarily operates in the US, Europe, Japan and Asia Pacific. It is headquartered in Saint Paul, Minnesota. See www.sjm.com.

13

Organizational Development

INTRODUCTION

The term "Organization Development" (OD) was coined by Richard Beckhard in the mid 1950s, as a response to the need for integrating organizational needs with individual needs. OD came into prominence in the 1960s. OD arose in response to needs. Organizational development is an intervention strategy that uses group processes to focus on the whole culture of an organization in order to bring about planned change. According to Harold M. F. Rush, OD "seeks to change beliefs, attitudes, values, structures, and practices so that the organization can better adapt to technology and live with the fast pace of change". It seeks to use behavioural science knowledge to help organization and to adjust more rapidly to change.

Organizational development is an intervention strategy that uses group processes to focus on the whole culture of an organizational development in order to bring about a planned change. It makes heavy uses of laboratory training approaches such as role playing, gaming and sensitivity training. It is important from the points of view of society, customers and workers themselves because overall costs are reduced that may be a result of reduction of wastage of human efforts and machine etc. In addition to that quality of the product improves and more effective organizational climate is developed. Wendell L. French and Cecil H. Bell Jr., traces the development of OD to the pioneering effort of The National Training Laboratories and Esso Standard Oil Company who began working on the problem of building better organizations and eventually OD evolved from their effort. There are mainly two causes that made OD necessary:

- The reward structure on the job did not adequately reinforce conventional training, so it often failed to carry over to the job.

- The second cause is the fast pace of change itself, which requires organizations to be extremely effective in order to survive and prosper.

OD attempts to develop the whole organization so that it can respond to change more uniformly and capable. OD is not without its shortfall Beckhard described the dilemma of integrating organizational needs with individual needs in the following words:* "If we are talking about the basic dilemma of managing work, the management problem has two horns, one horn is, how do you take all that human energy and channel it towards the organization's mission? The other horn is, how do you organize the work, the communication patterns, the decision-making, the norms and values, the ground rules so that people's individual needs for self-worth, achievement, satisfaction and so on are significantly met at the work place? A great deal of attention has been given to the second horn of the dilemma. But that alone does not solve the problem any more than the other way around. So the dilemma is, how do you manage the dilemma and not how you manage one horn of it. OD tries to work out and organize the interaction between the two".

DEFINITION

According to Wendell L. French and Cecil H. Bell, Jr. "Organization Development is a systematic process for applying behavioural science principles and practices in organizations to increase individual and organizational effectiveness". According to Cummings and Worly - Organization Development is "a systematic application of behavioural science knowledge to the planned development and reinforcement of organizational strategies, structures, and processes for improving an organization's effectiveness."

In the words of Burke "Organization development is a planned process of change in an organization's culture through the utilization of behavioural science technologies research and theory".

According to Schmuck and Miles "OD can be defined as a planned and sustained effort to apply behavioural science for system improvement, using reflexive, self-analytic methods".

According to Burk and Hornstien "Organization development is a process of planned change - change of an organization's culture from one which avoids an examination of social processes (especially decision making, planning and communication) to one which institutionalizes and legitimizes this examination".

According to Warren Bennis - "Organization development is a response to change, a complex educational strategy intended to change the beliefs, attitudes and structure of organization so that they can better adapt to new technologies, markets and challenges". American Society for Training and Development, defined OD as, "An effort (a) planned, (b) organization wide, (c) managed from the top, in order to (d) increase organizational effectiveness and health, through (e) planned intervention in the organizations "processes" using behavioural science knowledge".

From the above definitions we can say that organization development is an organizational improvement strategy. The term "Organization Development" (OD) may be defined as a technique for bringing change in the entire organization. In the late 1950s and early 1960s it emerged out of insights from group dynamics and from the theory and practice of planned change. Organization development is about how people and organizations function and how to get them to function better. OD programmes are long-term, planned, sustained efforts. It is based on knowledge from behavioural science disciplines such as psychology, social psychology, sociology, anthropology, systems theory, organizational behaviour, organization theory and management. The two major goals of OD programmes are:

i. To improve the functioning of individuals, teams and the total organization, and

ii. To teach organization members how to continuously improve their own functioning.

It is a modern approach to the management of change and the development of human resource. It is an organization wide planned change for improvement through the use of behavioural science techniques. Organizational Development programmes lead to improved organization performance through an improved decision making climate.

OBJECTIVES OF ORGANIZATIONAL DEVELOPMENT PROGRAMMES

The objectives of OD as given by Wendell French are given below:-

1. To build and enhance interpersonal trust, communication, co-operation and support among all individuals and group through the organization.

2. To encourage an analytical problem solving approach in a team spirit.
3. To enhance the sense of belonging of individuals to the organization so that the individual and organizational goals are synchronized.
4. To extend the process of decision making to the lowest operational level.
5. To increase personal responsibility for planning and implementing the plan.

BASIC ASSUMPTIONS OF ORGANIZATIONAL DEVELOPMENT

The assumptions underlying Organizational Development programmes are:

1. Assumptions of dealing with Individuals: The two basic assumptions about individuals in organizations are:-
   a. Most individuals have drives towards personal growth and development. They want to develop their potential and therefore should be provided with an environment that is both supportive and challenging. In other words, individuals want personal growth and development, which can be attained in a supportive and challenging work situation.
   b. Most people desire to make, and are capable of making, a greater contribution to attain organization goals than most organizational environments permit. The implication of this assumption is that people are experts. Organizations must remove obstacles and barriers and reward success.
2. Assumptions of dealing with Groups: These assumptions relate to the importance of work teams.
   a. The most psychologically relevant reference groups for most people are the work group. The work group greatly influences feelings of satisfaction and competence. Therefore, individual goals should be integrated with group goals.
   b. Most people interact co-operatively with at least one small reference group.
   c. Work groups are the best way to satisfy social and

emotional needs at work. Therefore, the growth of individual members is facilitated by relationships, which are open, supportive and trusting.

d. The suppression of feelings adversely affects problem solving personal growth and satisfaction with one's work. Attitudinal and motivational problems in organizations require interactive and transactional solutions. Such problems have the greatest chance of constructive solution if all parties in the system alter their mutual relationship, co-operation is always more effective than conflict.

3. Assumptions for designing Organizations: These assumptions relate to the importance of designing organizations.

   a. Traditional hierarchical forms of organizations are obsolete. Therefore, experimenting with new organizational structures and new forms of authority is imperative (very important/ essential). Creating cooperative rather than competitive organizational dynamics is a primary task of the organization.

   b. An optimistic, developmental set of assumptions about people is likely to reap rewards beneficial to both the organization and its members. Co-operation is always more beneficial.

   c. People are an organization's most important resource. They are the source of productivity and profits and should be treated with care. An organization can achieve higher productivity only when the individual goals are integrated with organizational goals.

GOALS OF ORGANIZATION DEVELOPMENT

Edwin B. Flippo has given the following seven specific goals of OD. They are:-

1. Decision-making on the basis of competence rather than authority.
2. Creatively resolving conflicts through confrontation designed to replace win-lose situations with win-win types.
3. Reducing dysfunctional competition and maximizing collaboration.
4. Increasing commitment and a sense of "ownership" of organizational objectives throughout the work force.

5. Increasing the degree of interpersonal trust and support.
6. Creating a climate in which an growth, development and renewal are a natural part of the enterprise's daily operation.
7. Developing a communication system characterized by mutual openness and condor in solving organizational problems.

The choice depends on the circumstances. Restrictions the managers have to take into account including limits on time and money and lack of skill at implementing a strategy. The choice of a strategy usually results from conferences and discussions involving those who will be most directly affected. The experiences, feelings and perceptions of conference participants help determine if their parts of the organization are ready for change and for OD techniques. The success of OD depends on a high level of receptiveness to change.

PURPOSE OF ORGANIZATIONAL DEVELOPMENT

The main purpose of OD according to Burton is "to bring about a system of organizational renewal that can effectively cope with environmental changes. In doing so, OD strives to maximize organizational effectiveness as well as individual work satisfaction". Organizational development is the most comprehensive strategy for intervention. It involves all the activities and levels of management in ongoing problems that respond to external and internal sources.

TYPES OF ORGANIZATIONAL DEVELOPMENT ACTIVITIES

The different types of OD activities may be divided into the following classification:

a. For the Individual
b. OD for two or three people
c. OD for Teams or Groups
d. OD for Inter-group Relations
e. OD for the total organization

Sensitivity Training: Sensitivity training was an early and fairly widespread OD technique. The purpose of sensitivity training sessions or T-groups (T for training) is to change the behaviour of the people through unstructured group interactions. In "T" groups, about ten participants are guided by a trained leader to increase their sensitivity and skills in handling interpersonal relationships. Members are brought together in a free and open environment, away from work places, in which participants discuss freely, aided by facilitator. No formal agenda is provided. The role of the facilitator is to create an opportunity for members to express their ideas, beliefs, and attitudes. The objectives of sensitivity training are to provide the participants with increased awareness of their own behaviour and greater sensitivity to the behaviour of others. Sensitivity training is less frequently used by organizations nowadays, and participants are usually screened to make sure that they can withstand the anxiety raised by a T group. Precautions are also taken to ensure that attendance is truly voluntary.

OD FOR TWO OR THREE PEOPLE

Transactional Analysis (TA): When two people interact with each other there results a social transaction. TA was pioneered by Eric Berne. TA encourages people to recognize the context of their communications. It encourages people to be more open and honest and to address the context of their messages. TA was popularised by Thomas Harris in the 1960s. Transactional Analysis concentrates on styles and content of communication (transactions or messages) between people. It teaches people to send messages that are clear and responsible. Transactional analysis attempts to reduce destructive communication habits or "games" in which the intent or full meaning of messages is obscured.

TA has found its acceptance everywhere because of several advantages associated with it. Eric Berne uses simple day-to-day language to explain the dynamics of personality and its application for human development. His theory has the following components: Structural Analysis: A personality according to Berne consists of three ego states. He defines an ego state as "a consistent pattern of feeling and experience directly related to a corresponding consistent pattern of behaviour". Berne calls these three ego states as: Parent, Adult, and Child.

The parent ego-state - is "a set of feelings attitudes and behaviour patterns which resemble those of the parental figure". The parent ego state is authoritative, dogmatic, overprotective, controlling, nurturing, critical, and righteous.

The Adult ego-state - is "an autonomous set of feelings, attitudes and behaviour patterns which are adapted to the current reality". The adult is the "thinking" ego state. In dealing with other people the adult state is characterised by fairness and objectivity.

The Child ego-state - is "a set of feelings, attitudes and behaviour patterns which are relics of the individual's own childhood". The child ego state represents the childish, dependent, and immature part of a person's personality.

i. Transactional Analysis: A transaction is the act of communication or interaction between two people. A transaction starts with a stimulus and ends with a response to the stimulus. Since each individual involved in the transaction has three egostates; the transactions are between the various ego-states. Depending on the kinds of ego states involved, the interaction can be complimentary, crossed or ulterior.

ii. Complimentary Transactions: These occur when the message sent or the behaviour exhibited by one person's ego state receives the appropriate or expected response from the other person's ego state. Since, these transactions meet the needs and expectations of the initiators, communications flow freely, interactions will continue as inter-personal relations will improve. There is, therefore, no scope for conflict in complimentary transactions. Examples of complimentary transactions are parent-parent, adult-adult, parent-adult, and child-child transactions.

iii. Crossed Transactions: Crossed transactions are the source of much inter-personal conflict in organization. The result can be hurt feelings and frustrations on the part of the parties involved and possible dysfunctional consequences for the organization.

iv. Ulterior Transactions: A message sent may have two targets (ego states). There may be an overt message (open and expressed), but it may also contain a covert message (a hidden one). Transactions with such messages are called ulterior transactions. Ulterior transactions cause much damage to inter-personal relations.

- Life-position Analysis: Life position comprises certain deeply ingrained convictions about the worth of the self and others. A person's conviction about himself/herself may either be 'I'm OK' or "I'm not OK'. Similarly he/she may look at others and think: 'You're OK' or "You're not OK'. Combining these, we have four life positions: Of the four life positions, the ideal one is I am OK, you are OK. It shows healthy acceptance of self and others.

This life position can be learnt. The other life positions are less psychologically mature and less effective. They have potential for interpersonal conflict.

- Games Analysis: A game is "a series of ulterior transactions with a gimmick, leading to a well-defined pay-off". Bern's in his book "Games People Play" describes more than 30 games people habitually play.
- Script Analysis: Script analysis is detailing of specific life dramas that people compulsively play out. Script analysis is a sophisticated and complex part of TA. The following four most popular elements in the script apparatus is discussed below: Pay-off or curse: This is the way the parents tell the child to end its life. According to Berne, the script pay-off will not take effect unless it is accepted by the child.
- Stoppers: Stoppers are injunctions or unfair negative commend from the parent.
- Counter script: Counter script messages are in the forms of slogans; proverbs for example, work hard. These counter scripts determine the person's style.

OD FOR TEAMS AND GROUPS

In process consultation, a consultant works with organization's members to help them understand the dynamics of their working relationships in group or team situations. The consultant helps the group members to change the ways they work together and to develop the diagnostic and problem-solving skills they need for more effective problem solving.

- Teams: Teams are also known by other terms such as empowered teams, self directed teams and self management teams. Katzenbach and Smith have defined a team as "a small number of people with complimentary skills who are committed to a common purpose, common performance goals, and an approach for which they held themselves mutually accountable". The most common types of teams are work teams, problem-solving teams, management teams and virtual teams.
- Work teams: Work teams are primarily concerned with the work done by the organization. Their principal focus is on using the organization's resources effectively.

- Problem-solving teams: Problem-solving teams are temporary teams established to attack specific problems in the work place. These teams generally offer recommendations for others to implement. In problem solving teams, members share ideas or offer suggestions on how work processes and methods can be improved.
- Management teams: The primary job of management teams is to coach and counsel other teams to be self managing by making decisions within the teams. These teams consist of managers from various areas and coordinate work teams.
- Virtual teams: Virtual teams are the teams that may never actually meet together in the same room - their activities take place on the computer via teleconferencing and other electronic information systems. Virtual teams use computer technology to tie together physically dispersed members in order to achieve a common goal.
- Groups: A work group is a group that interacts primarily to share information and to make decisions to help each member perform within his or her area of responsibility. The work group is an even stronger source of satisfaction when members have similar attitudes and values. The work group provides group members with opportunities for interaction with each other.
- Team Building: Team building utilizes high-interaction group activities to increase trust and openness among team members. Team building is a process of diagnosing and improving the effectiveness of a work group with particular attention to work procedures and inter-personal relationship within it. A related approach, analyzes the activities, resource allocations, and relationships of a group or team to improve its effectiveness. This technique can be used, for example, to develop a sense of unity among members of a new committee. Team building can be directed at two different types of teams or working groups: an existing or permanent team made up of a manager and his or her employees, often called a family group; or a new group that either has been formed to solve a specific problem or has been created through a merger or other structural change in the organization, which we will call a special group.

For both kinds of groups, team-building activities aim at diagnosing barriers to effective team performance, improving task accomplishment, improving relationship between team members, and improving processes operative in the team, such as communication and task assignment. The table below summarizes these activities for both family and special groups.

Diagnostic meetings may involve the total group or several subgroups and require only a brief time - a day or less - to identify strengths and problem areas. Actual team building requires a subsequent longer meeting, ideally held away from the workplace. The consultant interviews participants beforehand and organizes the meetings around common themes. The group proceeds to examine the issues, rank them in order of importance, study their underlying dynamics, and decide on a course of action to bring about those changes perceived as necessary. A follow-up meeting at a later time may then evaluate the success of the action steps.

ORGANIZATIONAL DEVELOPMENT FOR INTER-GROUP RELATIONS

Inter-group development seeks to change the attitudes, stereotypes and perceptions that groups have of each other. Such stereotypes can have an obviously negative impact on the coordinative efforts between the departments. To permit an organization's managers to assess the health of the organization and set up plans of action for improving it, the confrontation meeting may be used. This is a one-day meeting of all of an organization's managers in which they discuss problems, analyze the underlying causes, and plan remedial actions. The confrontation meeting is typically used after a major organizational change, such as a merger or the introduction of a new technology. Although there are several approaches for improving inter-group relations, the most sought after method is problem solving. In this method, each group meets independently to develop lists of its perception of itself, the other group and how it believes the other group perceives it. Differences are clearly articulated, and the groups look for the causes of disparities. Subgroups, with members from each of the conflicting groups, can now be created for further diagnosis and to begin to formulate possible alternative actions that will improve relations.

ORGANIZATIONAL DEVELOPMENT FOR THE TOTAL ORGANIZATION

OD attempts to develop the whole organization so that it can respond to change effectively. Change is so abundant in modern society that organizations need all their parts working together in order to solve problems. OD is a comprehensive programme that is intended to assure that all parts of the organization are well coordinated. The survey feedback technique can be used to improve the operations of the total organization. It involves conducting attitude and other surveys and systematically reporting the results to organization members. Members then determine what actions need to be taken to solve the problems and exploit the opportunities uncovered in the surveys. Everyone in an organization can participate in survey feedback. The data from the survey feedback is collected through a questionnaire and tabulated. The data so collected then become the springboard for identifying problems and clarifying issues that may be creating difficulties for people.

VALUES ORGANIZATIONAL DEVELOPMENT

Another source of individual differences is value. Values exist at a deeper level than attitudes and are more general and basic in nature. We use them to evaluate our own behaviour and that of others. Value is an enduring belief that a specific mode of conducts or end state of existence is personally and socially preferable to the alternative modes of conduct or end states of existence. Once it is internalised it becomes consciously or unconsciously, a standard or criterion for guiding action, for developing and maintaining attitudes toward relevant objects and situation, for justifying one's own and others' actions and attitudes for morally judging oneself and others and for comparing oneself with others. Value, therefore, is a standard or yardstick to guide actions, attitudes, evaluations and justifications of the self and others.

Ronald D White and David A Bednar have defined value as a "concept of the desirable, an internalised criterion or standard of evaluation a person possesses. Such concepts and standards are relatively few and determine or guide an individual's evaluations of the many objects encountered in everyday life". Values are tinged with moral flavour, involving an individual's judgement of what is right, good or desirable. Thus values:

- Provide standards of competence and morality.
- Are fewer in number than attitudes.
- Transcend specific objects, situations or persons.
- Are relatively permanent and resistant to change, and
- Are more central to the core of a person.

Individuals learn values as they grow and mature. They may change over the life span of an individual develops a sense of self. Cultures, societies, and organizations shape values.

IMPORTANCE OF VALUES

Values are important to the study of organizational behaviour because they lay the foundation for the understanding of attitudes and motivation and because they influence out perceptions. Individuals enter an organization with preconceived notions of what "ought" and what "ought not' to be. For example, If Jeevan enters IG Ferns and Curtains with a view that salary on piece-rate system is right and on time-rate basis is wrong. He is likely to be disappointed if the company allocates salary on time-rate basis. His disappointment is likely to breed his job dissatisfaction. This will, in turn, adversely affect his performance, his attitude and in turn, behaviour would be different if his values are aligned with the company's reward/pay policy.

FORMATION OF VALUES

Values are learned and acquired primarily through experiences with people and institutions. Parents, for example, will have substantial influence on their children's values. A parent's reaction to everyday events demonstrates what is good and bad, acceptable and unacceptable and important and unimportant. Values are also taught and reinforced in schools, religious organizations, and social groups. As we grow and develop, each source of influence contributes to our definition what is important in life. Cultural mores have influence of the formation of values. Basic convictions of what is good or bad are derived from one's own culture.

TYPES OF VALUES

Allport and his associates categorized values into six types.

1. Theoretical: Interested in the discovery of truth through reasoning and systematic thinking.
2. Economic: Interest in usefulness and practicality, including the accumulation of wealth.
3. Aesthetic: Interest in beauty, form and artistic harmony. Organizational Development
4. Social: Interest in people and love as a human relationship.
5. Political: Interest in graining power and influencing people.
6. Religious: Interest in unity and understanding the cosmos as a

whole

- Instrumental and Terminal Values: Rokeach distinguishes between two types of values: Instrumental and Terminal.
- Instrumental Value: Instrumental values reflect the means to achieving goals; that is, they represent the acceptable behaviour to be used in achieving some end state. Instrumental values identified by Rokeach include ambition, honesty, self-sufficiency and courageousness. Instrumental value refers to a single belief that always takes the form: It is believed that such and such a mode of conduct (example Honesty, courage, etc.) is personally and socially preferable in all situations with respect to all objects. An instrumental value is a tool or means for acquiring a terminal value.
- Terminal Value: Terminal values, in contrast, represent the goals to be achieved, or the end states of existence. Rokeach identified happiness, love, pleasure, self-respect, and freedom among the terminal values. Terminal value takes a comparable form: It is believed that such and such an end state of existence (example salvation, or world at peace etc.) is personally and socially worth striving for. A terminal value is an ultimate goal in a desired status or outcome.
- Work Values: Work values are important because they affect how individuals behave on their jobs in terms of what is right and wrong. The work values most relevant to individuals are:

1. Achievement: Achievement is a concern for the advancement of one's career. This is shown in such behaviours as working hard and seeking opportunities to develop new skills.
2. Concern for Others: Concern for others reflects caring, compassionate behaviour such as encouraging other employees or helping others work on difficult tasks. These behaviours constitute organizational citizenship.
3. Honesty: Honesty is accurately providing information and refusing to mislead others for personal gain.
4. Fairness: Fairness emphasizes impartiality and recognises different points of view.

ORGANIZATIONAL DEVELOPMENT INTERVENTIONS OR TECHNIQUES

OD interventions are sets of structured activities in which selected organizational units (target groups or individuals) engage in a task or a sequence of tasks with the goals of organizational improvement and individual development. The term organizational development (OD) essentially focuses on techniques or programmes to change people and the nature and quality of interpersonal work relationships.

The common thread in these techniques is that each seeks to bring about changes in or among organization's people's. Some of the O.D interventions are explained below:-

- Sensitivity Training: Sensitivity training is also known as laboratory training, encounter groups, and T-groups. It is a method of changing behaviour through unstructured group interaction. If individuals lack awareness of how others perceive them, then the successful T-group can affect more realistic self-perceptions, greater group cohesiveness, and a reduction in dysfunctional interpersonal conflicts.
- Survey Feedback: Survey feedback makes use of questionnaires to identify discrepancies among member perceptions and attempts to solve these differences.
- Process Consultation: The purpose of process consultation is for an outside consultant to assist a client (usually a manager) to perceive, understand and act upon process events. The consultant gives a client insight into what is going on around him (the client), within him, and between him and other people. The consultant then goes to identify the processes that need improvement.
- Team Building: Team building utilizes high-interaction group activities to increase trust and openness among team members. Team building can be applied within groups or at the inter-group level where activities are interdependent.
- Inter-group Development: Inter-group development seeks to change the attitudes, stereotypes, and perceptions that groups have of each other.
- Evaluating the Effectiveness of Organizational Development: Since OD requires an ongoing, long-term effort to bring about

lasting change in an organization's technology, structure and people, a successful OD programme takes a significant investment of money and time. Both are needed for managers to adequately diagnose the problem, select the strategy, and evaluate the effectiveness of the programme.

Managers can measure the effectiveness by comparing the results of the programme to the goals before it was implemented. Were the goals met? If not, why not? Perhaps they were too rigid and too hard to achieve. Perhaps the problems were inadequately defined, and the inadequate definition resulted in the choice of an inappropriate solution. Perhaps managers tried to institute changes before people were prepared for them. Regardless of the cause, the results of the OD analysis will provide feedback needed for later changes.

OD is an expression of manager's efforts to stay flexible. Managers recognize that events inside and outside the organization can happen quite suddenly and can create pressure for change. OD provides the personnel and mechanism to deal with change; control its evolution; and direct its impact on organizational structure, technology, and people.

The Future and Organizational Development: The environment in which organizations operate is increasingly turbulent in an era if global, national and regional commercial competitiveness. Yesterday's strategies are not likely to work in tomorrow's workplaces. Top-down autocratically directed, rigidly hierarchical, fear-generating organizations are giving way to something new. Increasingly, organizations will be flatter, with smaller groups and units. OD will be a major player in assisting organizations to shift to and sustain this new paradigm which proclaims that the most innovative and successful organizations will be those that derive their strength and vitality from adaptable, committed team players. Thus, the OD process should include:

- Careful tuning in to the perceptions and feelings of people.
- Creating safe conditions for surfacing perceptions and feelings.
- Involving people in diagnosing the strengths and weaknesses of their organizations and making action plans for improvement.
- Using qualified third parties consultants.
- Redesigning work so that it is more meaningful and motivating.
- Focusing on team work.

CHANGE MANAGEMENT

There is nothing permanent expect change. Change is induced by the internal and external forces. Meeting this challenge of change is the primary responsibility of management. An organization lacking adaptability to change has no future. Adaptability to change is a necessary quality of good management. Modern managers have the responsibility to devise the management practices to meet the new challenges and make use of the opportunities for the growth of the organization.

NATURE OF CHANGE

The environment of every business unit is influenced by two main factors:

- Internal Factors: Internal factors are activities that can be controlled by the management. Internal factors may be sub-divided into six categories:
  - — Managerial changes
  - — Operational changes
  - — Growth changes
  - — Plant changes
  - — Process changes and
  - — Design changes
- External Factors: External factors are activities that are uncontrollable. The success of an organization depends upon the adaptability of the firm to these factors. External changes may be sub-divided into five categories.
  - — Economic change
  - — Sociological change
  - — Governmental change
  - — Locational change
  - — Technological change.

Change may be warranted either by external stimuli or by an internal need. External change cannot be forecasted and may not be conducive to achieve the corporate goals. External changes are accepted with less resistance. In case of internal changes, the likelihood of resistance of all those affected by the proposed change is more.

CAUSES FOR RESISTANCE TO CHANGE

Change is an important feature of modern organizations. Significant changes take place every day in social, technological, political and other aspects of modern world. Changes may be perceived by people as threats to their jobs, the size of their incomes, promotion and so on. People strongly resist deprivation of what they possess, whether possession was justified or not in the first place. The important causes for resistance to change are:

1. Social Causes: People value established inter-personal relationship and their roles as group members. Establishment of new social equations necessitated by acceptance to change may be a painful and slow process. People would not like to experience such changes. Resistance to change develops among people if they believe that such change is likely to mean disruption of existing social relationships with which they are familiar.
2. Psychological Causes: In course of their working life, people get used to certain routines and ways of doing things. They develop familiarity and a measure of equilibrium with their established routines. A sort of inertia develops which induces them to disfavour changes. Therefore, people tend to behave in a rather conservative manner in relation to some types of changes. Resistance also springs from lack of trust and faith in those who initiate changes and due to inadequate information, knowledge and understanding.
3. Economic Causes: People meet their physical needs from their salary. They work because they need economic security. They tend to attach highest priority to protection of their jobs and income. If these are threatened by technological and other changes initiated by management, people naturally resist them.
4. Environmental Causes: Business environment have an impact on the growth of the organization. Change in government policy, entry of rivals in the market etc., will affect the growth of the organization. Many of the environmental factors are uncontrollable and therefore, organizations must visualize them and adapt to the changed circumstances.
5. Personal Reasons: Employees resist change for a variety of personal reasons. They are:
   - The proposed change may lead to greater specialization resulting in boredom.

- They may not fully understand the implications of the change.
- They may fear that the number of jobs may be reduced resulting in retrenchment.

PLANNED ORGANIZATIONAL CHANGE

Organizational change may be planned well in advance, or it may come as a quick reaction to an unexpected event in the business environment. Organizational change calls for a change in the individual behaviour of the employees. Any organizational change whether introduced through a new structural design or new technology or new training programme, basically attempts to make employees change their behaviour. But behavioural changes are the most difficult and marathon exercise. A commonly accepted model for bringing about change in people was suggested by Kurt Lewen in terms of three-phase process -

1. Unfreezing: It refers to making individuals aware that the present behaviour is inappropriate, irrelevant, inadequate and hence unsuitable to the changing demands of the present situation. According to Lewing, the first step in the change process is unfreezing, or preparing the situation for change by creating a felt-need for it. It is important to make sure that everyone understands that present behaviours are simply not effective. This action will minimize expressed resistance to the change process. Edgar Schien outlines the following elements which are vitally necessary during this unfreezing phase.
    - The physical removal of the individuals being changed from their accustomed routines, sources of information and social relationships.
    - The undermining and destruction of social support.
    - Demeaning and humiliating experience to help individuals being changed to see their old attitudes or behaviour as unworthy and then to be motivated to change.
    - The consistent linking of reward with willingness to change and to punishment with unwillingness to change.

    The essence of this unfreezing phase is that the individual is made to realize that his beliefs, feelings and behaviour are no longer appropriate or relevant to the current situation in the organization.
2. Changing: During the changing phase, the actual change is

implemented. It is the phase where new learning occurs. In order to change, it is not enough to sense that the current behaviour is inadequate. The necessary condition is that various alternatives of behaviour must also be made available in order to fill the vacuum created by the unfreezing phase. In the process it is critical for management to carefully identify the new, more effective behaviours to be followed as well as the associated changes in tasks, people, culture, technology and structure. During the changing phase, individuals learn to behave in new ways; the individuals are provided with alternatives out of which they choose the best one. Kelman explains the changing phase in terms of compliance, identification and internalisations.

- Compliance: Compliance or force occurs when individuals are forced to change either by rewards or by punishment.
- Internalisation: Internalisation occurs when individuals are forced to encounter a situation that calls for a new behaviour.
- Identification: It occurs when individuals recognize one among various models provided in the environment that is most suitable to their personality. The changing process follows good problem diagnoses and careful consideration of appropriate alternatives.

3. Refreezing: In this stage, the change is stabilized by rewarding appropriate new behaviours. During this phase, individuals internalise the new beliefs, feelings and behaviour learned in the "Changing" phase. It is also necessary that management provides the required resource support for the change. Performance - contingent rewards and positive reinforcement can be used to refreeze the new behaviour so that it is not easily forgotten or abandoned. It is very important for the manager concerned with the introducing change to visualize that the new behaviour is not extinguishable soon.

4. Management of Change: It is the responsibility of management to handle change in such a way that the employee's resistance is reduced to the least. Three methods available to management to cause people to accept change are:

   - Alteration in the environmental forces affecting the employees.

- Alteration in the person's perception of the forces which surround him.
- Alteration in the basic value system of the persons involved in the change.

CONCLUSION

Organizational development is an intervention strategy that uses group processes to focus on the whole culture of an organizational development in order to bring about a planned change. OD strives to maximize organizational effectiveness as well as individual work satisfaction." Organizational development is the most comprehensive strategy for intervention. It involves all the activities and levels of management in ongoing problems that respond to external and internal sources. OD interventions are sets of structured activities in which selected organizational units (target groups or individuals) engage in a task or a sequence of tasks with the goals of organizational improvement and individual development. The term organizational development (OD) essentially focuses on techniques or programmes to change people and the nature and quality of interpersonal work relationships. The environment in which organizations operate is increasingly turbulent in an era of global, national and regional commercial competitiveness. OD will be a major player in assisting organizations to shift to and sustain this new paradigm, which proclaims that the most innovative and successful organizations will be those that derive their strength and vitality from adaptable, committed team players.

Note: For a very good case study regarding this topic, reader can visit company's website of C.H. Robinson Worldwide Inc. C.H. Robinson Worldwide (CHRW) is a global provider of multimodal transportation services and logistics solutions. It also provides fresh produce sourcing and information services. The company primarily operates in the US. It is headquartered in Eden Prairie, Minnesota and employs about 7,961 people. www.chrobinson.com.

14

Organizational Culture

INTRODUCTION

When we talk about culture, we are typically referring to the pattern of development reflected in a society's system of knowledge, ideology, values, laws, social norms and day-to-day rituals. Accordingly, culture varies from one society to another. The word "culture" has been derived metaphorically from the idea of "cultivation" the process of tilling and developing land. Thus, culture can be considered as a constellation of factors that are learned through our interaction with the environment.

DEFINITION

The organizational culture is a system of shared beliefs and attitudes that develop within an organization and guides the behaviour of its members. There are clear-cut guidelines as to how employees are to behave generally within organization. The employees need to learn how the particular enterprise does things.

A few definitions on the term organizational culture are given below:-

According to Larry Senn, The corporate culture "consists of the norms, values and unwritten rules of conduct of an organization as well as management styles, priorities, beliefs and inter-personal behaviour that prevail. Together they create a climate that influences how well people communicate, plan and make decisions."

Joanne Martin defines cultures in organization in the following words "As individuals come into contact with organizations, they come into contact with dress norms ... the organization's formal rules and procedures, its formal codes of behaviour rituals .... And so on. These elements are some of the manifestations of organizational culture".

Edgar Schein defines organizational culture as "a pattern of basic assumptions - invented, discovered or developed by a given group as it learns to cope with its problems of external adaptation and internal integration - that has worked well enough to be considered valuable and, therefore to be taught to new members as the correct way to perceive, think and fell in relation to those problems".

According to Hersey, Blanchard and Johnson " Organizational culture is itself a complex phenomenon with many interpretations ... organizational culture is shared basic assumptions, or beliefs, about how to cope with the two fundamental problems that all groups and organizations face: survival and adaptation to the external environment and the internal integration and coordination of organizational functioning".

From the above definitions, culture may be considered as the general pattern of behaviour, shared beliefs, and values that organizational members have in common. Culture involves the learning and transmitting of knowledge, beliefs and patterns of behaviour over a period of time. Culture can be inferred from what people say, do, and think within an organizational setting. It often sets tight tone for the organization and establishes implied rules for the way people should behave. It is important to recognize that culture is learned and helps people in their efforts to interact and communicate with others in the society. When placed in a culture where values and beliefs are different, some people have a great deal of difficulty in adjusting.

BASIC ELEMENTS OF CULTURE

From the above definitions it is clear that culture is how an organization has learned to deal with its environment. It is a complex mixture of assumptions, behaviours, myths and other ideas that fit together to define what it means to work in a particular organization. Edgar H Schein suggests that culture exists on three levels: artefacts, espoused values and underlying assumptions. It mainly has the following three levels:

1. Artefacts: According to Schein, Artefacts are the first level of organizational culture. Artefacts are the things that come together to define a culture and reveal what the culture is about to those who pay attention to them. They include products, services, and even behaviour patterns of the members of an organization. Schein has defined Artefacts as things that "one sees, hears, and feels when one encounters a new group with an unfamiliar culture".

2. Espoused Values: Espoused values are the second level of organizational culture. Values are things worth doing, or the reasons for doing what we do. Values are the answers to the "why" questions. For examples, why are you reading this book? To know more about Organization Behaviour. Why is that Important? To be a better HR Manager. Why do you need more money? To fulfil my wife's desire to own a farm house. Such questions go on and on, until you reach the point where you no longer want something for the sake of something else. At this point, we have arrived at a value. Corporations have values, such as size, profitability, or making a quality product. Espoused values are the reasons that we give for doing what we do. Schein argues that most organizational cultures can trace their espoused values back to the founders of the culture.
3. Basic Assumptions: The third level of organizational culture, are the beliefs that organization members take for granted. Culture prescribes "the right way to do things" at an organization, often through unspoken assumptions. The influence of the leader on Organization Culture: Managers, especially top managers, create the climate for the enterprise. Their values influence the direction of the firm. Although the tern "value" is used differently, a value can be defined as a fairly permanent belief about what is appropriate and what is not that guides the actions and behaviour of employees in fulfilling the organization's aims. Values can be thought of as forming an ideology that permeates every day decisions. In many successful companies, value-driven corporate leaders serve as role models, set the standards for performance, motivate employees, make the company special, and are a symbol to the external environment.

CHARACTERISTICS OF ORGANIZATIONAL CULTURE

Organizational culture has a number of important characteristics. Fred Luthans has given six characteristics which is given below:

1. Observed behavioural regularities. When organizational participants interact with one another, they use common language, terminology, and rituals related to deference and demeanor.
2. Norms. Standards of behaviour exist, including guidelines on

how much work to do, which in many organizations come down to "Do not do too much; do not do too little."

3. Dominant values. There are major values that the organization advocated and expects the participants to share. Typical examples are high product quality, low absenteeism, and high efficiency.
4. Philosophy. There are policies that set forth the organization's beliefs about how employees and/or customers are to be treated.
5. Rules. There are strict guidelines related to getting along in the organization. Newcomers must learn those "ropes" in order to be accepted as full-fledged members of the group.
6. Organizational climate. This is an overall "feeling" that is conveyed by the physical layout, the way participants interact, and the way members of the organization conduct themselves with customers or other outsiders

CREATING AND SUSTAINING CULTURE

An organization's current customs, traditions and general way of doing things are largely due to what it has done before and the degree of success it has had with those endeavours.

The original source of an organization's culture usually reflects the vision or mission of the organization's founders. Because the founders had the original idea, they also may have biases on how to carry out the idea. Their focus might be on aggressiveness or it might be on treating employees as family. The small size of most new organizations helps the founders instill their vision in all organizational members. Organizational cultures can develop in a number of different ways, these steps are explained below:-

1. A single person (founder) has an idea for a new enterprise: Some organizational cultures may be the direct, or at least, indirect, result of actions taken by the founders. The founders of an organization traditionally have a major impact on that organization's early culture. They have a vision of what the organization should be.
2. Founders' creation of a core group: The founder brings in one or more other key people and creates a core group that shares a common vision with the founder. The founder's only hire and keep employees who think and feel the way they do. These

employees who form the core group believe that the idea is a good one, is worth the investment of time, money and energy. Sometimes founders create weak cultures, and if the organization is to survive, a new top manager must be installed who will sow the seeds for the necessary strong culture.

3. Indoctrinate and Socialize: The founding core group begins to act in concert to create an organization by raising funds, obtaining patents, incorporating, locating land, building infrastructure and so on. The core group indoctrinate and socialize employees to their way of thinking and feeling.
4. Build a Common History: The founders' own behaviour acts as a role model that encourages employees to identify with them and thereby internalize their beliefs, values, and assumptions. At this point, others are brought into the organization, and a common history begins to be built. When the organization succeeds, the founder's vision becomes seen as a primary determinant of that success. At this point, the founders' entire personalities become embedded in the culture of the organization. Most of today's successful organizations follow the vision of their founders.

SUSTAINING A CULTURE

Once a culture is in place, there are practices within the organization that act to maintain it by giving employees a set of similar experiences. Sustaining a culture depends on three forces. These forces are explained below:

1. Selection: The goal of the selection process is to identify and hire individuals who could make the organization successful through their services. Therefore candidates who believe in the values of the organizational have to be selected. Thus, the selection process attempt to ensure a proper match in the hiring of people who have values essentially consistent with those of the organization or at least a good portion of those values cherished by the organization. In this way, the selection process sustains an organization's culture by selecting those individuals who will fit into the organizations core values.
2. Top Management: Top management have an important role to play in sustaining the organization's culture. It is the top management who establish norms that filter down through the

organization. It is they through their conduct both implicit and explicit that shows what is desirable. They do this through pay raises, promotions and other rewards.

3. Socialization: Socialization is the process that adapts employees to the organization's culture. Organization wants to help new employees adapt to its culture. The adaptation is done through the process of "socialization". Socialization is made up of three stages:

   a. The Pre-arrival Stage: This stage encompasses all the learning that occurs before a new member joins the organization. The socialization process covers both the work to be done and the organization. The pre-arrival stage is the period of learning in the socialization process that occurs before a new employee joins the organization. For example, when students join a business school to pursue their MBA degree, they are socialized to have attitudes and behaviours that business firms want. This is so because the success depends on the degree to which the student has correctly anticipated the expectations and desires of those in the business school.

   b. Encounter Stage: In this stage of the socialization process, the new employee sees what the organization is really like and confronts the possibility that expectations and reality may diverge. In expectations prove to have been more or less accurate, the encounter stage merely provides a reaffirmation of the perceptions gained during the pre-arrival stage. Those employees who fail to learn the essential or pivotal role behaviours risk being labelled as "rebels" and face the risk of expulsion. This further contributes to sustaining the culture.

   c. Metamorphosis Stage: Metamorphosis stage is the stage in the socialization process in which a new employee changes and adjusts to the job, work group and organization. In this stage relatively long-lasting changes take place. The employee masters the skill required for his or her job, successfully performs his or her new roles, and makes the adjustments to his or her work group's values and norms. The metamorphosis stage completes the socialization process. The new employee internalizes the norms of the organization and his work groups and understands and accepts the norms of the organization and his work group. The success of this stage have a positive impact on the new employee's productivity and his commitment to the organization.

CULTURE FOR THE EMPLOYEES

Culture is transmitted to employees in a number of ways. The most significant are stories, rituals, symbols, and language.

- Stories: Organizational "stories" typically contain a narrative of significant events or people including such things as the organization's founders, rules breaking, reactions to past mistakes, and so forth. Lavinson and Rosenthal suggest that stories and myths about organization's heroes are powerful tools to reinforce cultural values throughout the organization and specially in orienting new employees. These stories provide prime examples that people can learn from. Stories and myths are often filtered through a "cultural network" and remind employees as to "why we do things in a certain way". To help employees learn the culture, organizational stories anchor the present in the past, provide explanations and legitimacy for current practices, and exemplify what is important to the organization.
- Rituals and Ceremonies: Corporate rituals are repetitive sequences of activates that express and reinforce the values of the organization, what goals are most important, and which people are important and which ones are superfluous. Ceremonies and rituals reflect such activities that are enacted repeatedly on important occasions. Members of the organization who have achieved success are recognized and rewarded on such occasions. For example, awards given to employees on "founders' day", Gold medals given to students on graduation day are reflections of culture of that institution.
- Material/Cultural Symbols: Symbols communicate organizational culture by unspoken messages. When you walk into different businesses, do you get a "feel" for the place - formal, casual, fun, serious, and so forth? These feelings you get demonstrate the power of material symbols in creating an organization's personality. Material artefacts created by an organization also speak of its cultural orientation and make a statement about the company. These material symbols convey to employees

who is important, the degree of equality desired by top management and the kind of behaviour that are expected and appropriate. Examples: - assigned parking space for senior executives in the company premises, large offices given to senior managers, luxury automobiles given to senior or successful officers of the organization.

- Organizational Heroes: Top Management and prominent leaders of the organization become the role models and a personification of an organization's culture. Their behaviour and example become a reflection of the organization's philosophy and helps to mould the behaviour of organizational members.
- Language: - Many organizations and units within organizations use language as a way to identify members of a culture. By learning this language, members attest to their acceptance of the culture and their willingness to help to preserve it.
- Managerial Decisions affected by culture: For any organization to grow and prosper, it is important that its mission and its philosophy be respected and adhered to by all members of the organization. Here managers play a significant role in building the culture of the organization. The manager plays continuous attention to maintaining the established standards and send clear signals to all the employees as to what is expected of them. Cultural consistency and strong adherence to cultural values become easy when the mangers themselves play strong role models. Good managers are able to support and reinforce an existing strong culture by being strong role models and by handling situations that may result into cultural deviations.

How the Environment Affects Managers: The environment affects managers

- Through the degree of environmental uncertainty
- Through the various stakeholders relationships.

Environmental Uncertainty:-The environmental uncertainty is the degree of change and complexity in an organization's environment.

Degree of Change: - If the components in an organization's environment changes to a minimum, we call it a stable environment. A stable environment is characterises by 1 No new technological breakthroughs by current competitors.

- No new competitors.

- Little activity by pressure groups to influence the organization.

We call it a dynamic environment, if the components in an organization's environment change frequently.

- Degree of Complexity: - The degree of complexity refers to the number of components in an organization's environment and the extent of the knowledge that the organization has about those components. Managers try to minimize uncertainty because it is a threat to organization's effectiveness. Given the choice, managers would prefer to operate in an environment which is simple and stable. However, managers rarely have full control over that choice.
- Stakeholders Relationship: - Stakeholders are any constituencies in the organization's external environment that are affected by the organization's decisions and actions.

  The few of the organizational stakeholders are explained below:
- Stockholders: The shareholders are the persons who provide the funds to the business enterprise. The business should be managed efficiently so as to provide a fair return on the investments of the shareholders. They should be provided with comprehensive reports giving full information about its working. In the same way, the shareholders should also meet the obligations of the business enterprise by supporting the efforts of the business so that continuous development of the enterprise is possible. They should encourage the business to follow a dynamic policy and to plough back profit for the purpose of development and expansion.
- Customers: Customers' satisfaction is the ultimate aim of all economic activity. This involves more than the offer of products at the lowest possible price. Adulteration of goods, poor quality, failure to give fair service, misleading advertising etc. are some of the violation by business towards its customers. A business enterprise has positive responsibility towards the consumers of its products. It has to provide quality goods to customers at the right time, right place, and at right price.
- Employees: Employees should be treated as human beings and their cooperation must be achieved for the realization of the business enterprises goals. The responsibilities of the business enterprises to its employees are - the security of employment

with fair wages, equal opportunity for growth and development within the organization, fair promotions, employee welfare, social security and profit sharing.

Further, the business enterprise should also provide the employee welfare, social security and profit sharing. Further, the business enterprise should also provide the employees scope for improvement of educational qualification, training and upgrading of skills so that they may get a chance to improve their prospects. Workers are poor and hence they cannot afford to remain without job for a long period. Most of them are ignorant and require advice and guidance from persons who have the genuine interest of the workers at heart. Each worker by himself is unable to fight against the injustice done to him. As such all the economists have recognized the right of the workers to organize themselves. As a group they can settle terms with the employers in a better way. In other words, the workers have been granted the right to bargain collectively. With a view to self-protection and self -help labour has organized itself under employee associations and unions. The associations formed by workers have come to be known as "Trade Unions".

- Suppliers: An important force in the environment of a business enterprise is the suppliers who supply the enterprise with inputs like raw materials and components. The importance of reliable source of supply is indispensable for the smooth functioning of a business enterprise. It is very risky to depend on a single supplier because the problems with that supplier are bound to seriously affect the business organization. Therefore, multiple sources of supply are often helpful. A business organization should deal with the suppliers judiciously. It should try for fair terms and conditions regarding price, quality, delivery of goods and payment. The dealings with the suppliers should be based on integrity and courtesy. The business must create healthy relations with its suppliers.
- Competitors: A firm's competitors include not only the other firms that market the same or similar products but also those who compete for the discretionary income of the consumers. Thus, competition among the different business organization should be such that the customer is helped to satisfy his desires and is better of buying the enterprises goods and services.
- Government: The business enterprise should take responsibility for providing amenities in the locality where it is located. It

should pay the taxes to the government regularly and honestly, so that the funds may be spent by the State for welfare activities. It should take measures to avoid bad effluent, fouling the air and condition of slum and congestion.

The business enterprise should extend full support to the Government in implementing its policies and programmes relating to the solving of the national problems such as the unemployment problem, food problem, wide disparity in income levels of the different sections of the society, regional imbalance in the economic development etc. It should also help the Government in the equitable distribution of commodities which are in scarce supply, in controlling prices and inflationary trend in the country and in the implementation of various development schemes of the Government. The business enterprise should realize that it cannot function without the support of the Government. If there is any difference between itself and the Government the same should be settled by mutual exchange of ideas and suggestions and not by restoring to non-cooperation with the Government.

From the above discussion, it is clear that the interest of the various Stakeholders interacting with the business enterprise is not identical. They are inflicting conflicting. The owners want highest dividend, the financial institutions want the highest interest, the workers the highest possible wages, the Government wants the highest possible revenue and the consumers want the lowest possible price. It is, therefore, the duty of the business enterprise to bring about a compromise among the interests of various groups. The enterprise is an arbiter among the various groups. It should endeavour to provide a fair dividend to the shareholders, fair pay and working conditions to the workers, good quality products at reasonable prices to the customers.

Stakeholders have a stake in or are significantly influenced by what the organization does. In turn, these groups can influence that organization. There are many reasons why managers should care about managing stakeholders' relationships. Some of the reasons are given below:-

- It can lead to other organizational outcomes such as improved predictability of environmental changes, more successful innovations, greater degree of trust among stakeholders, and greater organizational flexibility to reduce the impact of change.
- An organization depends on these external groups as sources of inputs (resources) and as outlets for outputs (goods and services) and organizations should consider their interests as

they make decisions and take actions.

Steps in Managing External Stakeholders Relationships:- There are four steps in managing external stakeholder relationships.

1. Identifying who the organization's stakeholders are. Those external groups that are to influence organizational decisions and be influenced by organizational decisions are stakeholders.
2. Determine that particular interests or concerns these stakeholders might have. For example -
   - Customers - product quality.
   - Shareholders - financial issues
   - Employees - safety/working conditions.
3. Decide how critical each stakeholder is to the organization's decisions and actions. For example, some stakeholders are more critical to the organization's decisions and actions than others.
4. Determine what specific approach they should use to manage the external stakeholder relationship. The more critical the stakeholder, the more uncertain the environment.

SUCCESSFUL ORGANIZATIONAL CULTURE

Research conducted by D.R Denison and A.K Mishra, show that organizational culture is related to organizational success. Organizational culture is a framework that guides day-to-day behaviour and decision making for employees and directs their actions toward completion of organizational goals. Culture is what gives birth to and defines the organizational goals. Culture must be aligned with the other parts of organizational actions, such as planning, organizing, leading, and controlling; indeed, if culture is not aligned with these tasks, then the organization is in for difficult times.

Organizational cultures are important to a firm's success for several reasons.

1. They give an organizational identity to employees - a defining vision of what the organization represents. When managers are uncertain about their business environments, the vision helps guide the discussions, decisions, and behaviour of the people in the company.
2. Organizational culture are an important source of stability and continuity to the organization, which provide a sense of security

to its members.

3. Knowledge of the organizational culture helps newer employees interpret what goes on inside the organization, by providing an important context for events that would otherwise seem confusing.
4. Culture helps to stimulate employee enthusiasm for their tasks by recognizing and rewarding high-producing and creative individuals, thereby identifying them as role models to emulate.

CORPORATE CULTURE AND ORGANIZATIONAL SUCCESS

Artefacts, espoused values, and basic assumptions form the basics of understanding organizational culture. Organizational culture is a framework that guides day-to-day behaviour of employees. Culture is what gives birth to and defines the organizational goals. John Kotter and James Heskett, researchers of Harvard Business School, tried to determine which factors make some organizational cultures more successful than others.

Kotter ahd Heskett identified two levels of culture.

Visible Level: are the behaviour patterns and styles of the employees.

Invisible Level: are the shared values and assumptions that are held over a long period of time.

Kotter and Heskett, argue that changes in the visible level (i.e., in behaviour patterns and styles) overtime can lead to change in the invisible level (i.e., more deeply held beliefs). The study had four main conclusions:

1. Corporate culture can have a significant impact on a firm's long-term economic performance.
2. Corporate culture will probably be an even more important factor in determining the success or failure of firms in the next decade.
3. Corporate cultures that inhibit strong long-term financial performance are not rare; they develop easily, even in firms that are full of reasonable and intelligent people.
4. Although tough to change, corporate cultures can be made more performance enhancing.

CHANGING ORGANIZATIONAL CULTURE

If organizations are to consciously create and manage their cultures they must be able to take their employees into consideration. There are problems that managers face when they go about the business of changing organizational culture. Changing organizational culture takes patience, vigilance, and a focus on changing the parts of an organizational culture that managers can control:

- Behaviours: one way of changing a corporate culture is to use behavioural addition or behavioural substitution to establish new patterns of behaviour among employees.
  - Behavioural Addition: Behavioural Addition is the process of having managers and employees perform new behaviours that are central to and symbolic of the new organizational culture that a company wants to create.
  - Behavioural Substitution: Behavioural substitution is the process of having managers and employees perform new behaviours central to the "new" organizational culture in place of behaviours that were central; to the "old" organizational culture.
- Visible Artefacts: Another way in which managers can begin to change corporate culture is to change visible artefacts of their old culture. Visible artefacts are visible signs of an organization's culture, such as the office design and layout, company dress codes, and company benefits and perks like stock options, personal parking spaces, etc. These need to change keeping the new corporate culture in mind.

CONCLUSION

Corporate cultures are very difficult to change. Consequently, there is no guarantee that behaviour substitution, behavioural addition or changing visible artefacts will change a company's organizational culture. Clearly, an open display of top management commitment and support for the new values and beliefs is critically important to enable employees to change.

Note: For further knowledge regarding this chapter, reader can visit Ryland Group Inc website. The Ryland Group (Ryland) is engaged in home building and mortgage financing activities. The company primarily operates in the US. It is headquartered in Calabasas, California and employs 1,303 people. Its website is www.ryland.com

15

Organizational Effectiveness

INTRODUCTION

Organizational effectiveness is the concept of how effective an organization is in achieving the outcomes the organization intends to produce. The idea of organizational effectiveness is especially important for non-profit organizations as most people who donate money to non-profit organizations and charities are interested in knowing whether the organization is effective in accomplishing its goals.

An organization's effectiveness is also dependent on its communicative competence and ethics. The relationship between these three are simultaneous. Ethics is a foundation found within organizational effectiveness. An organization must exemplify respect, honesty, integrity and equity to allow communicative competence with the participating members. Along with ethics and communicative competence, members in that particular group can finally achieve their intended goals.

Foundations and other sources of grants and other types of funds are interested in organizational effectiveness of those people who seek funds from the foundations. Foundations always have more requests for funds or funding proposals and treat funding as an investment using the same care as a venture capitalist would in picking a company in which to invest.

Organizational effectiveness is an abstract concept and is basically impossible to measure. Instead of measuring organizational effectiveness, the organization determines proxy measures which will be used to represent effectiveness. Proxy measures used may include such things as number of people served, types and sizes of population segments served, and the demand within those segments for the services the organization supplies.

For instance, a non-profit organization which supplies meals to house bound people may collect statistics such as the number of meals cooked and served, the number of volunteers delivering meals, the turnover and retention rates of volunteers, the demographics of the people served, the turnover and retention of consumers, the number of requests for meals turned down due to lack of capacity (amount of food, capacity of meal preparation facilities, and number of delivery volunteers), and amount of wastage. Since the organization has as its goal the preparation of meals and the delivery of those meals to house bound people, it measures its organizational effectiveness by trying to determine what actual activities the people in the organization do in order to generate the outcomes the organization wants to create.

Activities such as fundraising or volunteer training are important because they provide the support needed for the organization to deliver its services but they are not the outcomes per se. These other activities are overhead activities which assist the organization in achieving its desired outcomes. The term Organizational Effectiveness is often used interchangeably with Organization Development, especially when used as the name of a department or a part of the Human Resources function within an organization.

To be effective and achieve its goals, an organization must successfully respond to environmental factors. How can the effectiveness of an organization be measured? Various models of determining organizational effectiveness exist because organizations face different environments, they produce different products, their organizational members are made up of different kinds of people, and the organizations are at different stages of development. Each model is most useful to an organization having a particular combination of these environmental and organizational attributes.

Two different underlying dimensions may be considered to develop models of organizational effectiveness. The first is the organization's internal versus external focus. The second dimension is the organization's emphasis on flexibility versus control. Flexibility allows faster change, whereas control allows a firmer grasp on current operations. When these two dimensions are drawn at right angles to each other, the first four models of organizational effectiveness can be plotted. They are the rational goal, open system, internal process, and human relations models.

According to the rational goal model of effectiveness, an organization is effective to the extent that it accomplishes its stated goals.

With an open system model an organization is effective to the degree that it acquires inputs from its environment and has outputs accepted by its environment. The University of Alberta follows this model when it is concerned about the quality and number of students applying for admission and what jobs they receive on graduation.

The internal process model focuses on the effectiveness of the internal transformation process. When Hamilton's Stelco Inc. examines its steel-making methods to determine price and quality competitiveness, it is focusing on its internal processes.

The human relations model focuses on the development of the organization's personnel. Marlin Travel sends its agents on familiarization trips to expand their knowledge of specific hotels, cruises, and destinations. The competing values model requires that an organization scrutinize the balance among the above four effectiveness models. In this model there are three sets of competing values. The first is the tension between internal versus external focus. The more the organization focuses on one, the less it can concentrate on the other. For example Apple Computer has focused externally on its customers and making computers that are intuitive and easy to use. The computer chip maker Intel has had a more internal focus on how to make faster and more powerful central processing units at a low price. The second set of values in competition is flexibility versus control. Flexibility allows quick response to changing conditions and values innovation. Control values the opposite. Stability and predictability mean that routine activities are performed well but change is more difficult. The third set of competing values is the relative concern with the feelings, needs, and development of the people making up the organization versus the organization and its requirement to accomplish its tasks.

A private hospital, for example, is concerned with how patients are treated and the success rate of surgeries (the rational goal model). It is also interested in how hospital procedures are performed (the internal process model) and with the skills and abilities of hospital staff (the human relations model). Finally, because it is a private hospital and must make a profit to survive, it needs to take into account how many and what kinds of patients are admitted (the open system model). The hospital must balance the three sets of competing values in order to be effective.

With the strategic constituencies model an organization would aim to at least minimally satisfy the most important constituents (or stakeholders) in its environment. The owner of an A&W franchise must satisfy the customers and A&W head office management. Customers care about the quality and price of the food as well as the speed and friendliness of service. Head office cares about these issues along with financial reporting, product promotions, and the store's relationship with its community.

An organization seeking legitimacy survives by acting in a manner seen by other organizations as legitimate. An example would be producing a business plan and projected income statement in order to obtain a bank loan.

The organization adopting the fault-driven model of effectiveness seeks to eliminate traces of ineffectiveness in its internal functioning. The National Aeronautics and Space Administration (NASA) in the United States is a good example. Its systems are designed with backups to be reliable even if some components fail.

Finally, the organization as a high performing system compares itself to other similar organizations. The Vancouver Symphony Orchestra can measure ticket sales and customer satisfaction with performances. But to determine the quality of the orchestra itself, comparison is made to other orchestras in the world. Effectiveness is seen as the degree to which that comparison is positive. One method used by high performers to make such comparisons is to examine industry rankings. An example is the Maclean's magazine ratings of Canadian universities.

ORGANIZATIONAL LIFE CYCLE

What makes an organization effective varies with its stage of development. As organizations pass through common stages throughout their life cycle their structure changes, their basis of growth changes, and their goals change. It should be remembered that organizations may not grow continuously but may remain at one stage of development for long periods.

Most organizations are in operation for significantly fewer years than the average person lives. We know that failure is very common with new organizations. Restaurants, for example, are known to have high rates of startups and closures. This tendency is called the liability of newness. Older organizations die, too, though we often feel a sense of shock when we read of a well-established company that closes its doors. A recent example is Eaton's.

The first stage of an organization's development is its birth. Here growth is through creativity, the goal is survival, and the structure is non-bureaucratic. The organization's founder is often ruling the organization and does not rely on formalized rules and relationships. Predictable crises are encountered by growing organizations. The first crisis is that of leadership. Will the transition be made from being managed by the organization's founder to being managed by professional managers?

The next stage of development is the organization's youth. Growth now is by direction, as professional managers brought into the company start to impose organizational rules and bureaucracy. The goal is growth and management aims to provide a sense of mission to members of the organization. The crisis faced at this stage is that senior managers may not wish to relinquish control to more junior managers by delegating tasks and authority to them.

At the organization's midlife, growth is through delegation and coordination, the goal is efficiency, and the structure becomes more bureaucratic and departmentalized. To be able to change from a red-tape bureaucracy to a collaborative team-oriented organization is the crisis that will eventually arise. At maturity this collaboration will be achieved. The crisis at this stage is to avoid becoming stagnant and enduring a slow decline and eventual death. Instead, the organization must continually renew itself. In the final stage of decline and death some organizations cannot change because their management becomes a roadblock to change. Also, the organization's current structure can become a constraint on necessary change.

ORGANIZATION STRUCTURE

The founder of an organization has to make a series of decisions about what business to be in, what the organization's goals and objectives are, what work has to be performed to attain those goals, how the work will be divided and coordinated, and who will do the work. These decisions may be interdependent if the organization is small. Making one decision will affect others. For example, the skills and abilities of the particular people hired into the organization will then affect decisions about what the organization can do and how it will do it.

A small organization, for example a shoe store, would have a simple structure. Here everyone, including the managers, is involved in selling. Some specialized functions, such as accounting and advertising, may be contracted out to a bookkeeper and an advertising agency. A small travel agency would also have a simple structure. It could consist of only two divisions, one with two sales agents working exclusively with corporate clients and the other with two agents selling personal holidays to the general public. The manager (who may also be the owner) would sell travel packages to corporate and holiday clients, hire and train staff, pay the bills, and try to build agency sales by finding new corporate and holiday clients.

Another simple form of organization would be a restaurant whose manager has divided the staff into three groups: the bar, the food, and the service.

These simple forms could be much enlarged by adding more people to the basic structure. But as more people work in an organization, coordination becomes more difficult. There often isn't enough time for the manager to deal with every person individually on every issue. To solve this problem, more vertical division of labour would occur. In the travel agency an assistant manager could be hired to manage the Corporate Travel department. Those agents would report to the assistant manager, whose job would be to help them sell, deal with problems, and manage their work life (holidays, pay, training, etc.). The agency manager would then, in this example, manage the holiday travel agents as well as the assistant manager of corporate travel.

As a business grows, more people are hired to do the basic work of the organization. It often then creates new departments to perform specialized services that used to be contracted or hired out to other organizations or individuals. For example, a growing corporation that contracts its accounting to a public accounting partnership might set up its own accounting department and hire an accounting manager as its head. Such specialized services are known as staff functions.

The word staff refers to a person, group, or department that provides a service to the rest of the organization. For example, a cost accountant who studies the cost of making steel at Stelco is on the staff. The opposite of staff is the line. People, groups, and departments that are engaged in making or selling the organization's product, or managing those who do, are in the line. In a travel agency the travel agents are line personnel.

Besides accounting, other staff services might include public relations, advertising, finance, and legal services. However, whether these activities are staff or a line service depends on the basic work of the organization. For example, accountants working for a public accounting firm are line personnel, not staff.

As an organization grows it may become inefficient to have employees who each deal with many different products and/or a variety of clients. It begins to make sense for the organization to increase the amount of specialization of its personnel. The travel agency may assign its corporate travel agents to different teams. Each team might then deal with only a certain group of corporate clients or one large client such as a federal government department. The teams are therefore specialized by customer and would be managed by an assistant manager in charge of all corporate travel. Holiday travel agents may be divided by their specialty knowledge of a particular geographic region or type of travel (for example cruises, adventure travel). These agents would have their own assistant manager.

In the travel agency example the organization is growing. Sometimes organizations are created large at the outset, usually because size is an advantage or a necessity. For example, the owner of an independent supermarket does not open a small store in a newly built subdivision and then grow larger as demand warrants. Instead, a large store is designed and built that has the capacity to deal with the expected number of customers in the neighbourhood. A small grocery store could not compete effectively in price and selection with other nearby supermarkets.

A division by product is illustrated in the supermarket example. Work is split into bakery, meats, dry goods, and produce, the four classes of product provided. Employees would specialize in working with and knowing one type of product.

An organization can divide the work it does into geographic areas. This arrangement is employed when each unit operates relatively independently. Geographic departmentation is also used when a large territory needs to be divided into parts of manageable size.

In a manufacturing firm functional departments typically include production, marketing and sales, and research and development. Production makes the shoes; marketing and sales is responsible for advertising, distribution, and pricing; and R&D studies new designs and materials for shoes. Organizations often create a mixture, or hybrid, of the above-mentioned ways to departmentalize.

MEASURES OF STRUCTURE

Structure concerns more than the division of labour or the boxes on the organization chart. It is also about the reporting relationships between organizational members. These are the lines connecting the boxes, rules and regulations about how the work is performed, and whether organizational decisions are made at the top of the organization or lower down. In order to compare one organization's structure with that of another or to study the effects of structure on organizational performance, we need to have consistent ways to measure structure. Three important structure measures are complexity, formalization, and centralization.

Complexity refers to the number of separate parts in an organization's structure. The more tasks are divided among individuals and specialized, the more the organization is horizontally complex. As the vertical chain of command lengthens, more organizational layers are inserted between top management and production workers. The organization becomes more vertically complex. Vertical complexity is often also called the tallness of the organization. Organizations today are tending to move towards flatter organizations by eliminating whole levels of middle management. This downsizing increases the number of people supervised. Therefore the span of control increases for the managers that remain.

Formalization refers to the extent to which job activity is defined and controlled by rules. The more rules there are about how to do the work and how decisions are made, the more an organization is formalized. Police departments are often very formalized as the activities of officers are strictly controlled by rules that cover almost every situation that may arise. A campus radio station, on the other hand, may be much less formal, having only a few rules governing the broadcasting behaviour of station members.

Centralization concerns where in the organization decisions are made. When decision-making is reserved for top management, vertical centralization is high. Vertical centralization is low when lower-level employees in the hierarchy are given decision-making authority. Horizontal decentralization occurs when workers in many different organizational units are allowed to make decisions without referring to a more central authority.

These structural measures of complexity, centralization, and formalization may be combined into the two broad and descriptive categories of mechanistic and organic. Mechanistic organizations were so named because they can be seen to operate as machines. They are characterized by highly specialized tasks that tend to be rigidly defined, have hierarchical authority and control, and communications that primarily take the form of instructions and decisions issued by superiors to subordinates. Communication is mostly vertical from the top down. Further, loyalty to the organization and obedience to superiors is a condition of membership. Mechanistic organizations tend to be complex, formalized, and centralized. An automobile factory that uses a production line technology is a good example of an organization with a mechanistic structure.

Organic organizations act more as living things. They have tasks that are more interdependent and that are continually adjusted and redefined through interaction with organizational members. An advertising agency such as Saatchi & Saatchi needs to be flexible in dealing with customers and in creating concepts for television commercials and print advertisements. In an organic organization, control depends less on formal job position and more on expertise relevant to the particular problem being considered. Communication is both vertical (up and down the hierarchy) and horizontal (across different departments of the organization) depending on where the needed information resides. These communications primarily take the form of information and advice. Commitment in the organic organization is to the organization's tasks and goals. Members accept general responsibility for task accomplishment beyond their individual role definition. That is, they do not stick to a job description as a definition of the work they will do. Organic organizations tend to be simple, low in formalization, and decentralized. They adapt to and create change in their environments.

WEBER'S IDEAL TYPE OF BUREAUCRACY

Max Weber (1864-1920) was a German sociologist who studied organizations in the early 1900s. He was a first-hand observer of industrialization and a trend in Western society towards organizations that were run less on the authority of one person and more on a set of formalized rules and relationships. This form of organization can be called a bureaucracy, which means a set of related offices.

Weber described his ideal type of bureaucracy, the most perfect example of this type of organizing, as having the following components.

- Formalization. A continuous organization of official functions bound by rules.
- Records. Administrative acts, decisions and rules are formulated and recorded in writing.
- Office. The combination of written documents and a continuous organization of official functions constitute the office.
- Specialization. Each office has a clearly defined sphere of competence.

- Hierarchy. Each lower office is under the control and supervision of a higher one.
- Officials. Candidates are selected on the basis of technical qualifications. They are appointed, not elected. The office is treated as the sole, or at least the primary, occupation of the incumbent. The job constitutes a career. There is a system of promotion according to seniority or to achievement, or both. There is a complete absence of appropriation of official position by the incumbent.
- Ownership. There exists complete separation of the property belonging to the organization, which is controlled within the sphere of office, and the personal property of the official. Members of the administrative staff should be completely separated from ownership of the means of production or administration.
- Impersonality. The dominance of a spirit of formalistic impersonality, without hatred or passion, and hence without affection or enthusiasm. Everyone is subject to formal equality of treatment.

Bureaucratic theory makes the assumption that people are rational and can work within the rules. These guide behaviour, meaning that conflict would be avoided. Weber provides guidelines for how to structure an organization. This is the ideal type bureaucracy, as it should work. Non-rational behaviour and conflict between individuals were not anticipated. We now know that non-rationality and conflict are present in bureaucratic structures.

TECHNOLOGY

Technology is defined as the sequence of physical techniques, knowledge, and equipment used to turn organizational inputs into outputs. Joan Woodward conducted research into the connection between technology and structure by studying 100 manufacturing firms in the southern part of England. She identified three types of technology.

The first was small batch. This is the production of one or a few custom items by one person or a small team working closely together. An example of small batch technology would be custom cabinet making. Here the cabinetmaker produces a unique product or a few similar products.

Woodward's second technology type was large batch/mass production. This is the production of many units of an identical product. A common example of mass production is an automobile assembly line. When in operation, many units of the same product are made. An example of large batch production is the making of beer, which in a brewery is made in large fermentation kettles that may each hold many thousands of litres. Each kettle holds one batch of beer.

Woodward's third technology type was continuous process. This is the production of a standard product without pause. An example of continuous process technology is a nuclear power plant. Once started, electricity is generated without pause for a long period of time. A few highly skilled technicians monitor the nuclear reactor. Expended uranium fuel rods may even be replaced while the reactor is in operation. A second example of this type of technology is an oil refinery. Crude oil is continually input into the refinery's cracking and distilling apparatus and refined products such as gasoline are continually extracted.

Woodward and her colleagues found that organizations were more effective when their technology matched the organization's structure. Specifically, for small batch production, an organic structure was best because the production of custom items requires a good deal of informal communication and adaptation. Organizations using a mass production technology were more effective when using a mechanistic structure. The reason was that control over a complex and repetitive process could be effectively exerted by rules and regulations. When a continuous process technology was used, Woodward found that an organic structure was more effective. In this case highly trained technicians monitored machines producing the organization's output and needed to communicate freely about the production process and any irregularities that were noticed.

The concept that technology determines the best organizational structure was termed the technological imperative.

While it isn't limited to productivity, organizational effectiveness certainly encompasses it. Defined narrowly as the amount of physical output for each unit of productive input, productivity has been a human concern for centuries. The Chinese philosopher Mencius (372-279BC) wrote about conceptual models and systems that would qualify today as production-management techniques. Plato (427-347BC) spoke of the division of labour in The Republic: "A man whose work is confined to such limited task must necessarily excel at it."

Early thinking about productivity remains relevant to production today. Measuring it, however, has become more complex. The U.S. Bureau of labour Statistics (BLS) measures what it calls "multifactor productivity," in which "output is related to combined inputs of labour, capital and intermediate purchases. Labour is measured by the number of hours of labour expended in the production of output. Capital includes equipment, structures, land, and inventories. Intermediate purchases are composed of materials, fuels, electricity, and purchased services." The problem with measurement comes in defining output for non-manufacturing, service activities commonly thought of as "white collar" or "knowledge work" that the BLS labels "hard-to-measure." These include "transportation, communications, utilities, retail and wholesale trade, finance and insurance, and various additional services rendered to persons and businesses."

Measurement is an issue because a significant portion of the service sectors in the economies of developed nations relies on knowledge and human capital. Managers in these economies recognize that technology ultimately derives from human ingenuity. The challenge becomes to quantify, and more effectively manage, intangible components of the productivity mix.

In their book The Balanced Scorecard, Dr. Robert S. Kaplan and Dr. David P. Norton addressed the complexity of measuring and managing organizational performance: "The balanced scorecard retains traditional financial measures. But financial measures tell the story of past events, an adequate story for industrial age companies for which investments in long-term capabilities and customer relationships were not critical for success. These financial measures are inadequate, however, for guiding and evaluating the journey that information age companies must make to create future value through investment in customers, suppliers, employees, processes, technology, and innovation."

The authors argue that organizations must examine their business both internally and externally, expressing a vision and strategy and identifying objectives, measures, targets, and initiatives that address four questions.

- To succeed financially, how should we appear to our shareholders?
- To achieve our vision, how should we appear to our customers?
- To satisfy our shareholders and customers, what business processes must we excel at?

- To achieve our vision, how will we sustain our ability to change and grow?

Michael O'Neill, who leads a program of research into organizational effectiveness for Herman Miller, notes that the value of an approach such as the balanced scorecard is that it attempts to quantify the capacity an organization has to conduct work and ultimately create value. "In traditional productivity measures," O'Neill notes, "the unit of analysis is the individual. In terms of knowledge work, that may be irrelevant because increases in individual productivity, no matter how they're measured, do not automatically transfer to the productivity of the organization. Instead, the team, or functional group, becomes the unit of analysis. This requires managers to make a conceptual shift in their thinking, to understand that it's more relevant to measure activities that contribute to overall business goals and strategies, such as the speed of organizing around new opportunities and the quality of business processes." O'Neill says that in addition to the external factors that may affect a business, this perspective should take into account

- The design of the organization (for instance, centralized versus decentralized decision making).
- Its technology (information technology strategy and implementation).
- Its people (human resource issues, work styles, performance).
- The physical work environment (spatial dispersion of facilities, work environment design, facilities and real estate issues).

CONTRIBUTORS

Every employee contributes to organizational effectiveness. Taking into account skills, experience, motivation, and rank, some play a bigger role than others. Peter Drucker coined a term for one category of these high-level performers in his 1959 book Landmarks of Tomorrow. He wrote of "knowledge workers," defining them as anyone who works for a living at the tasks of developing or using knowledge. Richard Florida in his 2002 book Rise of the Creative Class says anyone whose work creates "meaningful new forms" is vital to the success of an organization. According to Florida, creative professionals "work in a wide range of knowledge-intensive industries such as high-tech sectors, financial services, the legal and healthcare professions, and business management. These people engage in creative problem-solving, drawing on complex bodies of knowledge to solve specific problems."

At a deeper level, Florida identifies a "super-creative core" that includes scientists, engineers, university professors, designers, and architects. This core, along with the "thought leadership" of cultural figures, think-tank researchers, analysts, and other opinion-makers, "produce new forms or designs that are readily transferable and broadly useful-such as designing a product that can be widely made, sold and used; or coming up with a theorem or strategy that can be applied in many cases." In other words, knowledge work falls somewhere on a continuum of complexity and difficulty. As Thomas H. Davenport, director of the Accenture Institute for Strategic Change, puts it, "Workers at the lower end of the continuum would possess less knowledge, would use knowledge more than create it, and would have less discretion in how to employ knowledge in the course of their work. Knowledge workers at the higher end of the continuum are more expert and experienced, and are in most cases knowledge creators as well as users."

Susan Conway of the Information Work Productivity Council, an independent group of companies and academics studying information work productivity and profitability, notes that knowledge work is actually part of "information work," a broader occupational category. "In sophisticated economies," says Conway, "the great majority of workers constantly use data, information and knowledge-each to varying degrees-in their jobs. They create, manage, share, receive and/or manipulate information. To accurately classify a particular type of worker as working with a particular type of information content is almost impossible."

Whatever the terminology, everyone from consultants to CEOs acknowledges the importance of this type of work to achieving organizational effectiveness. However, gauging the contribution of knowledge workers to overall organizational effectiveness poses several challenges because no single measure is likely to capture the outcomes.

MEASUREMENT

An old business adage says that whatever cannot be measured cannot be managed. Yet, as Susan Cantrell, research fellow at the Accenture Institute for Strategic Change, points out, knowledge workers resist being measured, "both because they have no history of being measured and because they believe it might take the 'magic' out of their work. Most high-end knowledge workers…tend to work on unique, one-off, highly specialized problems, making it impossible to have one measure for all such knowledge workers. Moreover, many knowledge workers...work interdependently, making it difficult to isolate one knowledge worker's contribution from another's. And, because the work performed is generally unobservable, a knowledge worker could be working for months, or sometimes even years, before an output is tangibly realized." Based on her analysis of several firms, Cantrell cites five best practices for measuring high-end knowledge work.

- Involve knowledge workers and top management in identifying measures. Sometimes the most obvious element is the one missed. If knowledge work is critical to the business, top management better be involved in setting measurements and making sure they align with corporate strategy. And if knowledge workers are really valuable to the organization, then they better have a say in setting their work practice and effectiveness measures so they have ownership.
- Identify only a few, simple measures that are "good enough." Complex measures confuse and frustrate both managers and knowledge workers. It is better to sacrifice accuracy for clarity when using measurements to guide the efforts of knowledge workers.
- Build a causal chain of evidence. Cantrell identifies four areas of measurement for high-end knowledge workers and says the goal is to implement measures in each of them:
  - — The impact of an intervention (such as a new workplace design) or multiple interventions (such as a change in organizational structure and an information technology implementation);
  - — The individual's work practices;
  - — The individual's effectiveness; and
  - — The overall impact on organizational effectiveness.
- Don't rely on measures alone. If the organization's goal is to guide, motivate, or even control knowledge workers' behaviour, it must supplement measurement with strong cultures and value systems. Measurements may be attractive for their apparent preciseness, but they must be tempered with the observations, experience, and common sense of managers.
- Compare apples to apples. Knowledge work is idiosyncratic, so avoid generalizing among groups, either in terms of what

measurements apply or what impact an intervention may have.

As an example of Cantrell's "causal chain of evidence," Michael O'Neill of Herman Miller conducted research to identify a "casual model" that shows the logical relationships between organizational, workplace, and technology design features, and subsequent effects on employee behaviour and business outcomes. This model was empirically tested as part of a long-term research project with a major customer in the shipping industry. The company wanted to examine the impact on collaboration and efficiency of business processes of a major consolidation of employees from four locations into one. The redesign project included some new furniture and improved adjacencies between key individuals and groups. Herman Miller researchers conducted detailed analyses of the steps and time involved, as well as the cost of business processes within the organization.

The research showed that as a result of the design interventions, the time required for "business project approvals" (involving interaction between four departments) decreased by about 20 percent, from 112 to 90 days. Cross-departmental ratings on quality of "responsiveness" to needs for information between departments increased by 32 percent. When these time savings were computed using employee compensation data, the cost savings equalled $710,000 for one process alone. These results, notes O'Neill, demonstrate the importance of understanding an organization's high-level business strategies and then creating measures that determine whether the contributions of knowledge workers are achieving the desired goals. "We do measure business-process efficiency," O'Neill says. "The cost side of the equation is still important; however, that is the only part of the issue. Effectiveness involves more than this. We want to increase the quality of output as well as the amount." Whether workplace design interventions or changes in work practices or processes are involved, consultant Cliff Grimes notes that no single measure, or single instance of measurement, is sufficient to give a clear picture of effectiveness. "A family of measures...related to the real objectives of the department, allows the level of performance to be measured and monitored over time to establish whether it is stagnating, declining, or improving. It allows the effect of productivity initiatives to be established and focuses managers' attention on the need to improve productivity, the only true way to improve a company's competitive position."

FOSTERING EFFECTIVENESS

As measurement allows management, management implies control, or at least the ability to guide and direct. Failing to foster the effectiveness of individuals in achieving overall organizational goals carries a high price. According to the Gartner Group, 50 percent of workplace investments through 2005 will focus on the productivity of knowledge workers. By the end of 2007, organizations will target 20 percent of all investment in information and communication technologies at improving knowledge worker productivity.

Yet, researchers at the Accenture Institute for Strategic Change found that among 40 firms they studied, "all of which had knowledge work at the core of their businesses, very few had made specific attempts to improve or enhance these workers' efforts. In fact, many organizations took affront to the idea of focusing on high-end [knowledge] workers (HEKW) at all. They argued that HEKWs were not treated differently because their firm had an inclusive, democratic culture, and it would be damaging to the culture to treat any group of workers in a privileged fashion. Yet several of these firms had distinct approaches for dealing with senior executives. We believe the primary reason is that executives don't know how to attack the problem of improving HEKW performance." Beyond identifying measures that relate to achieving overall business goals, efforts to increase organizational effectiveness by helping knowledge workers be more productive seems to involve three key areas:

- Establishing a culture of trust that gives people autonomy;
- Creating vital workplaces; and
- Providing healthful physical support for individuals.

ESTABLISH TRUST AND GIVE PEOPLE AUTONOMY

Corporate turnaround specialist John Whitney says that without trust people cannot or will not work together except under conditions of stringent control. According to Professor Rosabeth Moss Kanter, work environments that provide access to information, resources, support, and the opportunity to learn and develop empower employees to accomplish their work. As a result, employees are more satisfied with their work, and they sense that management trusts them to do whatever is necessary to achieve high-quality outcomes for the organization. In one example, researchers studying the effect of a trusting environment in healthcare found a direct link between empowerment and organizational effectiveness. They chose a random sample of nurses and used a variety of self-reporting scales to test two hypotheses: whether empowerment would have a direct effect on satisfaction and affective commitment (an individual's emotional attachment to, identification with, and involvement in an organization); and whether empowerment would lead to feelings of trust that, in turn, would enhance job satisfaction and organizational commitment.

Using structural equation modelling, the researchers first tested job satisfaction as the outcome variable, with formal power, informal power, and perceived access to work empowerment structures modelled as indicators of the latent variable "overall empowerment." The analysis found higher levels of empowerment associated with increased satisfaction. When testing affective commitment as the outcome variable, the data showed a direct link to empowerment and an indirect yet significant link to trust in management. Establishing a climate of trust is important for allowing knowledge workers to contribute their best efforts to achieving organizational effectiveness. Balancing an open, autonomous work climate with structures and measurements that tie information work to organizational goals is critical. Yet, researchers at the Accenture Institute for Strategic Change "found relatively few grand experiments for high-end knowledge workers (HEKW) in the companies we studied. Because firms don't want to risk alienating HEKWs, they've been somewhat conservative in adopting new organizational arrangements. They also realize that knowledge workers value autonomy and don't like heavy-handed programs imposed from above. Therefore, in the companies we studied we found little evidence of process reengineering, formal empowerment programs, or even quality improvement initiatives specifically targeted at high end knowledge workers."

CREATE A VITAL WORK ENVIRONMENT

Reluctance to take on cultural changes need not prevent an organization from undertaking physical changes that can improve organizational effectiveness. Office space is expensive, however, so there is a temptation to focus only on reducing its cost because that is much easier to quantify than the effect of giving knowledge workers a workplace redesign or more computing and communications tools. Weighing the benefit of reducing costs for space and work tools against the gains in effectiveness an organization can achieve with more productive knowledge workers shows just how important a vital work environment is. Michael O'Neill contends that vital work environments result from the amount of control provided to employees at the organization-wide, business unit, team, and even the individual levels. "If the corporate mission demands continual reorganization around customer or market needs (as is increasingly common), ease of facility adaptability and reuse will permit changes in space usage to occur incrementally on an as-needed basis. Thus, the integration of environmental control into facility design may enhance effectiveness at the organizational level."

At the work group or team level, O'Neill says, the potential for environmental control "is determined by the flexibility of the physical (and organizational) boundaries surrounding the team. Boundaries serve to control the flow of information to and from the group. Control may be exercised by the ability to determine and self manage the reconfiguration of workspace layout and boundaries as the current state of formation of the team, and overall mission, dictate. Organizational boundaries can be reinforced or made more permeable through the design of the physical workspace." Individuals exercise autonomy through the adjustability of the physical elements within their workstations, such as task lighting, shelves, storage, work surface height, level of enclosure, computer screen and keyboard, and HVAC system. O'Neill notes that "control over these elements may contribute to comfort, environmental satisfaction, privacy, communication, and other perceptions that are related to effectiveness and quality of work life." Researchers at Herman Miller recently studied the impact of the work environment on employee behaviour and work process, work effectiveness, and business productivity. Using a project that consolidated employees into one building, they analyzed the impact of workplace design issues, including departmental adjacencies, collaborative space, and assigned and unassigned space use, for an experimental group (employees who moved) and a control group (employees who did not move) both before and after the change occurred.

As part of this effort, researchers mapped three ongoing business processes within several departments and collected metrics on those processes, such as process cycle time before and after the move. Using data from almost 1,200 employee surveys, they created a statistical model that identified key workplace variables that predicted cycle time for those processes. Increases in quality of lighting, quality of internal group processes, design of interior space to support quickly shifting from individual to collaborative work, and amount of time spent in unassigned workstations were the main predictors of reduced cycle times.

To illustrate the impact of the move on process quality and efficiency, researchers plotted process cycle times for a repeatable business process against an independent assessment of the quality of output for the group responsible for that process. They found that the process cycle time decreased after the move, and the assessment of work product quality rose. Employees involved in the business process achieved efficiency gains that resulted in time savings of 7.5 percent.

PROVIDE HEALTHFUL SUPPORT

A comfortable worker is a happier worker and a more productive contributor to organizational effectiveness. A wealth of statistics exist to bolster the argument that ergonomic chairs and adjustable work and input surfaces, especially for people who spend long periods of time at a keyboard, reduce costs related to medical claims and absenteeism. The real news is that healthful support can increase productivity.

Working with a global management consulting and technology services company, Michael O'Neill and a team of researchers examined the effects of

- Moving employees from four buildings into one that had fewer workstations than people
- Giving them new furniture and interior design concepts intended to make interior space highly flexible for either individual work or group collaboration
- Providing them with training geared to improve ergonomic awareness and communicate new "rules of behaviour" for using the space.

The project involved a total of 1,135 employees representing three groups. The control group did not receive any changes in its workplace nor did it get any training. The first experimental group moved into the new workplace and received training. The second experimental group moved to the new space but did not receive training. Researchers studied each group before and after the move and the training.

Because job control is a reliable predictor of employee health and the reductions in the risk of coronary heart disease, the researchers wanted to test the hypothesis that the greatest reduction in pain and musculoskeletal discomfort would result from the combination of workspace flexibility and ergonomic training. The results of the study supported this premise. Employees who moved into the new work environment reported a statistically significant 2 percent increase in job control. Employees in the new environment who also received training reported a 13 percent increase in job control. "Work-related discomfort" decreased 27 percent for the group that moved, and 46 percent for the group that moved and received ergonomic training.

The study also showed significant results related to the relationship between workplace design, training, and business-process efficiency. Using a method called Business Process Analysis, the research team gathered information from the control and experimental groups to determine the time, resources, and steps involved in four repeatable business processes. The average across all four processes the researchers studied was a 5.62 percent reduction in process cycle times for the move-only experimental group and a 10.55 percent reduction for the group that received the move and the training). Further analysis showed that workplace design features, such as meeting rooms and flexible workstations, were significant predictors of the reduction in process cycle time. The researchers concluded that there is credible evidence that broad workplace strategies to support behaviours (such as collaboration), which managers intuitively believe lead to effective work, actually do increase performance and business success.

Information work and knowledge workers will be key contributors to organizational effectiveness for the foreseeable future. Recognizing that fact is merely one step toward enabling their best contributions. For that to occur, organizations must tackle the challenge of measuring their contributions and then supply them with an environment and tools that allow them to create value for their employers.

Note: Reader can visit OfficeMax, Inc. site www.officemax.com for a detailed study of connected to this chapter. OfficeMax (formerly Boise Cascade Corporation) is engaged in the distribution of office products. The company operates in the US, Puerto Rico, the US Virgin Islands, Mexico, Canada, Australia and New Zealand. It is headquartered in Naperville, Illinois and employs 33,000 people; this figure includes 11,000 part-time employees.

Bibliography

A. Balsa and T. G. McGuire, "Prejudice, Clinical Uncertainty, and Stereotyping as Sources of Health Disparities," *Journal of Health Eco-nomics*, January, 2003.

A. Bryman, "Leadership in Organizations," in *Handbook of Organization Studies,* ed. S. R. Clegg, C. Hardy, and W. R. Nord, Thousand Oaks, CA: Sage, 1996.

A. Mehrabian, *Silent Messages*, Belmont, CA: Wadsworth, 1971.

A. G. Dawson, "Administrators Settle into New Digs," *Delaware Coast Press,* July, 2003.

A. G. Schick, L. A. Gordon, and S. Haka, "Information Overload: A Temporal Approach," *Accounting, Organizations & Society*, 1990.

A. P. Hare, "Types of Roles in Small Groups: A Bit of History and a Current Perspective," *Small Group Research*, 1994.

B. M. Bass, "From Transactional to Transformational Leadership," *Organizational Dynamics,* Winter 1990.

B. W. Tuckman and M. A. C. Jensen, "Stages of Small-Group Development Revisited," *Group and Organization Studies,* 1977.

C. A. Beatty and B. A. Barker, *Building Smart Teams: Roadmap to High Performance*, Thousand Oaks, CA: Sage Publications, 2004.

C. E. Shannon and W. Weaver, *The Mathematical Theory of Communication*, Urbana: University of Illinois Press, 1949.

C. N. Macrae and G. V Bodenhausen, "Social Cognition: Thinking Categorically about Others," *Annual Review of Psychology*, 2000.

D. Goleman, R. Boyatzis, and A. McKee, *Primal Leaders*, Boston: Harvard Business School Press, 2002.

D. Hamermesh and J. E. Biddle, "Beauty and the Labor Market," *American Economic Review*, 1994.

D. Robb, "Global Workgroups," *Computerworld,* August, 2005.

D. Robey, H. M. Khoo, and C. Powers, "Situated Learning in Cross-Functional Virtual Teams," *Technical Communication,* February, 2000.

D. Rynecki, "Putting the Muscle Back into the Bull," *Fortune,* April,

2004.

D. Tannen, *That's Not What I Meant!*, New York: Ballantine, 1987.

D. Woodruff, "Crossing Culture Divide Early Clears Merger Paths," *The Asian Wall Street Journal,* May, 2001.

D. B. Simmons, "The Nature of the Organizational Grapevine," *Supervisory Management,* November, 1985.

D. C. Bamlund, *Communication Styles of Japanese and Americans: Images and Realities*, Belmont, CA: Wadsworth, 1988.

D. C. Feldman, "The Development and Enforcement of Group Norms," *Academy of Management Review,* 1984.

D. C. McClelland, *Power: The Inner Experience*, New York: Irvington, 1975.

D. C. Thomas and K. Inkson, *Cultural Intelligence: People Skills for Global Business*, San Francisco: Berrett-Koehler, 2004.

D. D. Dawley and W. P. Anthony, "User Perceptions of E-Mail at Work," *Journal of Business and Technical Communication*, April 2003.

D. D. Steiner and J. S. Rain, "Immediate and Delayed Primacy and Recency Effects in Performance Evaluation," *Journal of Applied Psychology*, 1989.

D. L. Miller, "The Stages of Group Development: A Retrospective Study of Dynamic Team Processes," *Canadian Journal of Administra-tive Sciences*, 2003.

D. V Day and R. G. Lord, "Executive Leadership and Organizational Performance: Suggestions for a New Theory and Methodology," *Journal of Management,* 1988.

E. Hart, "Manager of the Year: John Mang," *Iron & Steelmaker,* June, 2003.

E. Horwitt, "Knowledge, Knowledge, Who's Got the Knowledge," *Computerworld,* April, 1996.

E. Ulich and W. G. Weber, "Dimensions, Criteria, and Evaluation of Work Group Autonomy," in *Handbook of Work Group Psychology,* ed. M. A. West, Chichester, UK: John Wiley and Sons, 1996.

E. A. Locke, "Why Emotional Intelligence Is an Invalid Concept," *Journal of Organizational Behavior,* 2005.

E. M. Heffes, "Follow These Leaders," *Financial Executive,* April 2005.

F. Piccolo, "Brownie Points," *Atlantic Business,* October-November 2004.

F. Russo, "My Kingdom for a Door," *Time Magazine,* October, 2000.

G. Bethune, "From Worst to First," *Fortune,* May, 1998.

G. Evans and D. Johnson, "Stress and Open-Office Noise," *Journal of Applied Psychology*, 2000.

G. Hitt and J. D. McKinnon, "Cheney Takes Blame for Shooting but Defends How It Was Disclosed," *The Wall Street Journal,* February, 2006.

G. Johns, "Absenteeism Estimates by Employees and Managers: Divergent Perspectives and Self-Serving Perceptions," *Journal of Applied Psychology*, 1994.

G. Yukl and R. Lepsinger, "Why Integrating the Leading and Managing Roles Is Essential for Organizational Effectiveness," *Organizational Dynamics*, 2005.

G. Buckler, "Staking One for the Team," *Computing Canada,* October, 2004.

G. N. Powell, "One More Time: Do Female and Male Managers Differ?" *Academy of Management Executive,* 1990.

H. Lee, "Behavioral Strategies for Dealing with Flaming in an Online Forum," *The Sociological Quarterly*, 2005.

H. Mintzberg, *The Nature of Managerial Work*, New York: Harper & Row, 1973.

H. H. Kelley, "The Process of Causal Attribution," *American Psychologist*, 1973.

I. D. Steiner, *Group Process and Productivity*, New York: Academic Press, 1972.

J. Barling, T. Weber, and E. K. Kelloway, "Effects of Transformational Leadership Training on Attitudinal and Financial Outcomes: A Field Experiment," *Journal of Applied Psychology*, 1996.

J. Collins, *From Good to Great*, New York: Harper Collins, 2001.

J. Davidson, "Fighting Information Overload," *Office Solutions*, 2006.

J. Gordon, "Do Your Virtual Teams Deliver Only Virtual Performance?" *Training,* June, 2005.

J. Porterfiled and B. H. Kleiner. "A New Era: Women and Leadership," *Equal Opportunities International*, 2005.

J. Yang and K. W Mossholder, "Decoupling Task and Relationship Conflict: The Role of Intergroup Emotional Processing," *Journal of Organizational Behavior,* 2004.

J. B. Rosener, "Ways Women Lead," *Harvard Business Review*, November-December 1990.

J. G. Miller, "Living Systems: The Organization," *Behavioral Science*, 1972.

J. J. Dose and R. J. Klimoski, "The Diversity of Diversity: Work Values Effects on Formative Team Processes," *Human Resource Management Review,* Spring 1999.

J. M. Burns, *Leadership*, NewYork: Harper& Row, 1978.

J. M. Feldman "Beyond Attribution Theory: Cognitive Processes in Performance Appraisal," *Journal of Applied Psychology*, 1981.

J. P. Kotter, "What Leaders Really Do," *Harvard Business Review*, 1990.

J. R. Kelly and S. G. Barsade, "Mood and Emotions in Small Groups and Work Teams," *Organizational Behavior and Human Decision Processes*, September 2001.

J. V Bommel, "Rumors," *Journal of Finance*, 2003.

K. Griffiths, "KPMG Sacks 670 Employees by E-Mail," *The Independent*, London, November , 2002.

K. Jelin, "A Multimethod Examination of the Benefits and Detriments of Intra-group Conflict," *Administrative Science Quarterly*, 1995.

K.. M. Jackson, "Buzzword Backlash Looks to Purge Jibba-Jabba from Corporate-Speak," *Boston Globe,* April, 2005.

K. J. Krone, EM. Jablin, and L. L. Putnam, "Communication Theory and Organizational Communication: Multiple Perspectives," in *Handbook of Organizational Communication: An Interdisciplinary Perspective,* ed.

F. M. Jablin et al. , Newbury Park, CA: Sage, 1987.

K. T. Dirks and D. L. Ferrin, “The Role of Trust in Organizations,” *Organization Science*, July-August, 2004.

L. Adams, “Medrad Works and Wins as a Team,” *Quality Magazine,* October, 2004.

L. Coch and J. French, J. P. . R, “Overcoming Resistance to Change,” *Human Relations*, 1948.

L. Z. Tiedens and A. R. Fragale, “Power Moves: Complementarity in Dominant and Submissive Nonverbal Behavior,” *Journal of Personal-ity and Social Psychology*, 2003.

L. Z. Tiedens and A. R. Fragale, “Power Moves: Complementarity in Dominant and Submissive Nonverbal Behavior,” *Journal of Per-sonality and Social Psychology*, 2003.

M. Brandel, “Global CIO,” *Computer world,* November, 2005.

M. Fujio, “Silence during Intercultural Communication: A Case Study,” *Corporate Communications*, 2004.

M. McLuhan, *Understanding Media: The Extensions of Man*, New York: M-Graw-Hill, 1964.

M. L. Loughry, “Coworkers Are Watching: Performance Implications of Peer Monitoring,” *Academy of Management Proceedings,* 2002.

N. , Wasserman, B. Anand, and N. Nohira, *When Does Leadership Mat-ter?* Harvard Business School Working Paper, 2001.

N. L. Kerr and S. R. Tindale, “Group Performance and Decision Making,” *Annual Review of Psychology,* 2004.

O. E. Williamson, “Calculativeness, Trust, and Economic Organization,” *Journal of Law and Economics*, 1993.

P. Ekman and E. Rosenberg, *What the Face Reveals: Basic and Applied Studies of Spontaneous Expression Using the Facial Action Coding System*, Oxford, England: Oxford University Press, 1997.

P. Harris and R. Moran, *Managing Cultural Differences*, Houston: Gulf, 1987.

P. Haw, “Learning from Lean Principles,” *Business Day,* July, 2003.

P. Salovey, and J. Mayer, “Emotional Intelligence,” *Imagination,*

Cognition, and Personality, 1990.

P. Sullivan, J. and D. L. Feltz, "The Relationship between Intrateam Conflict and Cohesion within Hockey Teams," *Small Group Research*, June, 2001.

P. Tripp-Knowles, "A Review of the Literature on Barriers Encoun-tered by Women in Science Academia," *Resources for Feminist Research*, Spring/Summer 1995.

P. Winkielman and K. C. Berridge, "Unconscious Emotion," *Current Directions in Psychological Science*, 2004.

P. J. Taylor and J. L. Pierce, "Effects of Introducing a Performance Management System and Employees' Subsequent Attitudes and Efforts," *Public Personnel Management*, Fall 1999.

P. O. Northouse, *Leadership: Theory and Practice,* 3rd ed. , Thousand Oaks, CA: Sage, 2004.

R,M. Stogdill. *Handbook of Leadership*, New York: The Free Press, 1974.

R. Cross, "Looking before You Leap: Assessing the Jump to Teams in Knowledge-Based Work," *Business Horizons,* September, 2000.

R. Hallowell, D. Bowen, and C. -I. Knoop, "Four Seasons Goes to Paris," *Academy of Management Executive*, November 2002.

R. Jacobs, "Using Human Resource Functions to Enhance Emotional Intelligence," in *The Emotionally Intelligent Workplace,* ed. C. Cherniss and D. Goleman, San Francisco: Jossey-Bass, 2001.

R. Winters, "Harvard's Crimson Face," *Time,* January, 2005.

R. C. Liden et al. , "Social Loafing: A Field Investigation," *Journal of Management*, 2004.

R. D. McPhee, "Vertical Communication Chains," *Management Communication*, 1988.

R. E. Rice, "Task Analyzability, Use of New Media, and Effectiveness: A Multi-Site Exploration of Media Richness," *Organization Science*, 1992.

R. H. Lengel and R. L. Daft, "The Selection of Communication Media as an Executive Skill," *Academy of Management Executive*, 1988.

R. J. House and R. N. Aditya, "The Social Scientific Study of

Leadership: Quo Vadis?" *Journal of Management*, 1997.

R. J. House et al. , "Personality and Charisma in the U. S. Presidency: A Psychological Theory of Leadership Effectiveness," *Administrative Science Quarterly*, 1991.

R. J. House, "Path-Goal Theory of Leadership: Lessons, Legacy, and a Reformulated Theory," *Leadership Quarterly*, 1996.

R. L. Daft and R. H. Lengel, "Information Richness: A New Approach to Managerial Behavior and Organization Design," *Research in Organizational behavior*, 1984.

R. M. Belbin, *Team Roles at Work*, Oxford, UK: Butterworth-Heinemann, 1993.

R. S. Kaplan and D. P. Norton, *The Balanced Scorecard: Translating Strategy into Action*, Boston: Harvard Business School Press, 1996.

S. Beatty, "Bass Talk: Plotting Plaid's Future," *The Wall Street Journal,* September, 2004.

S. Keer and J. M. Jermier, "Substitutes for Leadership: Their Meaning and Measurement," *Organizational Behavior and Human Performance*, 1978.

S. Lieberson and J. F. O'Conner, "Leadership and Organizational Per-formance: A Study of Large Corporations," *American Sociological Review*, 1972.

S. Ohtaki, T. Ohtaki, and M. D. Fetters, "Doctor-Patient Communica-tion: A Comparison of the USA and Japan," *Family Practice*, June 2003.

S. Prashad, "Building Trust Tricky for 'Virtual' Teams," *Toronto Star,* October, 2003.

S. E. Nedleman, "Recruiters Repeal Their Top Interview Questions," *Financial News Online,* February, 2005.

S. H. N. Leung, J. W. K. Chan, and WB. Lee, "The Dynamic Team Role Behavior: The Approaches of Investigation," *Team Performance Management,* 2003.

S. J. Karau and K. D. Williams, "Social Loafing: A Meta-Analytic Review and Theoretical Integration," *Journal of Personality and Social Psychology*, 1993.

S. L. Bellar, M. Helms, and D. E. Arfken, "The Glacial Change:

Women on Corporate Boards," *Business Perspectives*, 2004.

S. M. Crampton, J. W. Hodge, and J. M. Mishra, "The Information Communication Network Factors Influencing Grapevine Activity," *Public Personnel Management*, 1998.

S. S. Webber and L. M. Donahue, "Impact of Highly and Less Job-Related Diversity on Work Group Cohesion and Performance: A Meta-Analysis," *Journal of Management*, 2001.

Staff reporter, "Exit Bad Guy," *The Economist,* June, 1998.

T. Koski, "Reflections on Information Glut and Other Issues in Knowledge Productivity," *Futures*, August 2001.

The NTSB and NASA studies are summarized in J. R. Hackman, "New Rules for Team Building," *Optimize,* July, 2002.

VL. Goodwin, J. C. Wofford, and J. L. Whittington "A Theoretical and Empirical Extension to the Transformational Leadership Construct," *Journal of Organizational Behavior*, November, 2001.

W. Bennis, *Why Leaders Can't Lead*, San Francisco: Jossey-Bass, 1989.

W. B. Scott, "Blue Angels," *Aviation Week & Space Technology,* March,. 2005.

W. C. Kim and Mauborgne, "Tipping Point Leadership," *Harvard Business Review*, 2003.

W. G. Dyer, *Team Building: Current Issues and New Alternatives,* 3rd ed. , Reading, MA: Addison-Wesley, 1995.

Index

H

I

J

K

L

M

O